infra 4 u.
plana. Foliis firmis, on-
las esse possunt.

153. Oerobris f.
Floruit octobri, sed in Pfarn-
quidem in medio exhibitae

Carduii genus in ембеstry non
Hans vertes salices, iuf donte Culmaerifs
hic sup, malis ocul-
mi aculeis,
Ab una radicibus ad-
genus saler Сandes in
divers, о аbibitos
Mustia fabulos.

26 a

Taken up in the Atlantic
Lat: 28° 56'. Oct. 14th 1825 MS—
Weed of the Gulf Stream.—

with 2 marine insects
the white minute shells on the faded
leaves & stalks appear to belong to Seaworms.

Botanical Sketchbooks

Helen & William Bynum

with 275 illustrations

in association with the Royal Botanic Gardens, Kew

On the cover: (front, clockwise from top left) details from illustrations on pages 271, 158, 49, 9 (The J. Paul Getty Museum, Los Angeles), 281, 39, 157, 280, 38, 267; (back, clockwise from top left) details from illustrations on pages 72, 63, 11, 37, 85, 139, 269, 11, 49, 281, 77. All illustrations © 2017 The Board of Trustees of the Royal Botanic Gardens, Kew, except where indicated.

Half-title: Conrad Gesner, nodding thistle (*Carduus nutans*).

Title page: Maria Graham Callcott, 'Weed of the Gulf Stream'. As she sailed home from South America to Britain, Callcott continued to botanize, sketching seaweed lifted from the sea on 14 October 1825.

Authors' note: The plant names the artists used in their sketches are given in inverted commas, with modern scientific names provided where identification is helpful or possible.

First published in the United Kingdom in 2017 by Thames & Hudson Ltd, 181A High Holborn, London WC1V 7QX

This second edition published in 2023
Reprinted 2024

Botanical Sketchbooks © 2017 and 2023 Thames & Hudson Ltd, London

Text and layout © 2017 and 2023 Thames & Hudson Ltd, London
Illustrations © 2017 The Board of Trustees of the Royal Botanic Gardens, Kew, unless otherwise stated on p. 295

No part of this publication may be reproduced or transmitted in any form or by any means, electronic or mechanical, including photocopy, recording or any other information storage and retrieval system, without prior permission in writing from the publisher.

British Library Cataloguing-in-Publication Data
A catalogue record for this book is available from the British Library

ISBN 978-0-500-29718-6

Printed and bound in China by C & C Offset Printing Co. Ltd

Be the first to know about our new releases, exclusive content and author events by visiting
thamesandhudson.com
thamesandhudsonusa.com
thamesandhudson.com.au

CONTENTS

Introduction: *a compulsion to record* 6

I Made on Location 12

adventurers 14
MARK CATESBY (1683–1749) 14
THOMAS BAINES (1820–1875) 16
JAMES AUGUSTUS GRANT (1827–1892) 22
JOHN KIRK (1832–1922) 26
JOHN MUIR (1838–1914) 30
FREDERICK ANDREWS WALPOLE (1861–1904) 32
MARGARET MEE (1909–1988) 36

collectors 40
WILLIAM BARTRAM (1739–1823) 40
FRANCIS MASSON (1741–1805) 42
WILLIAM BURCHELL (1781–1863) 44
MARIA GRAHAM CALLCOTT (1785–1842) 48
ALFRED RUSSEL WALLACE (1823–1913) 52
FRIEDRICH CARL LEHMANN (1850–1903) 54
HELEN FAULKNER (1888–1979) 60

botany on the side 66
RICHARD DREYER (1763–1838) 66
FRANCIS HALL (1791–1833) 68
JOHN EYRE (1791–1865) 72
ROBERT SCHOMBURGK (1804–1865) 76
JOHN CHAMPION (1815–1854) 78
CHARLES PARISH (1822–1897) 84
ISAAC DRÈGE (1853–1921) 90
SANTIAGO CORTÉS (1854–1924) 94

imperial projects 98
HENDRIK VAN RHEEDE (1636–1691) 98
NICOLAES WITSEN (1641–1717) 102
JUAN DE LA CERDA & ATANASIO ECHEVERRÍA (*fl.* 1787–1803) 104
JOHN REEVES (1774–1856) 108
WILLIAM SWAINSON (1789–1855) 110
JOHN CATHCART (1802–1851) 112

II Doing Science 116

primus inter pares 118
CARL LINNAEUS (1707–1778) & CHARLES DARWIN
   (1809–1882) 118

naturalists 120
CONRAD GESNER (1516–1565) 120
FABIO COLONNA (1567–1640) 126
MARIA SIBYLLA MERIAN (1647–1717), JOHANNA
   HELENA HEROLT (1668–1723/30) & DOROTHEA
   MARIA GSELL (1678–1743) 128
NICCOLÒ GUALTIERI (1688–1744) 132
HARRIET SCOTT (1830–1907) & HELENA FORDE
   (1832–1910) 136
CHARLES DORAT (*fl.* 1850s–1860s) 142
BEATRIX POTTER (1866–1943) 144

from the botanical garden 146
FRANCIS (FRANZ) BAUER (1758–1840) 146
JOHN TYLEY (*fl.* 1790s–1800s) 150
WILLIAM JACKSON HOOKER (1785–1865) 152
WALTER HOOD FITCH (1817–1892) 156
NICHOLAS BROWN (1849–1934) 160
MARY GRIERSON (1912–2012) 162

botanists 166
JOHN STEVENS HENSLOW (1796–1861) 166
WILLIAM GRIFFITH (1810–1846) 168
JOSEPH DALTON HOOKER (1817–1911) 172
MARY ANNE STEBBING (1845–1927) 180
CHARLES MARIES (1851–1902) 184
OTTO STAPF (1857–1933) 186
ARTHUR HARRY CHURCH (1865–1937) 190

III Making Art 192

nature in art 194
LEONARDO DA VINCI (1452–1519) 194
ALBRECHT DÜRER (1471–1528) 196
JOHN CONSTABLE (1776–1837) 198
YOSHIKAWA KOKEI (*fl.* 1820s–1850s) 200
SAMUEL PALMER (1805–1881) 204

JOHN RUSKIN (1819–1900) 206
CHARLES RENNIE MACKINTOSH (1868–1928) 208

patrons' dependents 212
SEBASTIAN SCHEDEL (1570–1628) 212
SHAFI' 'ABBÁSÍ (*fl.* 1628–1660s) 218
GEORG DIONYSIUS EHRET (1708–1770) 220
PIERRE-JOSEPH REDOUTÉ (1759–1840) 222

in print 224
ALFRED RIOCREUX (1820–1912) 224
OKADA SEIFUKU (*fl.* 1820s/1830s) 226
OLIVE COATES PALGRAVE (1889–1963) 230
MURIEL DAWSON (1897–1974) 234
ANNE TODD DOWDEN (1907–2007) 236
VIOLET EMILY GRAHAM (1911–1991) 238

jobbing 240
JOHN HILL (*c.* 1716–1775) 240
SYDNEY PARKINSON (*c.* 1745–1771) 242
JOHN DOODY (*fl.* 1790s) 244
FERDINAND BAUER (1760–1826) 246
CONRAD MARTENS (1801–1878) 250
EDWARD LEAR (1812–1888) 252
EDWARD MINCHEN (1852–1913) 256

IV A Pleasing Occupation 258

JOHN JAMES (*fl.* 1680s) 260
FRANCIS NICHOLLS (1699–1778) 262
HELLEN SHELLEY (1799–1885) & MARGARET SHELLEY
   (1801–1887) 264
JOHN DAY (1824–1888) 266
ANNE STEBBING (1841–1925) 272
JOHN TRAHERNE MOGGRIDGE (1842–1874) 274
MARIANNE HARRIET MASON (1845–1932) 278
LAURA KING (1847–1918) 282
ANNIE MORSE (1855–1940) 284

finding out more 288
index of people and places 291
index of plants 293
note on plant names 295
illustration credits 295
acknowledgments and *about the authors* 296

433

Cyrthandracea. Novum genus Hackia nominandum.

Introduction: *a compulsion to record*

It is all the same, drawing, painting, modelling, the irresistible desire to copy any beautiful object which strikes the eye. Why cannot one be content to look at it? I cannot rest, I must draw, however poor the result ...

So wrote the teenage Beatrix Potter as a troubled adolescent, fascinated with the natural world. The happy culmination would be her famous illustrated children's stories, but along the way she produced skilful botanical sketches with nothing 'poor' about them. In voicing her compulsion to make a record of what she saw, Potter could have spoken for all the artists featured here. Young or old, amateurs or professionals, scientists, illustrators, collectors and adventurers – all shared the urge to sketch plants. They drew to engage with the plant world, by looking, understanding, capturing and recording its details in an image. If the ephemeral beauty of plants, the sheen of a petal, a detail of dusty pollen or tilt of a leaf lent themselves to sketching, so too did the enduring and rugged form of root and branch or the texture of bark. Some hoped to find fame by their art, or at least make a living. Others were scientists, travellers and plant collectors who needed an aide-mémoire. Sketching is also about pleasure; there need be no other impetus.

While Beatrix Potter might not be the most obvious person to find in a book of botanical sketches, she is certainly one of a series of fascinating characters who sketched for different reasons, in different times and in many different places. It is the results of such endeavours, the motivations and adventures of the makers, and the plants that fired their imagination, that are celebrated in *Botanical Sketchbooks*.

What makes a botanical sketch?

An effective sketch can consist of simply a few minimalist pencil marks, or perhaps a more deliberate pen and ink drawing, in sepia or bold Indian ink. English-speakers only began 'sketching' officially in the late 17th century, at least that's when the word 'sketch' (from German *skizze* or Dutch *schets*) enters the English language. German *skizze*, from the early 17th century,

WILLIAM GRIFFITH
William Griffith's sketch of '*Slackia*', as he travelled from Assam to Ava (Inwa, Myanmar) on 20 March 1837; he wondered if he had discovered a new genus.

captured the sound of the Italian *schizzo*, meaning quickly splattering or splashing. It seems to express the dynamism and immediacy of many of the sketches seen here. French had its *esquisse* and Spanish *esquicio*, going all the way back to the Latin *schedius*. The popularity of the act was in part dependent on the availability of the materials. Drawing became much more widespread, indeed a recognized activity in itself, as paper became cheaper and more plentiful in 15th-century Europe. Sketches became a way of accumulating and storing visual information.

Colour added complexity: washes, watercolours, opaque body colours, perhaps small-scale studies in oil. The printmaker and artist Martin Schongauer created one of the earliest recognized botanical sketches with his study of three peonies in the early 1470s. Crucially, these were drawn direct from life not from memory or copied from elsewhere, and were reproduced in his *Madonna of the Rose Garden* of 1473. Because the boundaries between a hasty drawing, a pondered study (such as Schongauer's) and an almost finished picture are matters of degree, we have cast the net widely and brought together a varied and fascinating range of styles, materials and purposes. Formal botanical art can be constrained by convention – both artistic and scientific – while sketches give the artist freedom to explore and express ideas.

Before the late 18th century sketchbooks were generally bespoke items, but artists have also made their marks on writing pads, account books, field notebooks, school exercise books, vellum, loose sheets of paper, sometimes pasted or bound into albums, partly worked manuscripts, letters, herbarium sheets and as marginalia. Carl Linnaeus drew on the back of an envelope and Mark Catesby on a playing card – reminders that for each carefully prepared session, people also improvised and used whatever was available. Sketches often went hand in hand with the expansion in note-taking, as records of thoughts and observations. Among the most famous notebooks must be those of Renaissance polymath Leonardo da Vinci; filled with words and images these are repositories of the way he worked through and mused on many subjects. While very few reach his intellectual and artistic heights, we can all use a notebook.

Private sketches were often consigned to the artist's folder or the studio floor and were not intended for public consumption or to last beyond their creators' needs. Just such tiny sketches, from the final year of the great Pierre-Joseph Redouté, were gathered up, collected and revered because of his renown. Some works lay between private and public worlds and were admired within domestic circles, by groups of virtuosi or networks of plant obsessives. Such potential riches can fall prey to the vicissitudes of time, and the uncertainties of preservation and accessibility for searchers today. Francis Nicholls's 18th-century parchment manuscript was rescued from the wreckage of the London Blitz. William Griffith's papers from India were dumped in the basement of the East India Company's offices. Santiago Cortés's 19th-century Colombian flora came to Kew via Cyprus – no one knows how. But we are fortunate that sketches not made for posterity or designed to last are now appreciated in collections around the world. Transitory and vulnerable as they are, the experience of bringing them into the light again has been a privilege.

MARTIN SCHONGAUER
Details of this watercolour study of peonies (*Paeonia officinalis*) were used as models for flowers in his painting *Madonna of the Rose Garden* (1473).

Ordering the parts

High botanical art is sumptuous. Its history is generally told as the intertwined importance of naturalism in art and the pressing need for accurate plant identification. Added to this are the developments in the naming of plants (taxonomy), the recognition of the relationships between species (classification), and, as the science of botany matured, a deeper understanding of the structure and function of the parts of the plant. Art and science. Beauty in utility. Botanical sketches are part of the back story. Many sketches in these pages support these narratives, but we have tried to find new ways of looking at them and feature more botanist-artists such as the pre-eminent Joseph Dalton Hooker.

Drawing has rules, but also allows for individual expression. The same concept has been applied to the way we have shaped this book. Chronologically the sketches begin with the rise of naturalism in the 15th century and effectively stop in the later 20th century since we include only the dead. Encounters between cultures, such as when western naturalism came into contact with the very different artistic interpretation of the natural world in the east, produced a fascinating melding of styles. Material from Japan, China and India captures this coming together and reflects the global nature of the aesthetic, scientific and commercial interest in plants.

Sketches have been made in the field and the studio, in the wilderness and in the garden, and for a vast range of motives. We have arranged them into four chapters: 'Made on Location', 'Doing Science', 'Making Art' and 'A Pleasing Occupation'. Each section unfolds chronologically by date of birth; each also combines familiar with less familiar artists, and professionals sit next to amateurs. Of course, different sketches could put their makers into more than one of these chapters and sections. The guiding principle has been to look at the material itself rather than the reputation of the artist. There are images from the rudimentary to the more complete, although one criterion was that the plants featured should be for the most part recognizable and identifiable. The aim has been to offer a broad selection of the many wonderful possibilities.

Sketchers create an image from the blank page up. Despite photography's many virtues, the early cameras in unskilled hands could not approach the vivid freshness of a sketch, producing images often of poor quality in uninspiring shades of grey. But the photograph quickly assumed the role of the sketchbook, especially in the field. Learning to draw, once regarded as an important accomplishment, fell out of fashion. Perhaps the ready availability of sketching apps will reverse this trend, although still nothing feels like pencil or brush and paper in the hand. Botanical art, always appreciated in science, is flourishing again, thanks to both patrons and practitioners. Sketching is an inseparable part of this. The 19th-century German botanist Julius von Sachs was right: 'If you haven't drawn it, you haven't seen it.'

JOSEPH DALTON HOOKER
Sheltering from heavy rain on an excursion from Darjeeling, Hooker sketched this immense climbing pseudovine *Wightia speciosissima*, first in pencil (above right) then in more detail in ink (above left). (Below) 'The Cholera Tree' (*Ficus religiosa*).

Introduction

Wightia.

Wightia.

The Cadera Tree
Burkutta

I Made on Location

For as long as we have used and cherished plants we have transported them around the globe. Amassing plant collections, growing living samples in botanical gardens, curating dried ones in herbaria and creating paper museums of images – all have involved people moving about, too, and working on location. This resulted in camaraderie and competition. *Adventurers* often came across plants by default, as they fulfilled their desire to travel and see the world first-hand. *Collectors* made searching for plants their livelihood, seeking a living commodity in foreign floras. Passionate amateurs practised *botany on the side* whenever and wherever their occupations allowed. For those charged with the exploitation of new lands for trade and empire, the understanding and assimilation of plant knowledge were part of their *imperial projects*. All used sketches to help them achieve their aims.

FRANCIS HALL
Hall was able to begin to identify some of the plants he found on his perambulations around Quito, Ecuador. The orchid (top left) is probably *Otoglossum palaciosii*, which was only formally described in 1996 by orchidologists at Kew; (top right) *Loasa tricolor*; (below) *Bauhinia forficata*.

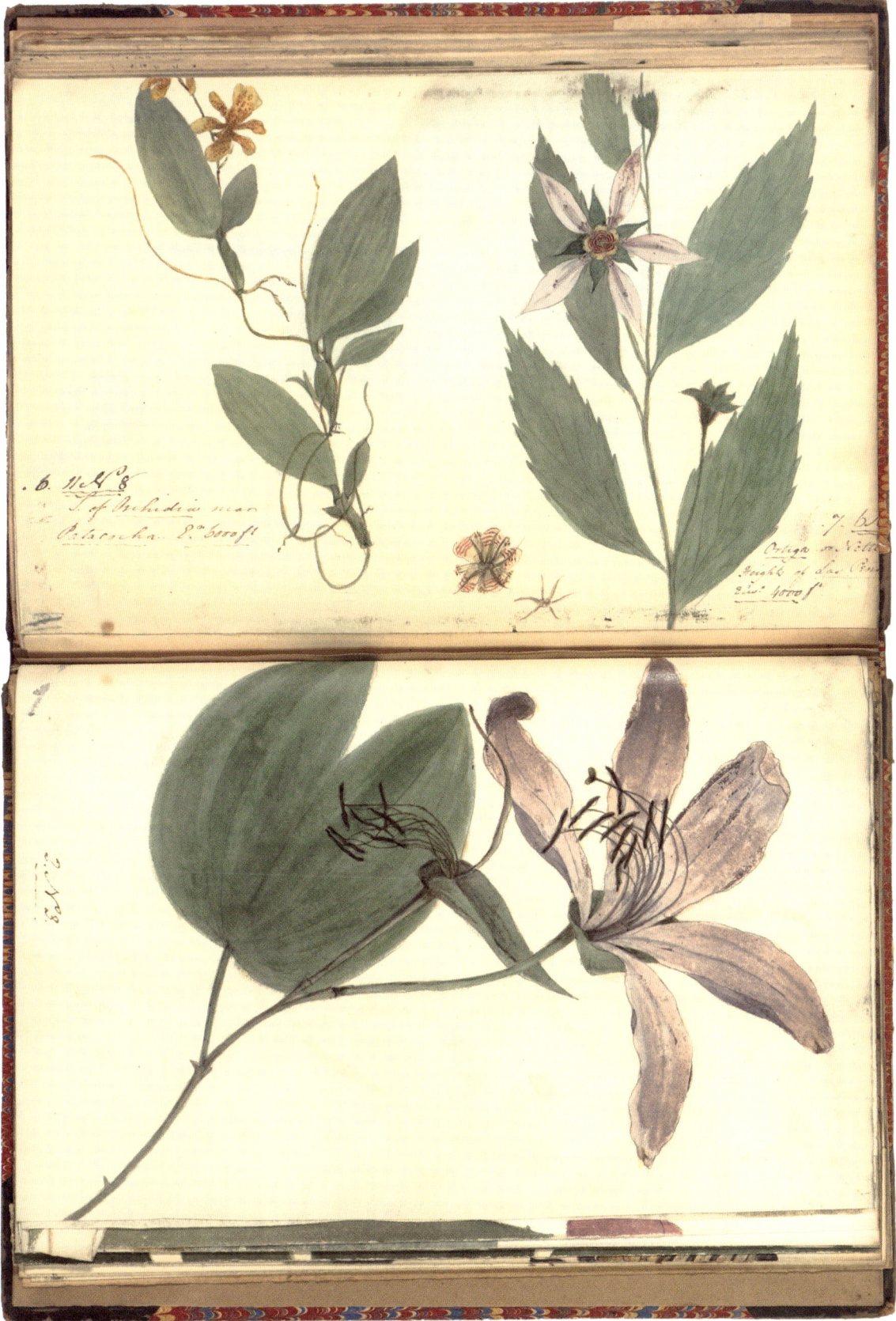

adventurers

People who are afflicted with wanderlust willingly put up with privation and danger in order to experience the thrill of exploration, and they are prepared to do it again and again. All the adventurers here made multiple journeys. Mark Catesby surveyed the southeastern states of America, while John Muir and Frederick Andrews Walpole traversed the western side of the continent. Thomas Baines, James Augustus Grant and John Kirk ranged through sub-Saharan Africa before modern, colonial-era boundaries were imposed. Margaret Mee navigated the waterways of the Amazon Basin, where the magnificent rainforest was already under threat. All were explorers whose fascination with nature, appreciation of ecology and understanding of the living world made their plant sketches a vivid and lasting record of their journeys.

MARK CATESBY

Sometimes called 'the colonial Audubon' because of his pioneering bird paintings, Mark Catesby (1683–1749) was above all a plants man. He grew up on the Suffolk–Essex border, near the eminent naturalist John Ray, a friend of his uncle. Although of middle-class stock, Catesby did not go to university, working instead for the successful nurseryman Thomas Fairchild in Hoxton, east London. Taking advantage of his sister's marriage, Catesby spent seven years in Virginia, USA, from 1712. He explored in a gentle way and sent new plants and seeds back, but he considered this initial trip unfruitful.

Catesby underestimated his success, however, and his reputation took him back to North America in 1722, with the support of several well-connected naturalists and botanists. His brief was to explore thoroughly, and record and collect in the southeastern regions of the continent, travelling as far as the Bahamas. This was adventure with a purpose. Back in England again, he spent the rest of his life turning his sketches and more finished drawings into his magnum opus: *Natural History of Carolina, Florida and the Bahama Islands* (1729–47); 'Florida' here refers to what is now Georgia. He drew ecological inspiration from the art of Maria Sibylla Merian (p. 128), while from Georg Ehret (p. 220) he learnt improved three-dimensionality. The book was widely acclaimed and contributed to Catesby's election to the Royal Society in 1733.

In the field, Catesby sketched mostly with pen and ink, sometimes adding watercolour or using colour notes. He then elaborated his drawings in his lodgings, where he also drew from specimens. In London, after settling in Fairchild's employ again in 1726, he continued to draw from plants cultivated in various nurseries and gardens from his own introductions.

Catesby's fresh renderings of skunk cabbage (*Symplocarpus foetidus*) (left), and the interlocking sprigs of sweet bay (*Magnolia virginiana*) and sassafras (*Sassafras albidum*) (opposite above) became much more elaborate in the published plates. (Opposite below) Ancient plants preserved in amber were highly collectable curiosities, and Catesby sketched two views of this example on the back of a playing card.

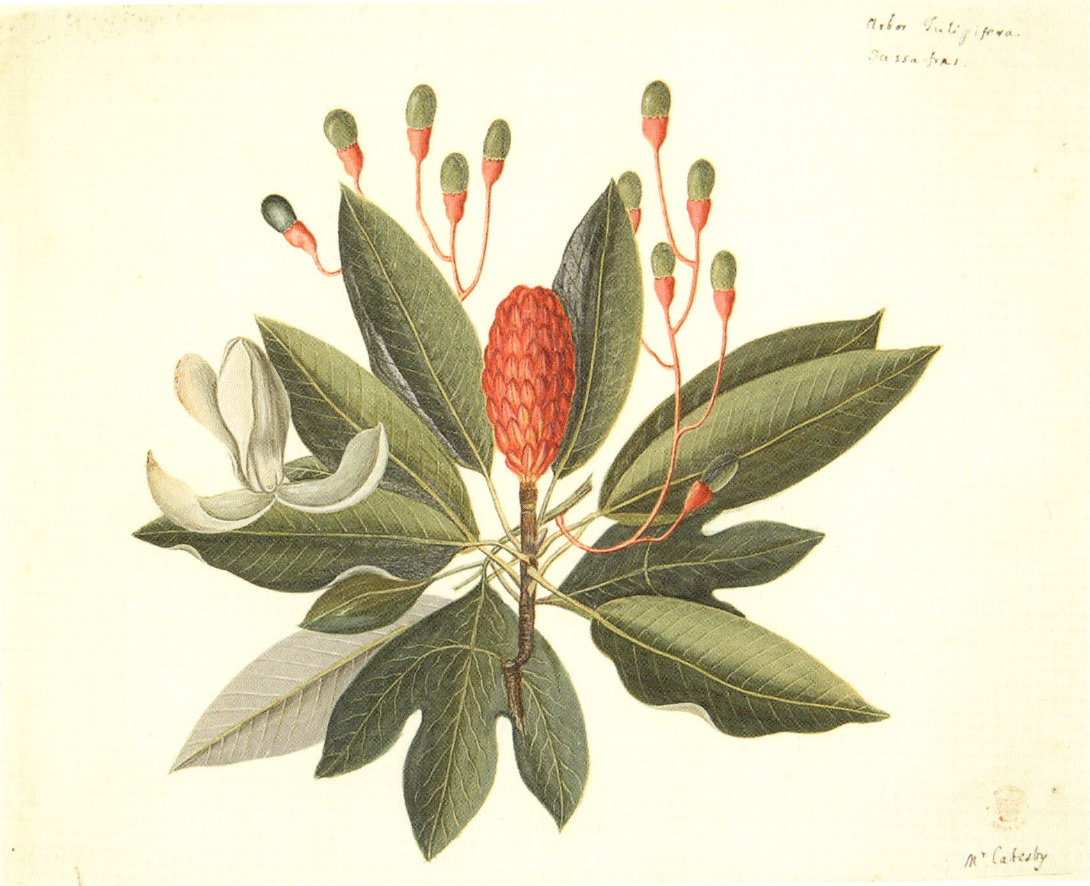
Arbor Tulipifera
Sassafras
Mr Catesby

A piece of amber found in Prussia now in the cabinet of Mr. Kleyn Secretary or Recorder of Dantzig.
BRITISH MUSEUM

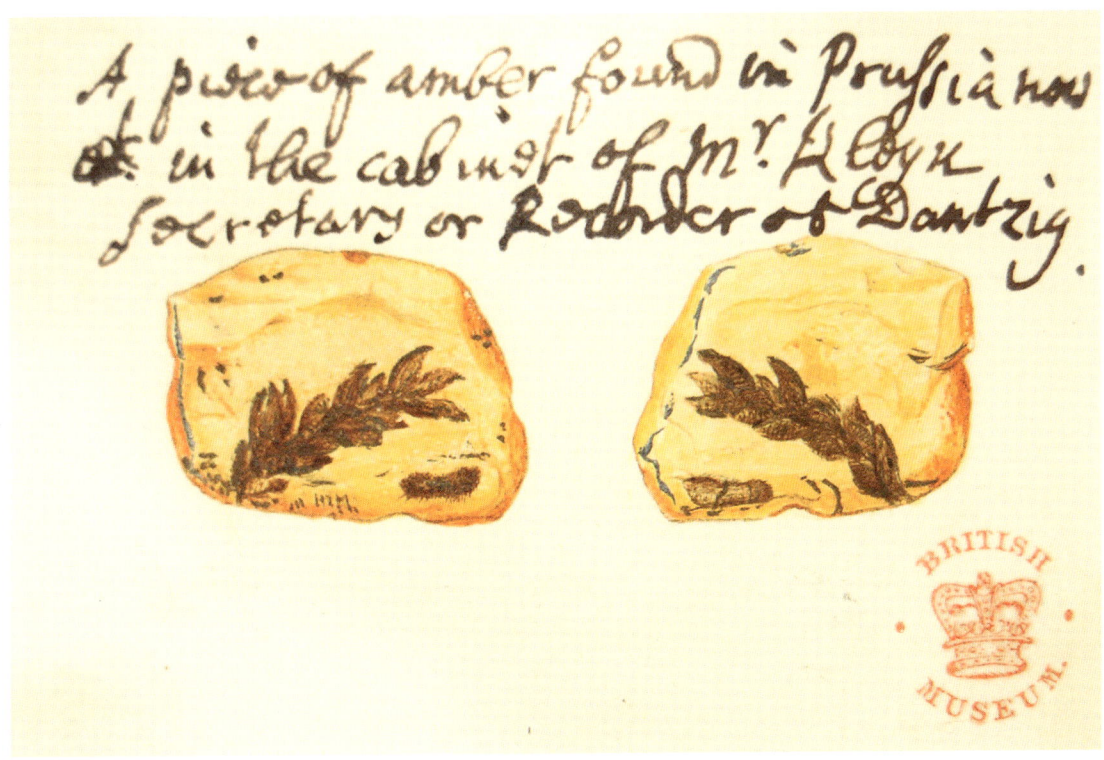

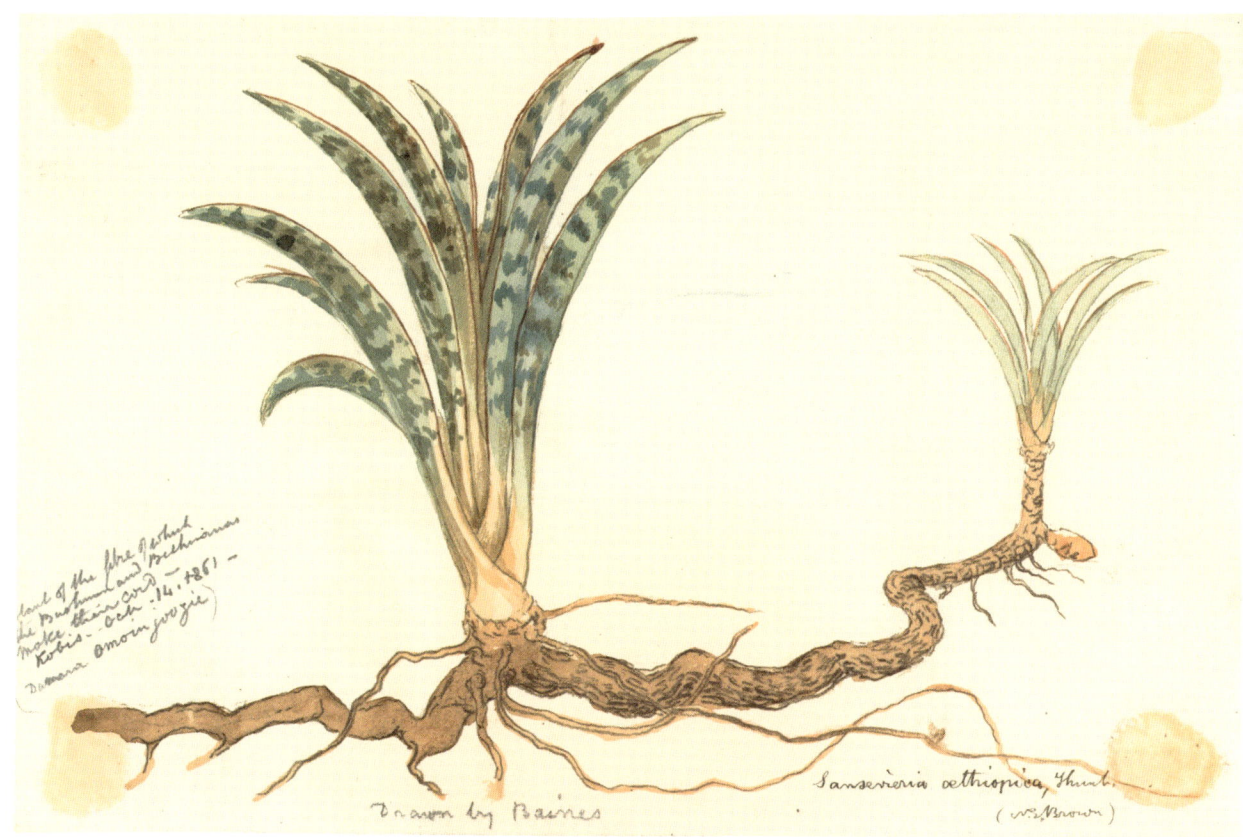

THOMAS BAINES

Thomas Baines (1820–1875) was an artist who explored rather than an explorer who drew. He grew up on the north Norfolk coast of England in a talented family – his brother Henry became a professional artist – and after an apprenticeship as a painter of heraldic arms on coaches began his career painting portraits and maritime subjects. He also painted battlefield scenes, and in the early 1850s was official war artist during the Cape Frontier Wars in South Africa. On his return to England he became attached to the Royal Geographical Society. From then on, the urge to trek never seemed to leave him, despite a pronounced limp ('Cripple Thigh' was a cruel nickname) caused by an improperly set fracture.

Baines went first to northwest Australia in 1855 and then to Africa in 1858 in an abortive association with David Livingstone as storekeeper and artist. For most of the rest of his short adult life he travelled back and forth between Africa and Britain. In 1861 he set out with South African explorer James Chapman on an expedition to the Victoria Falls, and finally searched for gold mines in the Transvaal, dying of dysentery at Durban aged 54. He financed his travels through lectures, books and his art, his mother acting as his chief publicist and agent.

Wherever he went, Baines always sketched, drew and painted, in watercolours as well as oils, and was curious in equal measure about the people, landscapes and flora and fauna of the places he explored. His artist's eye made him a good topographer – he produced valuable maps – and he collected plants as well as drawing them. He also revisited his sketches, noting how the spectacular rains of the African drylands affected the plants. In a process akin to time-lapse photography he built up his drawings, recording the form of short-lived flowers as they changed over the course of a few hours. Often he included himself in his paintings, which helped to provide a sense of scale, but also hints at how at home he felt in these alien landscapes.

On 14 October 1861 at 'Kobis' near Lake Ngami (now in Botswana) Baines sketched the seeds of 'stinkwood' (*Terminalia prunioides*, opposite below) and a fibre-producing succulent (*Sansevieria aethiopica*, above) as he attempted to cross Africa with Chapman. (Opposite above) The strange fruit and leaves of *Sterculia africana*.

adventurers 17

I   Made on Location

(Previous pages) *Pancratium tenuifolium* (page 18), sketched first between 3 and 4 p.m. in bud, and again between 6 and 7 p.m. in flower. 'The flower showed signs of opening about sunset and burst or rather exploded into full bloom immediately after', noted Baines. (Page 19) Magnificent *Crinum crassicaule*.

(Above) Baines painted himself into this remarkable landscape dominated by the tree aloe, *Aloe barberae*, in May 1861. (Opposite) 'A Palmyra tree' (*Hyphaene petersiana*).

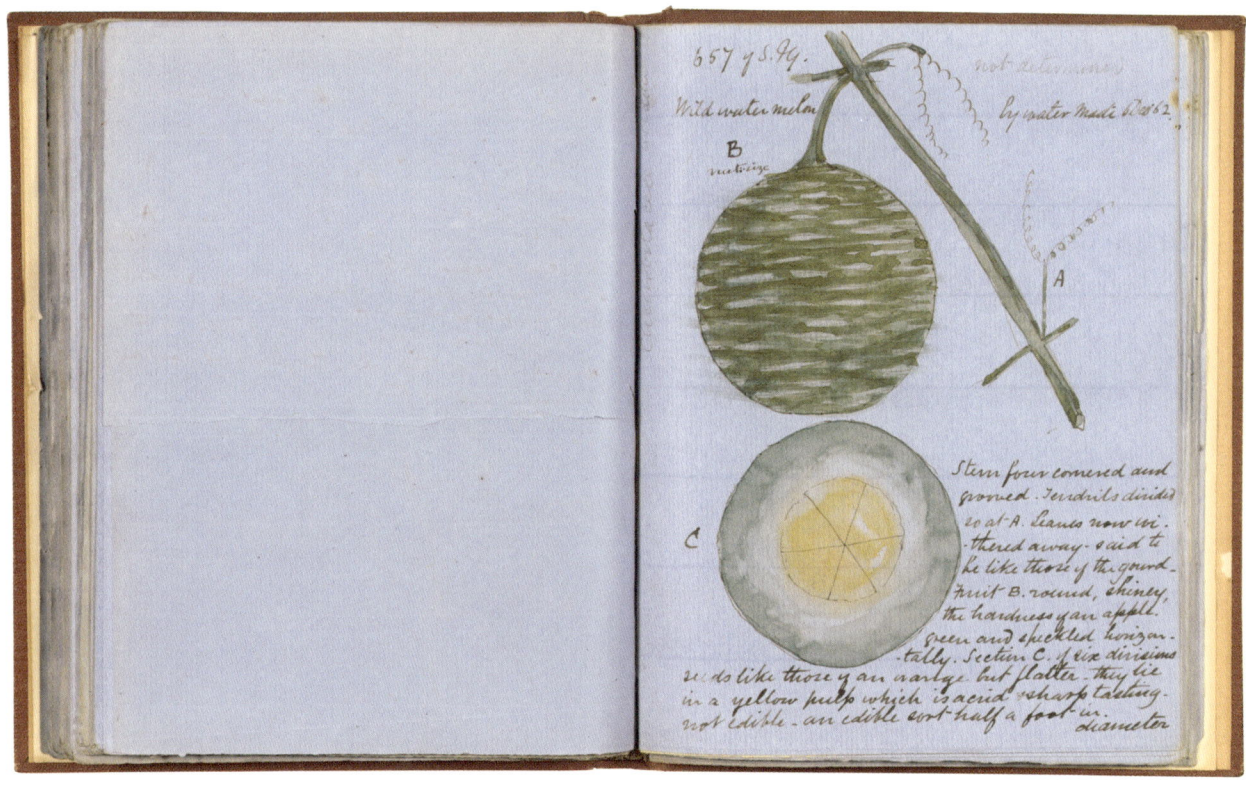

JAMES AUGUSTUS GRANT

While an army officer in India, James Augustus Grant (1827–1892) energetically pursued his passion for shooting. But he was also a keen watercolourist and botanist, having studied botany and natural history at Marischal College, Aberdeen, and taken drawing and perspective lessons from a local artist. At the end of his ten years in India, during the relief of Lucknow in the Indian Rebellion of 1857, he lost his right thumb and forefinger and was invalided home.

Grant's next adventure was in Africa. He volunteered for the expedition of 1860–63 sponsored by the Royal Geographical Society and led by his old shooting companion John Hanning Speke, who was determined to confirm Lake Victoria (Nyanza) as the primary source of the White Nile. But at the crucial stage of the journey, Grant was unwell and couldn't verify Speke's report, which remained contentious for several years.

Grant was able to paint, however, and his 250 watercolours provide a striking record of their famous expedition. And despite the weather, terrain and a brush with robbers, the potential for botanizing also appealed to Grant: 'it occurred to me that many a pleasant hour might be spent in collecting plants'. He collected 761 African plants, 113 of which were new to science, and thanks to the African porterage they arrived at the coast to be shipped home. Although some of Grant's drawings enlivened Speke's published account of the journey, his own *A Walk Across Africa* (1864) is curiously unillustrated.

With the help of Grant's detailed notes and field drawings, others, including Thomas Thomson at the Linnean Society and Daniel Oliver at Kew, were able to identify and classify some of his finds. Walter Hood Fitch (p. 156) illustrated a volume on the expedition's botany, with Grant paying for the engravings. Grant's real fascination lay with ecological relationships, and the indigenous people and their use of so much of the African flora for food, medicine and practical, material goods. It was a new way of seeing the world.

This 'Notes & Sketches' album holds copies Grant made from his field notes when they were sent to Thomson to identify. Most are marked 'undetermined' and were not included in the publications, but notes added later (see opposite top) reveal that Grant continued to ponder the expedition's botany.

460 of S.Ay. Undetermined?
~~Composite~~ plant- foot-high. Root A a bulb
not-scaled, inside it is of the colour of boiled
beet-root. A" shoots S rise from its
crown. 20S. March 4 - 16? Leaves thick
sessile, opp., linear or
like the leaves of an orchid & her-
-baceous like the whole plant
& clasping round
the stem B.
Inflorescence as in
fig C. a corymb of
deep brown flowers
each of which has a
small flat bractea.
calyx of five equal,
green parts deeply
divided and seemingly
attached to the corolla. Corolla of five equal, brown
parts having five smaller ones or filaments
between the chief petals, in this way I mean D
stamina five, of the form of a seed E and only
got at by squeezing them out of the flower - too
diminutive to examine the pistil.

Banana sp?
Village near Lake Shirwa, at 3000ft elevation. Lat.15°
Seeds worn by women as charms for purification.
(Grows also on the mountains of Gorongozo in Lat. 18°S.)

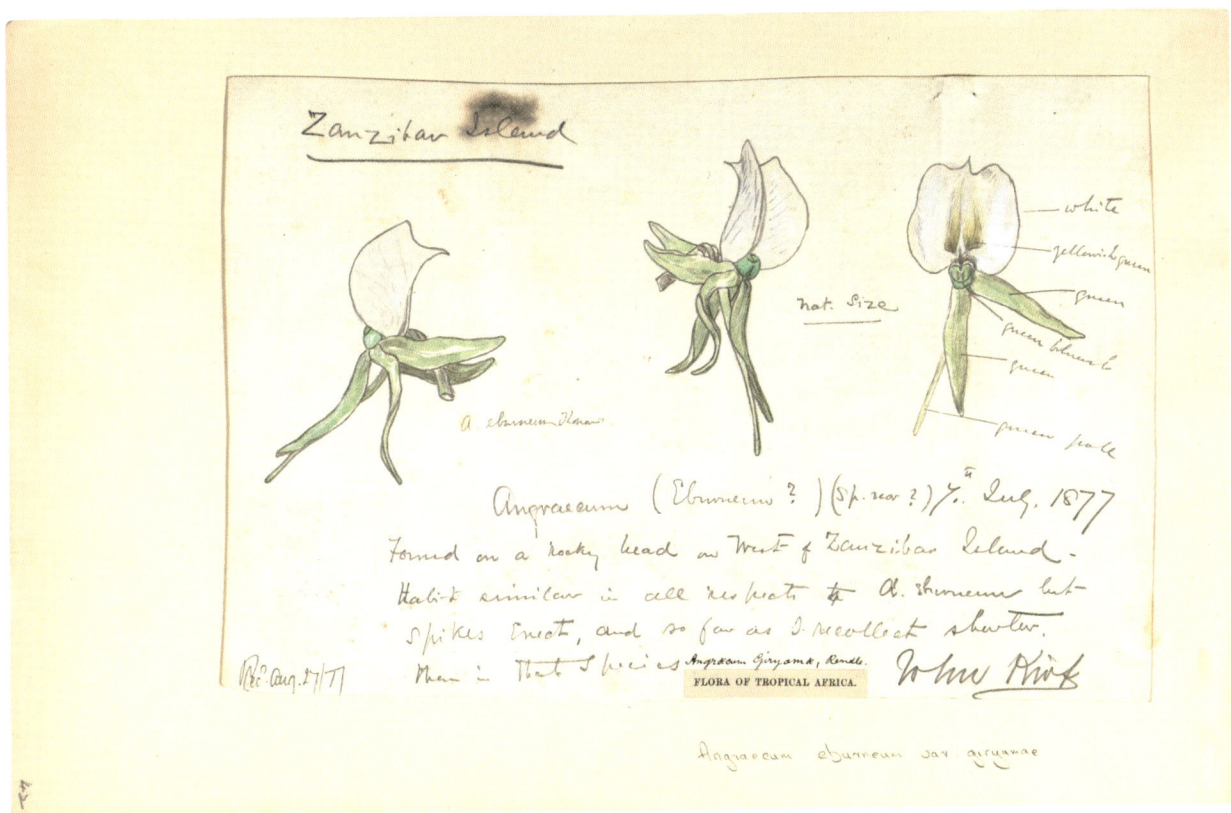

JOHN KIRK

Like many would-be biologists of his era, John Kirk (1832–1922) settled for medicine as a safer career option, but botany was his first love. After medical school at Edinburgh University he volunteered for the Crimean War, working in a hospital but finding time to roam the countryside of Asia Minor in search of plants (and animals). He returned to England just as David Livingstone's second Zambezi expedition (1858–63) was being organized. As his interests and qualifications fitted the ill-fated expedition's requirements perfectly, Kirk was taken on as medical officer and botanist.

His diaries reveal how much of his time was taken up in tending to Dr Livingstone's repeated attacks of diarrhoea, haemorrhoids and teeth problems, and Kirk himself suffered several bouts of fever and serious illness, but he revelled in the new plants and vistas. He sketched useful details of the leaf and fruit of the 'most singular palm' *Hyphaene coriacea*, noting how its topmost fans gave an 'effect to the landscape seen in no other country'.

Many of his botanical specimens and drawings were lost when his canoe capsized (and almost drowned him), but Kirk emerged with credit from the expedition. In 1866 he was appointed as vice-consul and medical officer on the island of Zanzibar, where he pursued his botanical researches and worked towards the abolition of the African slave trade. He was also able to aid Livingstone in his later African explorations. During his long retirement in England, Kirk continued to be involved in African affairs and was active in both the Royal and Linnean societies.

Kirk published many of his finds among the African flora, and also sent plant material and descriptions to colleagues at Kew and elsewhere. His detailed field sketches and notes were appreciated in his lifetime and continue to assist the work of botanists today.

(Above) Flower details with colour notes of the orchid *Angraecum eburneum* var. *giryamae* from Zanzibar.
(Opposite) The false banana *Ensete livingstonianum*.

(Overleaf) *Nauclea* sp. and '*Ipomoea pterygocaulis*' (*Merremia pterygocaulos*) (left), and *Hyphaene coriacea* (right), all from Livingstone's second Zambezi expedition.

adventurers 27

Mandea sp? M'Kindu Kindu
Opposite Senna [J. Kirk]
28 Dec 1860

Choisy
Ipomoea pterygocaulos
= Merremia pterygocaulos, Hall. f.

J. Kirk
Hyphaene Coriacea
Leaf of much = Doom Palm. Kongone
3d March 1860

Hyphaene Coriacea
J. Kirk
Hyphaene coriacea

J. Kirk
Hyphaene Coriacea Glistrini
(Ripe fruit. See Museum Kew)
Zambezi May 23 1859

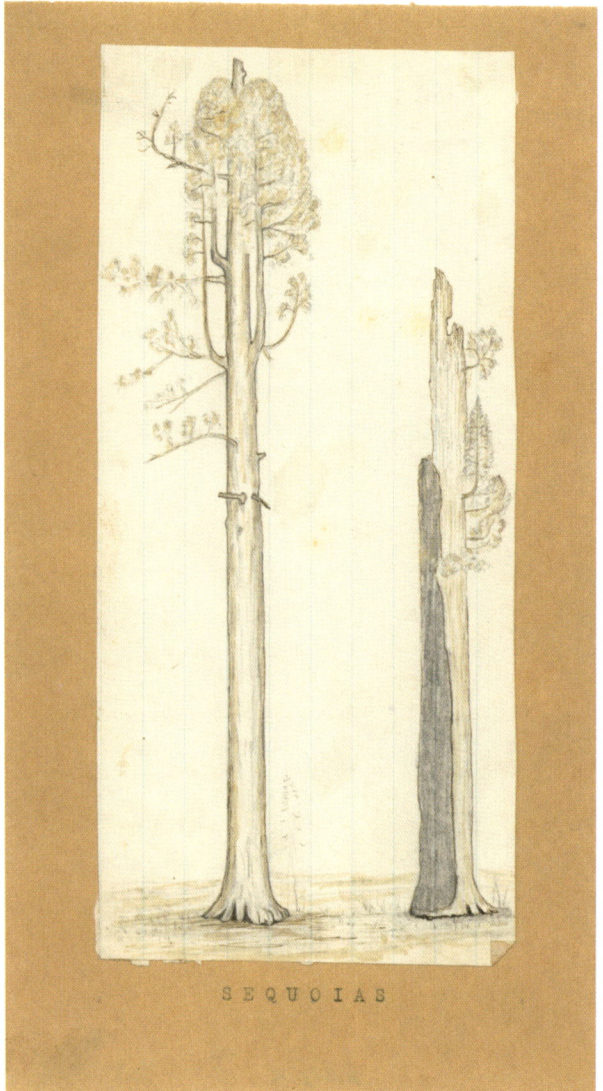

SEQUOIAS

JOHN MUIR

'I gazed and gazed and longed and admired … made hurried notes and a sketch, though there was no need for either, for the colours and lines and expression of this divine landscape-countenance are so burned into mind and heart they surely can never grow dim.' For John Muir (1838–1914), sketching took second place to experiencing. Even so, he sketched prolifically, and his drawings, mostly in pencil or ink, grace the many books he published.

Muir discovered his love of nature in his native Scotland, before moving with his family to Wisconsin in 1849. He managed to escape a dominant, religiously obsessed father, and received a scientific training at the University of Wisconsin. A clever inventor, Muir could have made his fortune. Instead, he loved to walk alone in nature, including a thousand-mile trek in the eastern United States before heading west. Arriving in San Francisco, he asked the first person he saw for the road out of town and never looked back.

Although his nature worship followed in the footsteps of American writers Henry David Thoreau and Ralph Waldo Emerson, he was always his own man, with his own style. Seemingly impervious to discomfort, he needed only bread and water to survive. Much of his wilderness time was spent in northern California, but he also trekked in Canada (from 1864) and Alaska (from 1879). He made serious contributions to the study of the glacial origins of the Yosemite Valley, and discovered a number of new species of plants and animals. Trees especially delighted him, but so too did plants of all kinds, as well as insects, mammals, clouds, streams – indeed the whole world, especially in its pristine state.

Muir's permanent legacy lies in his promotion of the American National Parks and the conservation movement – he maintained that such tracts of land needed to be preserved from human greed and exploitation. He also helped found the Sierra Club as an advocacy group.

(Opposite) A sketch in the Tuolumne River canyon of the Sierra Nevada Mountains, California, around 1872, where common coniferous trees are sugar, ponderosa and grey pines, incense cedar and sequoia (redwood; also left). Muir referred to the latter as the 'King': 'Do behold the King in his glory, King Sequoia!'

FREDERICK ANDREWS WALPOLE

Anyone who walks the final 285 km (177 miles) to Trail, Oregon, to find a site for a homestead certainly has something of the adventurer in him. Frederick Andrews Walpole (1861–1904) left Chicago and headed west in 1882. He had probably studied art with the landscape and portrait artist Junius R. Sloan, an academician at the Chicago Academy of Design, who took his students on paid sketching trips and advocated the 'Gospel of Nature'. Sloan was a devotee of John Ruskin (p. 206), an enthusiasm Walpole shared. How and when Walpole learnt his botany is less clear, but the annotations on his 800-odd drawings and sketches are evidence of his botanical literacy. Evident, too, is his appreciation of subtle differences in the colour and form of fruit and leaves on the same plant, and between different plants of the same species in various locations.

By 1896 Walpole had been working for ten years as a lithographic artist in Portland, where he had moved. In September that year his work was noticed by Frederick V. Colville, chief botanist of the Department of Agriculture and curator of the National Herbarium in Washington, DC, who was investigating the medicinal plants used by the Klamath people in Oregon. Congress had voted in 1889 to provide funds for botanical exploration and collecting in little known areas of America, and good artists were valuable assets. With Colville's encouragement, Walpole successfully applied for a post as botanical artist for the Department of Agriculture.

Walpole liked to sketch plants from life in their natural surroundings. Field sketches, often drawn in graphite, watercolour and very fine ink, could then be worked up in the studio. These preferences were also practical in the northern latitudes, with a busy part of the year spent in the field in the warmer months and the remainder in the herbarium in Washington, DC. Here Walpole also sketched from preserved specimens, making comparisons with his field work. In 1900 and 1901 he made two trips to Alaska, searching for specimens of medicinal plants and appreciating the way of life of the indigenous people. A few years later he died of typhoid in the field, sadly echoing his wife's death in 1898 from the same disease.

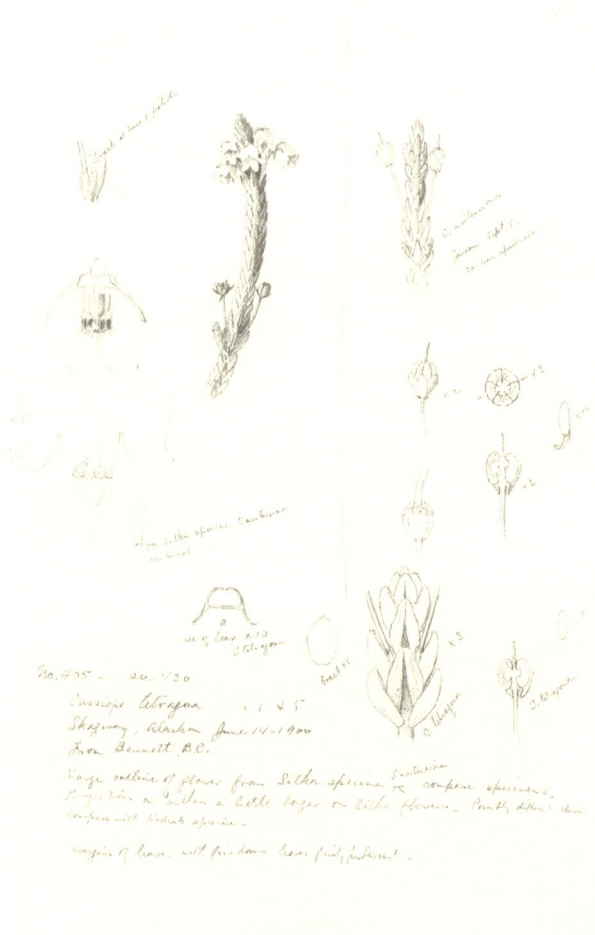

(Above right) Pencil sketch of the white mountain Arctic heather, *Cassiope tetragona*, illustrating Walpole's practice of comparing specimens in the field and studio. (Right) *Pinus attenuata*, the knobcone pine. (Opposite) '*Scirpus lacustris occidentalis*' (*Schoenoplectus acutus*) or tule: its stems and red roots were used in basket-making by the Klamath people. The rootstock was sketched on a second visit to the Klamath Falls.

adventurers 33

(Opposite) The harebell, *Campanula rotundifolia*, Kodiak, Alaska, 16 July 1900. (Above left) Details of the flower spike of *Dasylirion glaucophyllum*, an early sketch from 1897. (Above right) Fruit of '*Nymphaea polysepala*' (*Nuphar polysepala*), the yellow water lily found in enormous tracts of the Klamath marsh. The mature seeds, or *wokas*, were an important food source for the Klamath people.

MARGARET MEE

For Margaret Mee (1909–1988), essentials for plant sketching on her fifteen forays on the rivers of the Amazon Basin were drawing materials, plant baskets and a hammock – these were her priorities should her boat sink. This was a world little known to outsiders, and through her art, sketched first on these adventures, Mee helped reveal its flora to a growing global audience. Her repeated visits were overshadowed by a realization that the forests, home to perhaps a fifth of the world's plant species, were being destroyed at an alarming rate by the rapacity of the modern world and its hunger for minerals, rubber, timber and land for grazing and crops. Mee became a potent voice for the preservation of this wilderness and its indigenous people.

All this occurred in the second half of Mee's life, after she had trained as a mature student under British artist Victor Pasmore. From Pasmore's abstraction she acquired an understanding of the importance of shape, and carried this into her plant portraits, catching the wonderful forms of the Amazonian flora with an artist's eye. In time she would develop a botanist's eye, too, and became adept at recognizing new species.

In 1952 Margaret and Greville Mee moved to São Paulo, Brazil, which became the base for Margaret's local and long-distance sketching trips, from 1956 to 1988. She travelled with various, usually female, friends, local crews and a loaded revolver. In 1968 the couple moved to Rio, and Margaret strengthened her links with Brazilian botanists and artists. An early commission led her to concentrate on bromeliads, an association that was celebrated in the 1994 Rio Carnival. Almost inevitably, the multiplicity of orchids became another favourite. Since Mee drew only from life, gathering the precious specimens involved precarious scrambles in trees. Insects, from stinging ants and wasps, to biting flies and malaria-carrying mosquitoes, were a constant menace.

Her 1988 journey to capture on paper the night-flowering moonflower cactus (*Selenicereus wittii*) was both a final quest and a deliberately public affair to raise awareness for projects dear to her. Tragically, Mee died in a car crash in England that same year. Part of her legacy has been the preservation of her sketchbooks, the intimate record of an amazing talent and an equally amazing flora.

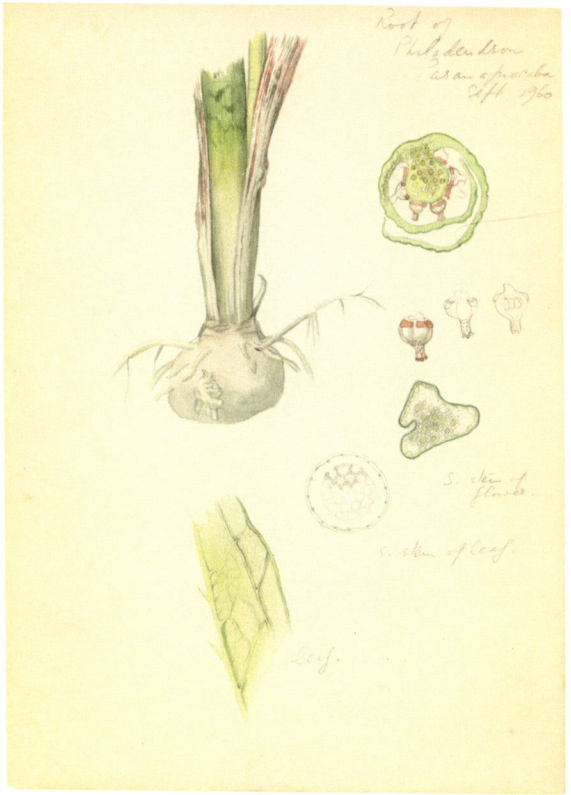

Nidularium innocentii bract from 1961 (above left) and root and sections of *Philodendron* sp., 1960 (left). (Opposite) Female flowers of the orchid *Catasetum macrocarpum*, 1981.

(Overleaf) *Aristolochia* sp. and *Mucuna urens* from Mee's first Amazonian adventure, Gurupí River, 1956–57.

collectors

Novelty in the garden can be created by patiently breeding new plants, or by searching elsewhere among the floral riches of another country or continent. Plant hunting could be a lucrative activity, but was often fraught with unforeseen problems. Independent collectors such as William Bartram in North America or Alfred Russel Wallace and Friedrich Carl Lehmann in South America needed contacts and agents for commercial success. Francis Masson went to South Africa with a stipend, but had to satisfy his paymasters. Maria Graham Callcott and Helen Faulkner were fortunate in being able to collect as a service to others. William Burchell, like his massive, unsorted collection, is difficult to categorize, and demonstrates how collecting can be compulsive and all-consuming.

WILLIAM BARTRAM

Important botanical networks were established between Britain and her American colonies before the American Revolutionary War; happily, they continued after its conclusion. An early interchange involved Peter Collinson, a Quaker merchant in London with a passion for plants, and John Bartram, also a Quaker, with a large garden near Philadelphia. Collinson acted as Bartram's contact in England, distributing to subscribers the shipments of plants and seeds that Bartram sent. Bartram collected further and further afield, and in 1765 took his son William (1739–1823) with him to the American south.

Although he was completely untaught, William's artistic talents emerged early, and he was always happiest wandering in the wilderness, observing and drawing plants and animals, especially birds. His natural dreaminess put paid to efforts to set him up as a shopkeeper and his own attempt to establish himself in Florida as a grower of indigo, then much in demand in England. However, his nature drawings impressed John Fothergill, a London physician who had become John Bartram's agent after Collinson's death. Fothergill offered to fund an expedition into South Carolina, Georgia and Florida. Bartram roamed for four years, from 1773, mostly alone and with the blessing of Native American tribes, who called him *Puc-puggy*, the 'Flower Hunter'. He did not publish his resulting journal, *Travels through North & South Carolina …* until 1791, but Wordsworth, Coleridge and other Romantic poets prized the London edition for its lyrical descriptions of the flora and fauna of the American South.

Whatever Bartram's superb drawings illustrated, they all reflect a deep feeling for nature. He spent the last decades of his life working in the nursery his father had established in Kingsessing, Philadelphia, where his fame ensured a steady stream of high-profile visitors including many naturalists, as well as Thomas Jefferson (no mean naturalist himself). Bartram declined an offer of a chair in botany at the University of Pennsylvania and although elected to the American Philosophical Society, he never attended a meeting.

Bartram referred to the large-flowered evening primrose *Oenothera grandiflora* (left) as 'the most pompous and brilliant herbaceous plant yet known to exist'. He sent seeds and dried plants of it to London in 1775, along with the oak-leaved hydrangea, *Hydrangea quercifolia* (opposite).

FRANCIS MASSON

If it was the result of the vision of the well-connected Joseph Banks that so much of South Africa's unique flora came to Britain, the groundwork was performed by his humble emissary, Francis Masson (1741–1805). Masson, who hailed from Aberdeen, was under-gardener to William Aiton at Kew and was sent by Banks on HMS *Resolution* as far as Cape Town on James Cook's second voyage in 1772.

From this base, Masson made short forays, becoming accustomed to the landscape. He then ventured three times into the interior on more extended collecting trips, twice with the Swedish naturalist Carl Peter Thunberg, using local ox-carts and drivers. The journeys were often uncomfortable, with extremes of heat and occasional cold, and the constant threat of danger from hippopotami, hyenas and snakes, but they did provide the modest Scot with breathtaking botanical vistas. He wrote of 'an infinite variety of plants peculiar to this country', with luxuriant 'meadows ... enriched with great variety of *ixiae*, *gladioli* and *irides*' and desert 'succulent plants ... never seen before ... which appeared to us like a new creation'. Masson kept journals on his travels and sketched his botanical discoveries, and later published a book on his finds among the *Stapelia* succulents.

His drawings were also a feature of his later expeditions to the West Indies, Canaries and Azores, Portugal and Algeria. While in Grenada in 1779 he was effectively press-ganged for the unsuccessful defence of the island against French attack, losing his papers and plant collections in the mêlée.

Masson returned to the Cape in 1785 and stayed for ten years. His foraging was circumscribed by tensions between the Dutch and the British, and Banks also wanted more thorough surveys of a smaller region. The restriction allowed Masson to cultivate as well as collect, and his garden became an important staging post. Here he could sketch, too, aware that images were sometimes the best means of documenting plants difficult to transport or cultivate, or which were so exotic people might otherwise doubt they actually existed.

Masson was particularly fascinated by succulents, as seen here: '*Mesambryanthemum simplex*' (above right) from the Karoo desert region of South Africa and '*Dactylopsis digitata*' (opposite above). (Opposite below) '*Stapelia reticulata*' – Masson published a book with his own illustrations, entitled *Stapeliae Novae: or, A Collection of Several New Species of that Genus* ... (1796–97).

I Made on Location

Dactylopsis digitata (Ait.) N.E.Br.
Mesembryanthemum digitatum Ait
(Drawn by Masson)
Rec'd from Brit Mus. 9/1888.

Stapelia reticulata. 6
Fr. Masson pinxit

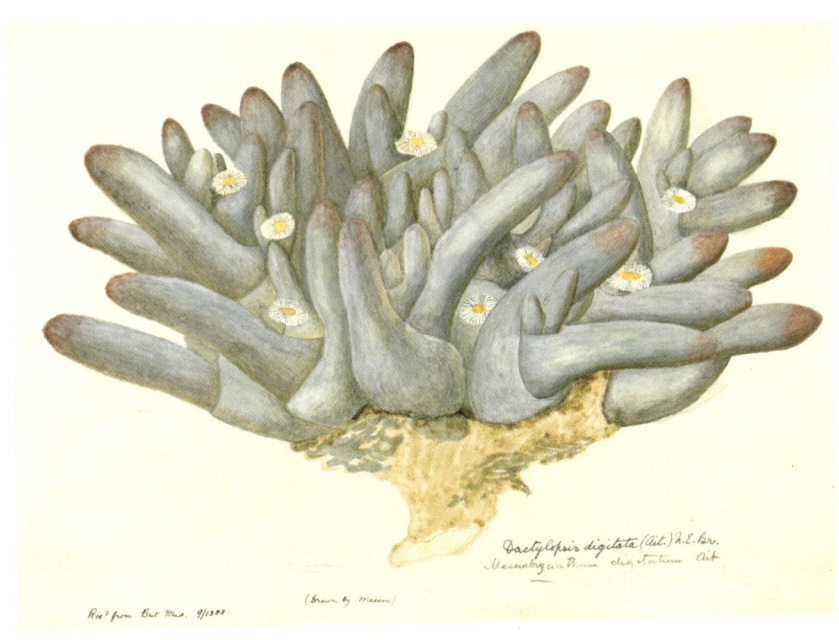

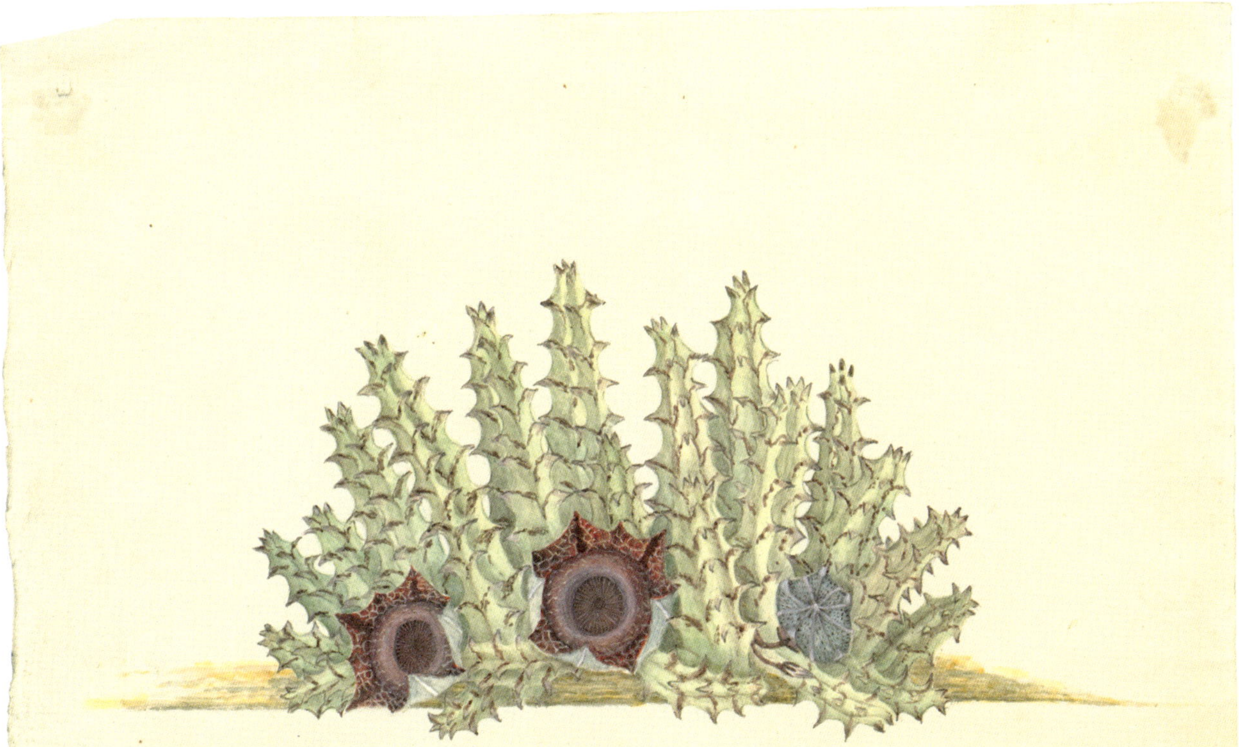

WILLIAM BURCHELL

'I now possess about 15,000 species of plants, all gathered by my own hand in their natural places of growth', wrote William Burchell (1781–1863) on his return to England from Brazil in 1830. There can be no doubt that he was an indefatigable collector. Born in Fulham to a nurseryman father, Burchell later spent some fifteen years of his life overseas, amassing natural history specimens and drawing. Wherever he went he recorded what he saw in its totality – plants, animals, people, landscapes. This comprehensive approach was all-embracing: he adapted a wagon for travel and as a studio in South Africa, and used astronomy and trigonometry to fix precisely plant locations and the dimensions of landscape features.

After study at Kew and election to the Linnean Society, Burchell's first experience of botany on foreign soil came on St Helena (1805–10). The governor, an agent of the East India Company, employed him as schoolteacher and naturalist, and Burchell was the first botanist to live for an extended period on this remote South Atlantic island. His botanizing there was significant: it revealed the endemic flora's uniqueness and its fragility. Burchell realized careless cutting of the giant gum trees threatened them with extinction, while generalized plant loss precipitated soil erosion. Enthused by the Romantic movement, he experienced, and captured in his sketches, 'the most peculiar gratification' in the St Helena landscape.

He followed this up with extensive exploration in South Africa (1810–15) and finally journeys in Brazil (1825–30), collecting voraciously everywhere he went. When, after his death, his sister donated his herbarium of dried plants to Kew, it comprised 57,000 specimens.

With so much material, Burchell's inevitable problem was handling, arranging and cataloguing the fruits of his omnivorous gathering. Potential publications could have been illustrated by his superb artwork. *Travels in the Interior of Southern Africa* (1822, 1824), with its fold-out landscape panoramas, ethnographic plates and botanical vignettes, hints at what might have been. After Brazil, however, Burchell gradually withdrew from society, and antagonisms clouded professional relationships; sadly, he took his own life after a period of invalidism.

Burchell's sketches were eclectic, including plant and nature studies and landscapes: (left) *Wahlenbergia burchellii*; (opposite) 'A group of plantains from nature' and a spider and hermit crab.

(Overleaf) A morning glory '*Ipomoea biloba*' (*I. pes-caprae*) and 'A view in St Helena' (left), and 'View of Lot's Wife', where he twice included himself, and 'Pencil sketch of tree ferns' (right).

A group of Plantains from nature.   20.2.1807.   49.   14.

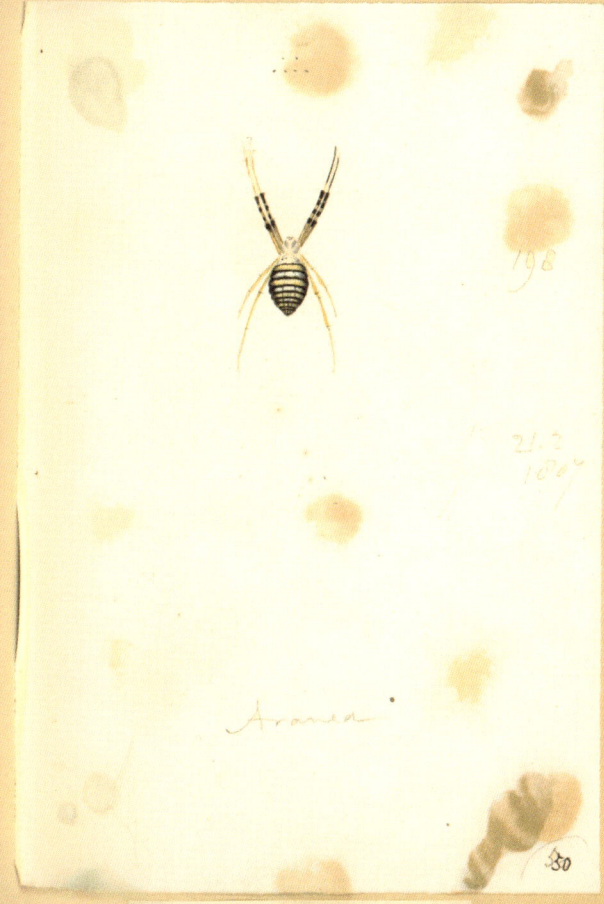

Aranea.   21.2.1807.   50.   198.

[Hermit Crab, Pagurus bernhardus?]   52.   197.

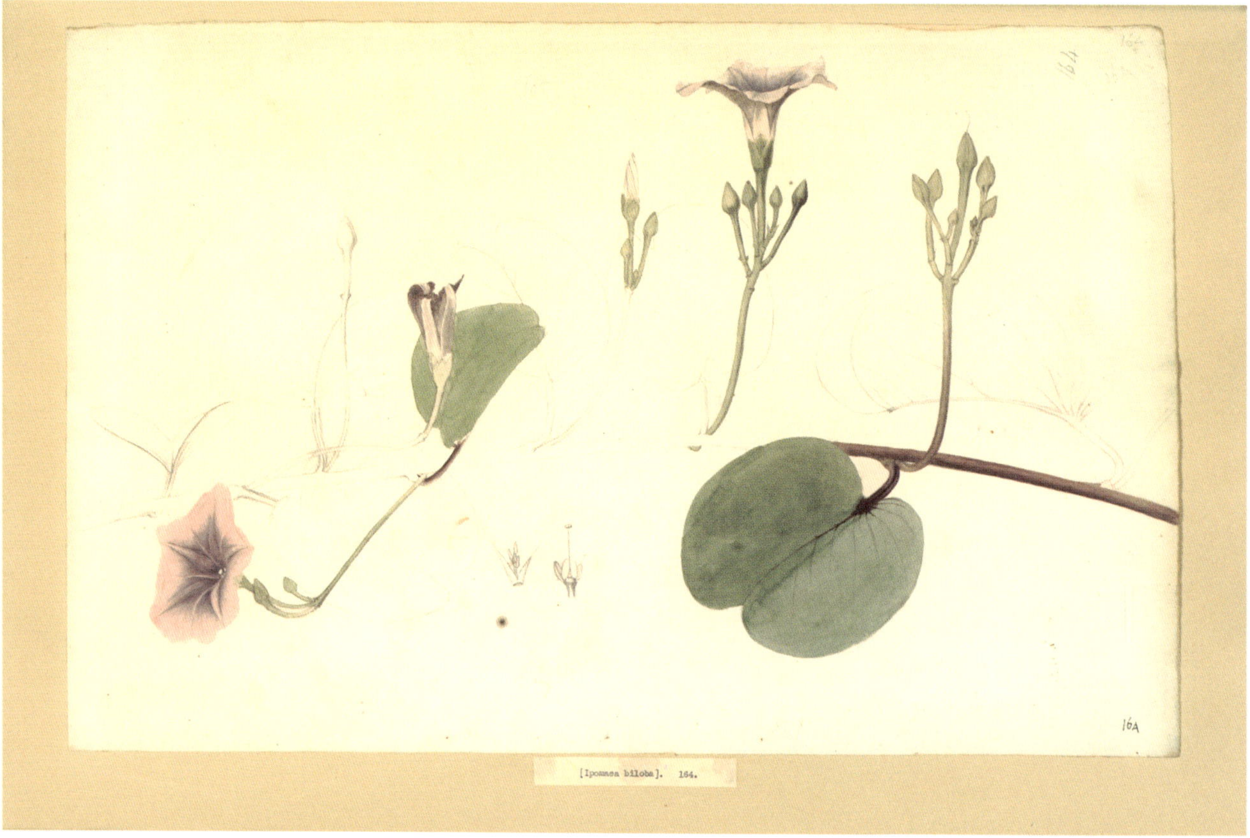
16A
[Ipomaea biloba]. 164.

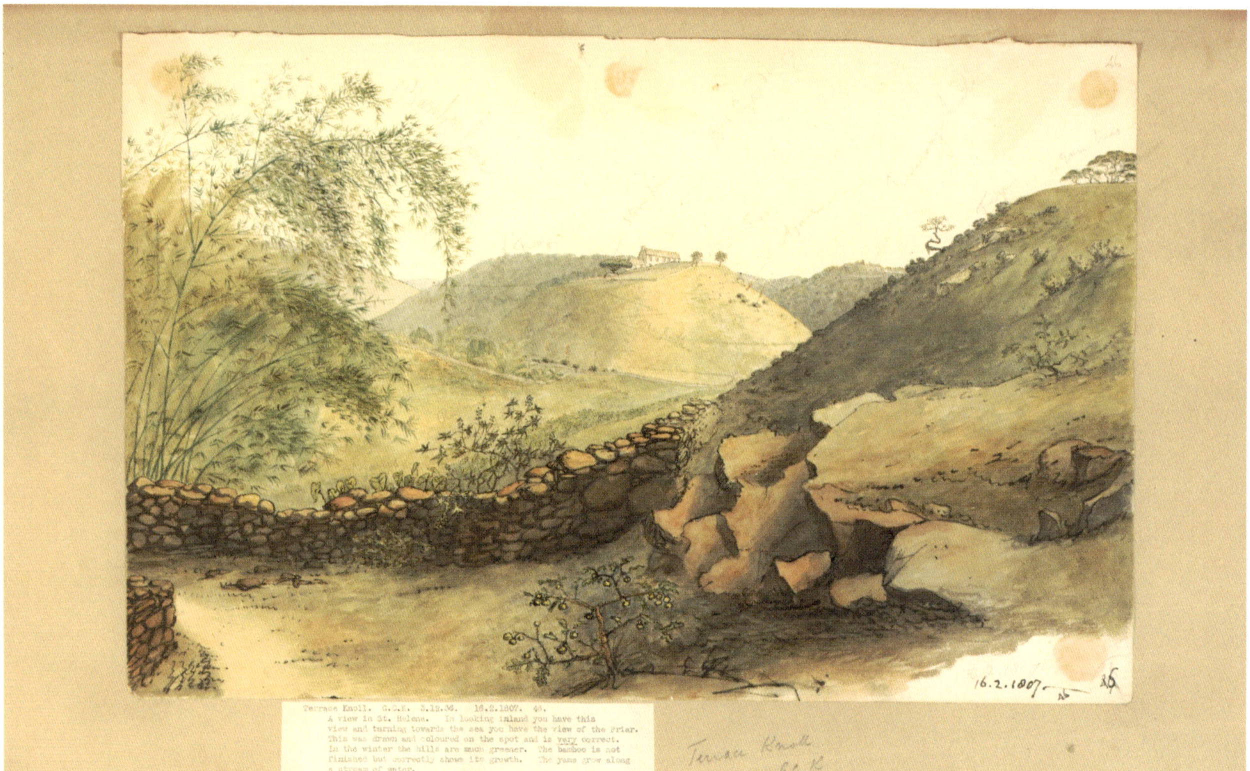
16.2.1807
Terrace Knoll. G.C.K. 3.12.36. 16.2.1807. 46.
A view in St. Helena. In looking inland you have this
view and turning towards the sea you have the view of the Friar.
This was drawn and coloured on the spot and is very correct.
In the winter the hills are much greener. The bamboo is not
finished but correctly shows its growth. The yams grow along
a stream of water.
Terrace Knoll
G.C.K

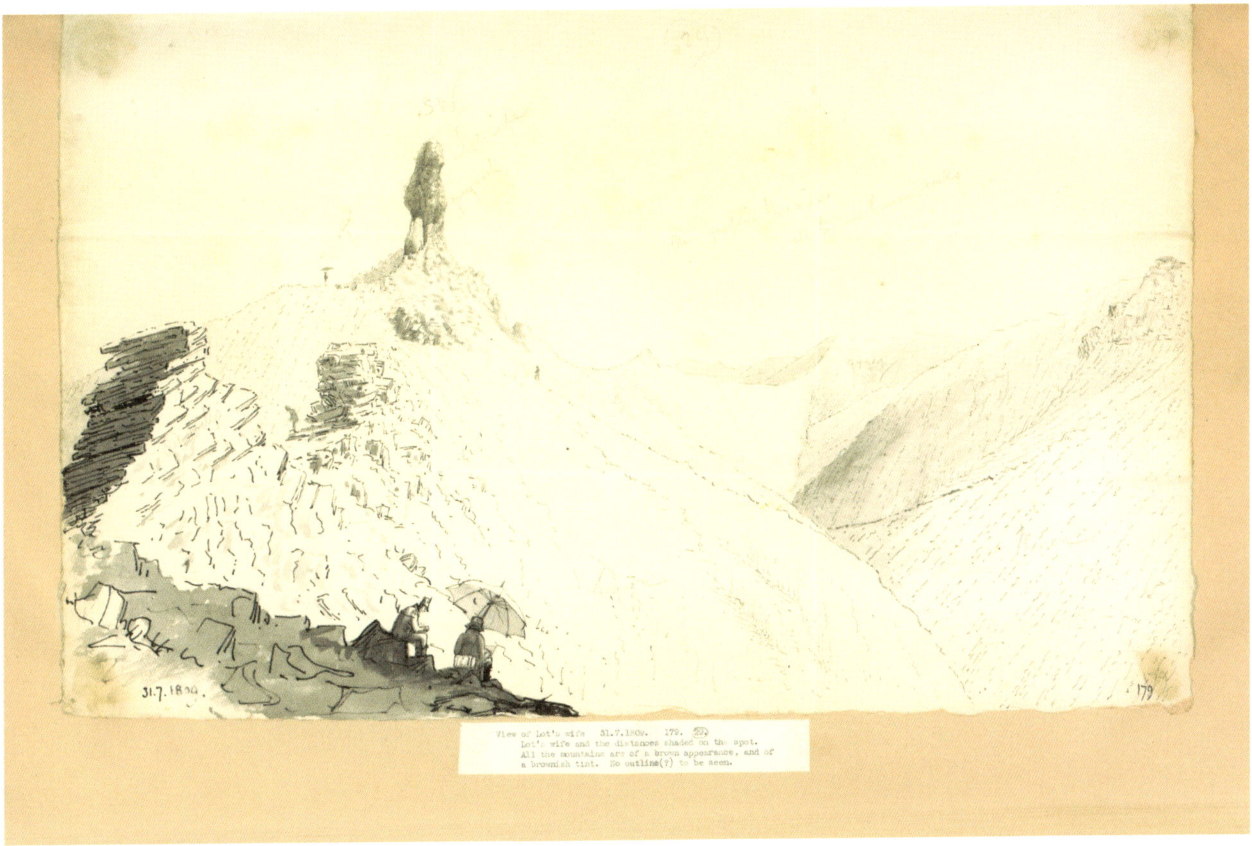
31.7.1809.
179
View of Lot's wife 31.7.1809. 179.
Lot's wife and the distances shaded on the spot.
All the mountains are of a brown appearance, and of
a brownish tint. No outline(?) to be seen.

87
[Pencil sketch of tree ferns]. 14.1.18 87. 51

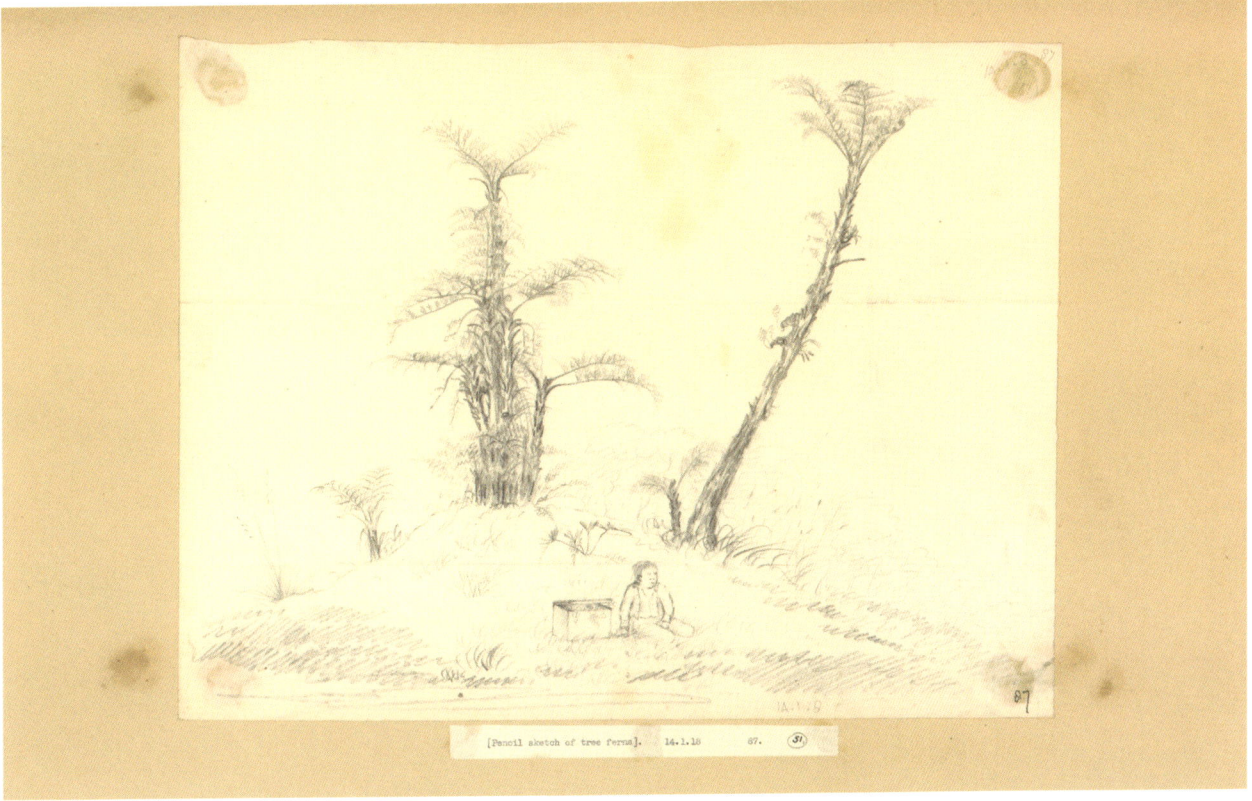

Callcott's approximately 100 sketches were annotated to explain sizes and proportions. She included the location she had collected the specimen and used a microscope to better reveal the small floral parts. Above is '*Bombax pentandium*' (*Ceiba insignis*) with 'old flowers' and 'flower newly opened'.

I   Made on Location

MARIA GRAHAM CALLCOTT

'I narrowly escaped becoming a slattern for life.' So the more mature Maria Graham Callcott (1785–1842) described her former self. She grew out of her tomboy stage but never lost her feistiness; the leading intelligentsia of Edinburgh nicknamed her 'metaphysics in muslin'. Although she showed signs of tuberculosis at an early age (and would later die from it), she travelled widely and published accounts of her experiences. A typically accomplished woman of her period, she was a keen sketcher and appreciated landscapes with an artist's eye; she also wrote books on art history. Maria fell in love with her husband, Thomas Graham, on board the ship taking her and her family to India. There she visited different parts of the country and enjoyed the company of the leading botanists; her journal became her first book.

In 1821 she accompanied her husband, now a ship's captain, to South America. When he died at sea en route from Brazil to Chile in 1822, she buried him, grieved, but resisted pressure to return to home. She stayed for another three years in South America, and again published a journal of her adventures. It was an exciting, if unnerving time to be in South America. She experienced a severe earthquake in Chile in 1822. Both Brazil and Chile were gaining their independence from Portugal and Spain, and territories less accessible to British naturalists were opening up. Little wonder that William Hooker (p. 152) was only too pleased that she collected plants and seeds for him. She reported that preparing dried specimens was a battle against the moisture and insect life of the tropics, and sensibly asked him on 11 April 1824: 'Pray in case of the fading of the colours of dried specimens might it not be advisable for me to add enough [coloured] sketches – say just an outline with the real colour of a petal and a leaf?'

Back in England she married the landscape painter (later Sir) Augustus Wall Callcott in 1827. A stroke in 1831 left her very frail, but she continued to write prodigiously. Her *Scriptural Herbal* (1842) was the product of her sick bed.

'Bromelia', a pencil sketch (above right), and 'Heliconia formerly Musa' (right). Callcott sometimes presented her plants in scenic landscapes to capture the full effect of the exotic flora.

(Overleaf) Callcott noted on one sketch (left), 'Many headed pineapple excellent flavour weighed near 30 lbs'; (right) *Senna alata*.

collectors 49

ALFRED RUSSEL WALLACE

Many people may be aware that Alfred Russel Wallace (1823–1913), independently of Charles Darwin (p. 118), discovered the role of natural selection in the evolution of new species. Fewer probably know that, as a young schoolmaster, Wallace taught drawing, a skill he used while working as a surveyor with his brother. His sketching and map-making abilities were also put to good effect in his two long exploratory expeditions, first to the Amazon, in 1848–52, and then to the Malay Archipelago (now Indonesia and Malaysia), in 1854–62. Wallace was already thinking about species and evolution before he set out for Brazil, but it was among the Southeast Asian islands that he formulated his theory of natural selection. By writing to Charles Darwin about it, he nudged the older naturalist towards publishing *On the Origin of Species* (1859). The 'Wallace Line' (marking the separation between species of Asiatic and those of mixed Asiatic/Australian characters) commemorates his crucial understanding of the geographical distribution of plants and animals.

With limited financial means, Wallace travelled by collecting and selling natural history specimens, mostly animals, especially insects and birds. But while still on the Rio Negro in Brazil in December 1851 he was already planning a book on plants, *Palm Trees of the Amazon and Their Uses* (1853), which would be illustrated from his own sketches. Wallace's adventures demonstrated his remarkable resilience, good eye and natural talent, but they also highlighted the potential perils. He had sent back early consignments to his agent, but the majority of his better specimens and drawings were lost on his return journey, when shipwreck almost cost him his life as well. The palm notebook survived – in it he tried to capture the strange new world of 'huge trees with buttressed stems, tangled climbers of fantastic forms, and strange parasitical plants' that 'everywhere meet the admiring gaze of the naturalist fresh from the meadows and heaths of Europe'.

'Forest giant sketched near Para.' Wallace wrote to his contemporaries in the Mechanics' Institute, Neath, Wales in 1849: 'There is one natural feature of [Amazonia], the interest and grandeur of which may be fully appreciated in a single walk: it is the "virgin forest".'

FRIEDRICH CARL LEHMANN

'The Cattleyas in question cost me (as coming from quite a new field) a great deal of money, hard work and exposure.' Friedrich Carl Lehmann (1850–1903) was writing from Colombia to the renowned orchid growers Sander's & Co. of St Albans, England. He informed them that the cattleyas had been shipped to them in error. He often dealt with fellow German, Frederick Sander, but this consignment had been for direct sale at the natural history auctioneers J. C. Stevens in Covent Garden, and, if they failed to reach their reserve, should have gone to rival nursery, Hugh Low & Co. This episode highlights the difficulties plant hunters faced in making a profit thousands of miles from their market. To the intrigue and skulduggery between competitors in the field must be added the physical demands of the hazardous territory and the need to pay skilled local collectors.

Lehmann had arrived in South America in 1870 as a prospector. He married and settled in Popayan, Colombia, eventually becoming the German consul. In 1876 he sent a well-prepared collection of orchids to the great German orchidologist Heinrich Gustav Reichenbach. In return for this unique material, Lehmann hoped for identifications that would allow him to present new plants to both the learned and the commercial world.

This pattern served Lehmann well, and he repeated it with other orchidologists and with botanic gardens from Glasnevin to Kew to Berlin. He made the most of the incredible array of plants in the coastal and montane border regions of Colombia and Ecuador, one of the most orchid-rich and biodiverse areas on the planet. To accompany his plant sales and sets of prepared herbarium specimens, Lehmann also sketched, brilliantly, even decorating his letters with orchids.

(Opposite) *Pescatoria Lehmannii*; (above) *Oncidium mirandum*.

(Following pages) *Masdevallia callichroma* (page 56); *Dracula radiosa* (page 57); a letter to Sander, 30 May 1886, on Lehmann's hand-decorated writing paper (page 58); *Epidendrum* sp (page 59).

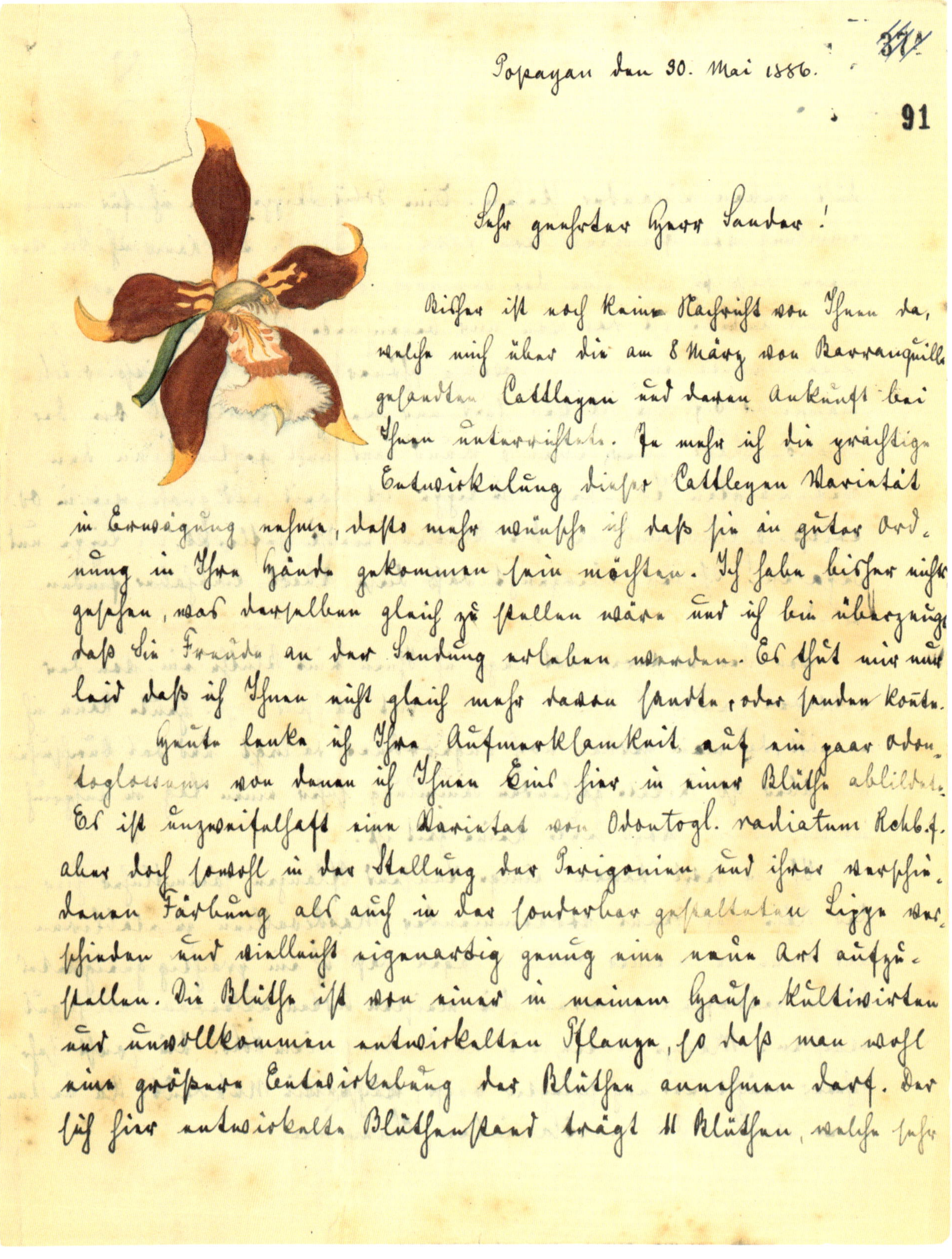

Popayan den 30. Mai 1886.

Sehr geehrter Herr Sander!

Bisher ist noch keine Nachricht von Ihnen da, welche mich über die am 8 März von Barranquilla gesandten Cattleyen und deren Ankunft bei Ihnen unterrichtete. Je mehr ich die prächtige Entwickelung dieser Cattleyen Varietät in Erwägung nehme, desto mehr wünsche ich daß sie in guter Ordnung in Ihre Hände gekommen sein möchten. Ich habe bisher nicht gesehen, was derselben gleich zu stellen wäre und ich bin überzeugt daß Sie Freude an der Sendung erleben werden. Es thut mir nur leid daß ich Ihnen nicht gleich mehr davon senden, oder senden konnte.

Heute lenke ich Ihre Aufmerksamkeit auf ein paar Odontoglossums von denen ich Ihnen Eins hier in einer Blüthe abbilde. Es ist unzweifelhaft eine Varietät von Odontogl. radiatum Rchb.f. aber doch sowohl in der Stellung der Perigonien und ihrer darauf dann Färbung als auch in der sonderbar gestalteten Lippe verschieden und vielleicht eigenartig genug eine neue Art aufzustellen. Die Blüthe ist von einer in meinem Hause kultivirten und unvollkommen entwickelten Pflanze, so daß man wohl eine größere Entwickelung der Blüthen annehmen darf. Der sich hier entwickelnde Blüthenstand trägt 11 Blüthen, welche sehr

HELEN FAULKNER

In 1954, from Mwambeni, Tanganyika Territory (Tanzania) on the Indian Ocean, Helen Faulkner (1888–1979) wrote: 'We are most comfortably and happily settled in our new home … I think there will be some interesting collecting here … so I hope I'll be sending you something worth while.' The Faulkners had been in sub-Saharan Africa since the early 1920s. After the First World War, Britain had gained various German colonies in East Africa, and along with the territory came the sisal plantations. These Mexican agaves (*Agave sisalana*) were an important fibre crop, and Hamlyn Faulkner managed plantations in Tanganyika and the Portuguese colonies of Angola and Mozambique. Helen's relationship with plants was different.

Born in Yorkshire, she had been educated in Paris before war broke out. The ballet classes were now redundant, but the art lessons came into their own. Enchanted by the landscape of the Alto Catumbela uplands, she began to sketch the wild flowers and then augmented her art with plant collecting, learning how to prepare herbarium-standard specimens from the government botanist, John Grossweiler. When the Faulkners were transferred across the continent in 1942 to Mocuba, Mozambique, Helen had completed 400 sketches.

She began to correspond with herbarium staff in Pretoria, South Africa, and Salisbury (Harare, Zimbabwe), as well as with Edgar Milne-Redhead at Kew. Milne-Redhead and 'La' developed a close working relationship after her visit to Kew in 1947. Plant specimens and sketches flowed to Kew, and back came long lists of names, increasing Faulkner's botanical knowledge. In the early days, her plants were often from places that didn't appear on Kew's maps, so she simply described her route. Aged 88, and without her own transport, she hitched lifts with local truck drivers to continue the plant collecting that had become such an important part of her life.

Helen Faulkner's eighteen sketchbooks were compiled between 1940 and 1967, and she also prepared over 5,000 dried plants for various herbaria. From sketchbook XIII, Namagoa, Mozambique, and Tanganyika, are (left) '*Hymenocardia mollis*' (*H. acida* var. *mollis*), the flowers drawn in October 1948 and the fruit in February 1949, and (right) '*Phialodiscus unijugatus*' (*Blighia unijugata*).

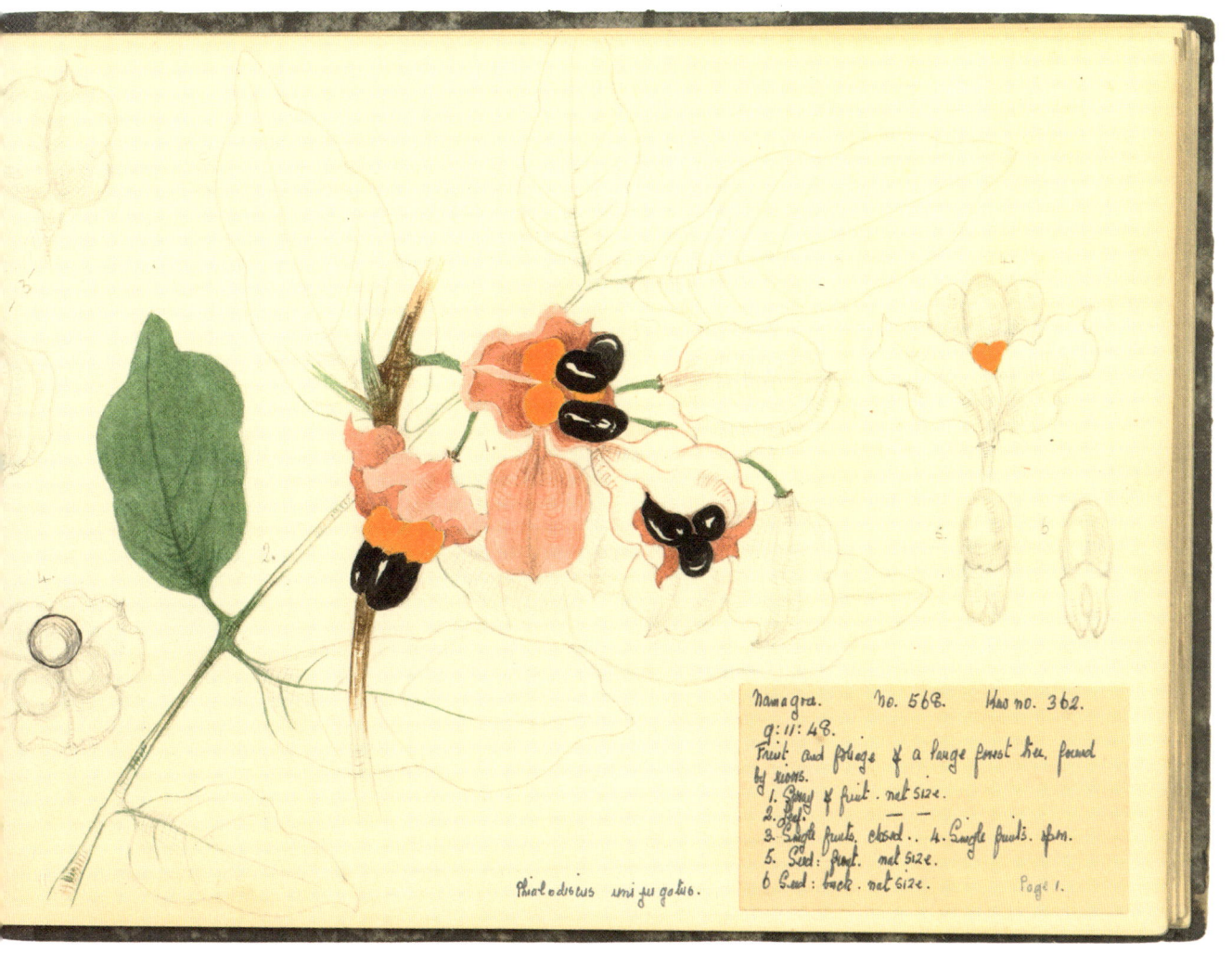

(Above) From sketchbook IV, 1940, Alto Catumbela, Angola, comes this unnamed plant (*Rothmannia* sp.), number '1' of Faulkner's Pretoria herbarium sequence. The detailed notes reveal that she found these 'Small trees or bushes' with 'Flowers large, shiny and strong scented' again in 1942. Although the plant specimens were for Pretoria, she made copies of this drawing and those featured opposite (*Strophanthus* sp., from VI) and overleaf (*Protea* sp., from VII), after loaning her sketchbooks to Edgar Milne-Redhead at Kew.

botany on the side

Plant fanatics have always found innovative ways to pursue their passion on the side. Service overseas provided exciting opportunities, while dedicated amateurs successfully exploited their domestic locations. Clergyman-naturalists were part of the English landscape. Richard Dreyer remained rooted, but Charles Parish carried his vocations with him to Asia. Though they couldn't chose their postings, their military careers took John Eyre and John Champion into the little-known landscapes of Hong Kong (China) and Sri Lanka. Francis Hall fought for Ecuador's independence and stayed on to see the new state emerge. Establishing clear boundaries in unfamiliar territory was an essential part of statecraft, and Robert Schomburgk and Santiago Cortés helped mark out the boundaries of Guyana and Colombia. Isaac Drège was a successful pharmacist, but made the time to increase his, and our, knowledge of Eastern Cape flora.

RICHARD DREYER

In Dreyer's lifetime it was common for books about the natural world to be issued in various formats. Large and expensive titles had glorious hand-coloured plates, whereas smaller, cheaper books, which included many descriptive floras, were often unillustrated. Richard Dreyer (1763–1838), rector of Bungay, Suffolk, ingeniously combined elements of both.

Dreyer was a Cambridge University graduate who spent his entire career in English country parishes. Although he published little save a couple of sermons, he obviously took his botanizing seriously, becoming a fellow of the Linnean Society in 1817. Its founder, Sir James Edward Smith, had purchased the manuscripts and herbarium of Carl Linnaeus (p. 118). Perhaps this, rather than expense, was why he adhered to Linnaeus's belief that proper Linnaean descriptions were unambiguous, and botanical publications using them did not need illustrations. When Smith published his *Flora Britannica* (1800–04) it contained no pictures.

Dreyer improved his copy of Smith's work with his own watercolour sketches, introducing these delightful images into the margins of the text. Many were taken direct from nature during botanizing trips, and he annotated the text to say where the plants had been found. Others, however, were copied from other books, mostly James Sowerby's beautiful *English Botany* (1790–1814), as well as a few from William Curtis's *Flora Londinensis* (1777–98). Dreyer carefully inserted his images into the space around and between the printed text, and included the important characters – the details of flowers and fruiting parts – used for classification.

That Dreyer clearly valued the finished product is indicated by his will, in which the volumes are singled out and left to the Linnean Society. For unknown reasons, he revoked the gift in a later codicil, but his wife, who outlived him by eleven years, donated them to the Society.

(Opposite above) *Viola tricolor, V. lutea* 'plentiful in all its varieties on old walls in Scotland: particularly at Oban' and *Verbascum thapsus*. (Opposite below) *Thalictrum flavum, Adonis annua* and *Ranunculus flammula*. Dreyer seems to have marked the printed description of the illustrated plants with a coloured +.

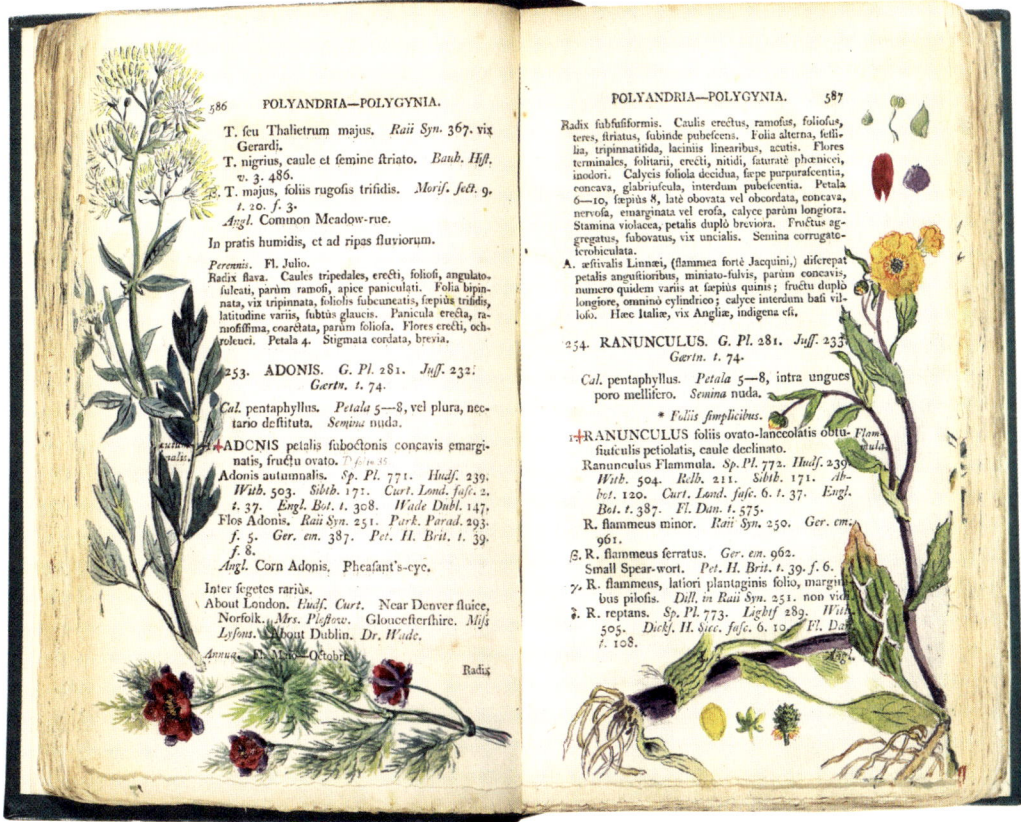

FRANCIS HALL

Quito, the capital of Ecuador, today stretches up the eastern slopes of the Pichincha volcano. In 1822 this was the site of a famous battle in the struggle for Ecuador's independence. It also became a favourite botanizing place for Colonel Francis Hall (1791–1833), a former British mercenary, who had fought with distinction at Pichincha.

After serving in the Napoleonic wars, Hall travelled in France, Canada and the USA and published his adventures. Inspired by Simón Bolívar's Enlightenment ideas, he then returned to military life. After Pichincha he settled in Venezuela, but subsequently moved to Quito, where he became professor of modern languages at the university. In his garden, he cultivated plants collected on trips with William Jameson, professor of chemistry and botany.

In July 1831 Hall welcomed the French chemist Jean-Baptiste Boussingault, who had also served with Bolívar. Over the following months they climbed several volcanoes, including Chimborazo (6,310 m/20,700 ft high), inspired by the great German explorer-naturalist Alexander von Humboldt. Hall drew the plants he found, and, Humboldt-like, noted the altitude at which they grew. He also described the plant communities and their aggregation in vegetation zones, and noted the soils and orientation of the slopes, the regional climate and microclimates. Recognized today as areas of great biodiversity, the mountains yielded plants which delighted Europe. Hall sent them to William Hooker (p. 152) via Jameson, who had introduced them, while Boussingault provided the same service for Humboldt.

Hall supported the *El Quiteño libre* newspaper and its call for liberal, transparent and representative government, and opposed the power of the Church. He was arrested and exiled in 1832. On his way to Payta on the Peruvian coast he continued to botanize and sketch. Allowed to return home, the respite was brief: he was assassinated on 10 October 1833.

(Opposite) *Oncidium hallii*. (Above) *Rubus nubigenus*, the giant Colombian blackberry (left), which Hall found 'dry and uneatable', and (right) *Hypericum laricifolium*.

(Overleaf) Hall collected near the snowline on Chimborazo and found *Draba aretioides* (left); on the right is *Talipariti tiliaceum* var. *pernambucense* from Esmeraldas.

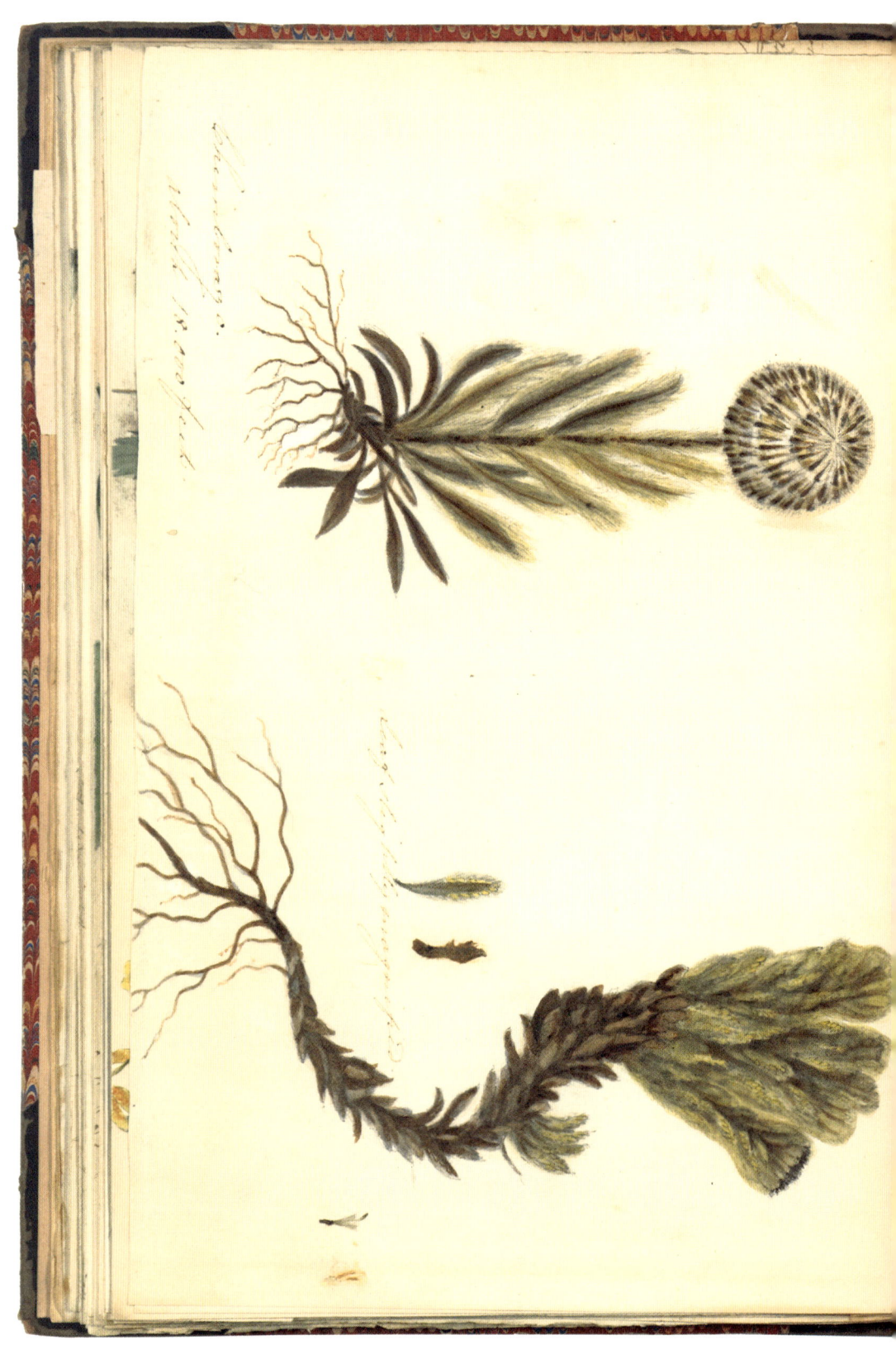

JOHN EYRE

'My friend Colonel Eyre is a great collector of seeds of all kinds … he is constantly in the hills, which is the only way to get the curious plants of the country'; moreover 'he possesses besides a considerable Herbarium, a beautiful set of coloured drawings of Hong Kong plants chiefly executed by himself'. In the late 1840s the new British colony of Hong Kong was a little-explored plantsman's paradise, and John Eyre (1791–1865) of the Royal Artillery (RA) was held in high regard by his brother botanists John Champion (p. 78) and Berthold Seemann, as shown by their praise of him.

Eyre was a career soldier. He was involved in the early Peninsular War in Europe before spending eighteen years in the West Indies. There are subsequent references to his familiarity with the tropical plants of the Caribbean, but his botanical exploits there are elusive. For Hong Kong, however, he created a vivid and lasting record of the plants that grew there at that time. Many have since disappeared, leaving mere fragments of a richer floral past.

Hong Kong, a rugged subtropical island off the southeast coast of China, was dominated by its steep slopes but also blessed with a fine natural harbour. After the British had gained the island following the First Opium War (1839–42) and opened it as a free-trade port, defence was crucial and batteries were quickly established. In 1847 Eyre assumed command of the RA in China at Hong Kong.

The greatest immediate threat was disease, especially malaria. Eyre did not escape illness, but still managed to spend his off-duty hours clambering up the sides of the Happy Valley and Wong Nai Chung Gap, which divided the island, seeking cooler air and seeds and plants for his watercolours. He also took advantage of the gardens of his prominent merchant friends, including David Jardine, head of the thriving commercial house Jardine, Matheson & Co.

Eyre retired to Chichester and his cherished drawings of the flora of Hong Kong stayed in the family after his death. His daughter's financial circumstances forced her to sell them to Kew in 1904.

(Above) Eyre found this orchid, *Renanthera coccinea*, growing wild in a ravine near the Royal Artillery's barracks. It is now extinct on Hong Kong, but that it once grew there is confirmed by Eyre's drawing of it. (Opposite) A ginger (*Zingiber* sp.).

(Overleaf) *Callicarpa tomentosa* (left) and '*Magnolia odoratissima*?' (*M. championii*; right) – Eyre may not have been certain of the name of this plant, but he noted that he was 'absolutely led to it by the nose'.

botany on the side 73

botany on the side 75

Alexandria Imperatricis
height from 10 to 12 feet

The above representation may be only considered as a hasty sketch
as it is rather too flat in its general appearance.
Schomburgk

ROBERT SCHOMBURGK

The maps accompanying the accounts by Robert Schomburgk (1804–1865) of his journeys in the interior of British Guiana (Guyana) are both richly detailed and full of unknowns. The watercourses he travelled from 1835 to 1839 are replete with tributaries, falls, cataracts and rapids, but little beyond is represented. He noted areas of 'dense forest' and 'savanna forest', hinting at the wider landscape. Yet everywhere there were new and fascinating plants. In October 1838 he recorded that 'almost impenetrable forest, rich in all the exuberant verdure and wildness of a virgin soil and a tropical sun' bounded the lower Essequibo. And on the upper Orinoco near La Esmeralda his party came 'unexpectedly on a granite platform of vast extent overgrown with ... vegetable productions of high interest to a botanist. They were remarkable for their gigantic size.'

Beyond their intrinsic interest, the plants mattered greatly to the Prussian-born Schomburgk. After his business in the West Indies had failed, he sought to combine his love of natural history with paid employment as a surveyor, and gained the support of the British Royal Geographical Society (RGS). This august body underwrote the cost of the expedition to Guiana, while Schomburgk covered his expenses by selling plants to British and German subscribers. It proved to be gruelling. He had to contend with savannah fires, snake bites, sickness, internecine warfare between indigenous people and slaving parties from Brazil. Adequate drying of plants was also challenging, and when the packages were opened in Europe many had rotted. But new species were found, and he did successfully send to England seeds of the 'vegetable wonder', the giant water lily *Victoria amazonica*.

Despite the problems, Schomburgk sufficiently impressed the RGS for them to ask him to serve again. From 1841 to 1844 he worked as boundary commissioner, delineating the British colonial territories in Guiana. His movement of the border westward, creating the 'Schomburgk line', would, he claimed, both protect British commercial interests and bring more of the indigenous people under protection, and it helped earn him a knighthood.

Schomburgk's 'hasty' sketches, as he called them, were in fact invaluable, and revealed a fascinating range of plants, from (above) parasitic *Langsdorffia hypogaea* found high in the 'upper region of the Orinoco' to (opposite) '*Alexandria imperatricis*' (*Vellozia tubiflora*).

JOHN CHAMPION

Rather than spend his time idling in the officers' mess, John Champion (1815–1854) botanized. He would have preferred the church to soldiering, but followed his family's wishes. His progress through the ranks of the 95th Regiment of Foot at least gave him the chance to indulge his passion for natural history in far-flung locations. Along with a keen eye, alert to new species, he possessed a growing understanding of the connectedness of the plant world.

Champion's first posting was to the Ionian Islands, which yielded more insects than plants. When he then left Europe behind for Ceylon (Sri Lanka), he encountered unfamiliar, luxuriant landscapes. Observing individual species such as the famed banyan trees, as well as *Dalbergia championii* and *Xylopia championii* (both named after him), he sketched them all. Near the artificial Kandy Lake (Kiri Muhuda), he described the massed effects of hills 'mounted by trees, bamboos, and cocoa-palms bewitchingly intermingling their plumage'. He wrote of vegetation zones created by soil, climate and topography. He pondered why plants other than those visible in the neighbouring jungle would spring up around the newly introduced coffee bushes. And he noticed how, on abandoned land, regeneration would progress through a succession of species adapting to changes in light levels and water availability.

Before he sailed for Ceylon in 1839, Champion had made contact with William Hooker (p. 152) and asked him for advice on books and equipment so he could set himself 'up as a botanist'. In return, he became an eager correspondent, and his letters included what he termed his 'rough daubs' – ink and watercolour sketches of the plants he collected.

Champion continued botanizing in Hong Kong in the late 1840s. Before setting out for the Crimea in 1854 he left his herbarium of dried plants with Hooker at Kew for safekeeping. It was a prescient act. Champion was shot in the chest at the battle of Inkerman and died of his wounds, aged 39, in the Scutari Barracks where Florence Nightingale had arrived to take charge. Hooker incorporated the dried specimens and sketches into his own fine collection, preserving Champion's enthusiasm and valuable observations for posterity.

(Opposite) '*Monocera Hookeriana*' (*Elaeocarpus montanus*): in a letter on 8 March 1843, Champion offered to name this plant, found on Adam's Peak, Sri Lanka, after his mentor. (Above) Herbarium sheet for the small plant *Burmannia championii*, with Champion's specimen and his characteristic sketches.

botany on the side 81

Champion consistently sent home news of plants he thought might be new to western science, with detailed drawings and copious notes on flimsy writing paper. All here (previous pages and above) are from his botanizing in Sri Lanka, including (page 80) a *Desmodium* sp. and (page 81) *Ilex buxifolia*, collected on 'Pedro table galla' (Pidurutalagala), the highest peak on the island. (Opposite) *Aeschynanthus ceylanicus*, a trailing epiphyte; (above) *Artabotrys zeylanicus*.

I   Made on Location

CHARLES PARISH

Botany and the Victorian British clergyman formed an important synergy, yielding a remarkable number of herbarium specimens, bountiful knowledge of local and regional floras, and beautiful images. The rootedness of a rural parish allowed for an extended study of the surrounding plants, which those so inclined could indulge as their religious duties permitted. The Reverend Charles Parish (1822–1897) epitomized this trend, except he was fortunate to have as his hunting ground the fascinating and then little botanized landscape of Burma (Myanmar).

Parish was born in India, and followed his father's vocation as a chaplain for the East India Company. Ordained and already a keen botanist, Parish arrived in Burma in June 1852 during the Second Anglo-Burmese War. After the war's end in 1853, Parish served the garrison and European school at the then capital Moulmein (Mawlamyine) until 1858. Once a year he travelled by boat to Tavoy (Dawei) and Mergui (Myeik) on the isthmus in the south. Here, the narrow coastal strip quickly gave way to steep, wooded hills abounding with the mosses, ferns and orchids that Parish collected with the assistance of Burmese locals. He was happy to contribute to the greater scientific good, writing up and sharing his finds with the leading botanists at the botanical gardens of Calcutta and Kew. But Parish was financially astute too. He sold his orchids to Messrs Hugh Low & Co. of Upper Clapton, east London, one of the world's leading orchid nurseries.

In 1854 Parish married Eleanor Johnson. In addition to caring for their large family, the Parishes shared a love of cultivating and sketching plants. Their garden hosted 150 species of orchids, and the two albums of some 300 orchid drawings are an archive of Parish's life, when 'hardly a day passed on which I did not either draw or examine microscopically one orchid or another'.

(Opposite) '*Vanda teres*' (*Papilionanthe teres*): Parish described this as 'One of the most lovely orchids'.
(Right) A first sketch of *Eria ornata*.

(Pages 86–87) A letter from Parish with drawings of *Lygodium microphyllum*, a 'delicate fern of graceful twining habit growing at an elevation of about 2500ft'. Though he had been told that Moulmein was not a place to find ferns, he sent a steady stream of them to Hooker at Kew.

(Pages 88–89) Parish used sketches to build a history of his orchids. On page 88 the coloured drawing of *Pholidota advena* was by 'Mrs P.' in 1870, when he was ill; he then added other details to his main pencil drawing in 1875. On page 89 are layers of sketches of Dendrobiums including *D. formosum*, 'The first orchid I ever drew'.

botany on the side 85

Lygodium ———?

a delicate fern of graceful twining habit growing at an elevation of about 2500 feet. It abounds in Wynaad where it is always to be found in swampy places. It appears to be confined to Wynaad, as I have not seen it elsewhere. It is a straggling plant twining loosely round the paire & other plants near wh. it may be growing - forming often entangled masses of yellowish green. The fertile fronds give a peculiar & an ornamental appearance.

Stalk slender & wiry. Shaft giving off alternately & distantly partial stalks of about ½ of an inch in length, each of wh. is surmounted by a pair of opposite frondlets, & a tuft of reddish brown tomentum terminates the stalk in the axil of the frondlet. Occasionally the partial stalks are prolonged beyond the frondlets-bearing other leaves & forming secondary branches or partial stalks.

Frondlets given off at right angles from the shaft - all the lower pairs barren - the rest fertile - have a jiggy or alternate stalked somewhat distant pinnæ wh. when fertile are broad somewhat heart shaped at base & blunt at apex - when barren elongated, bluntly acuminate at apex, & cordate at base. Frondlets occasionally come off in pairs or from the shaft. Margin of pinnæ scalloped & contracted into distinct bodies on the back of which the fructification is situated. Front or upper surface of scallop has the appearance of a double platting - produced by the arrangement of the veins - each cleft at the extremity. Segments acute. The upper of wh. is folded down & uniting itself by its lower margin to the vein and along parallel with the base of the theca, forms the indusium.

Spore cases in a double row on each scallop - varying in number from 4 to about 12 - partially covered by the indusium. Somewhat egg-shaped - **sessile** - with a complete terminal contracted ring - bursting by a longitudinal slit thro' the ringed extremity - Spores conical.

Fructification.

Spore-case.

Front of scalloped margin on w[hich] fructification is arranged

fertile pinna

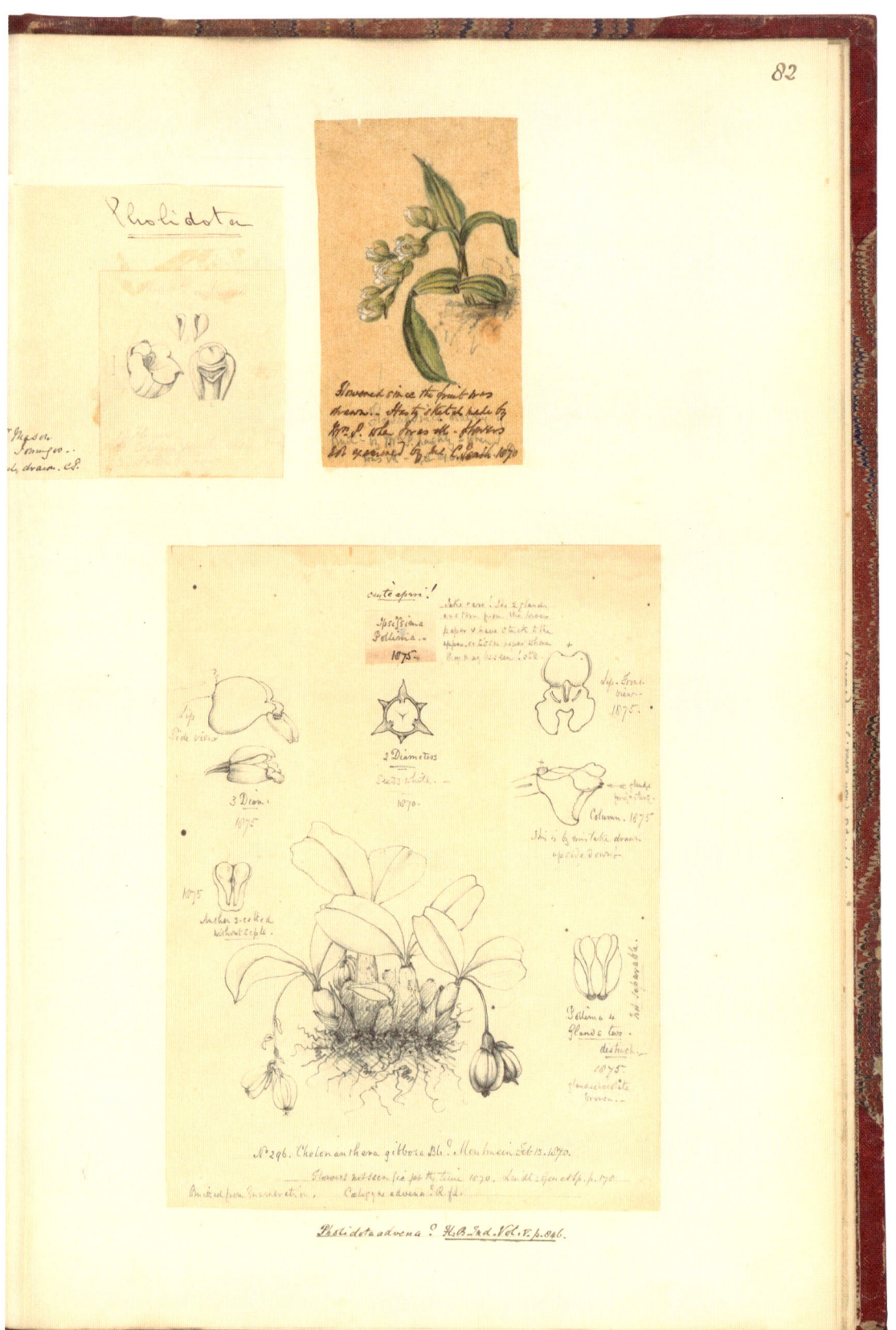

I Made on Location

ISAAC DRÈGE

For Isaac Drège (1853–1921), tramping through the Cape Provinces was in his blood. His father Carl and uncle Johann had established themselves in South Africa in the 1820s as professional collectors of natural history, ethnography and botanical specimens. Before yielding to his wanderlust, his father had trained as an apothecary, and Isaac followed this more practical career path. He established a business in Port Elizabeth on the Eastern Cape's coast and found a niche importing familiar drugs and medical sundries for German settlers, using family connections with the home country.

In the 1880s, Drège emerged from behind his counter, becoming involved with the Eastern Province Naturalist's Society and the Port Elizabeth museum. He clearly enjoyed collecting and botanizing, helping to swell the museum's insect holdings and offering plants to the important Albany Museum, Grahamstown, in 1905, where another German, botanist, Selmar Schönland, was building up the herbarium.

He began to use Winsor & Newton sketchbooks for his botanizing in 1901. The sketches are a visual record of the plant life of Port Elizabeth (on which he subsequently published), but the notes also delineate a network of amateurs and professionals that Drège was able to tap into. Among them was Robert Broom, who would later discover the famous Australopithecine fossils at Sterkfontein; he practised medicine briefly in Port Elizabeth, and made a noticeably more adept pencil sketch of a dianthus in Drège's sketchbook in 1908.

Drège worked in pencil and watercolour, initially sketching flowers and then returning to add details of dissections, seeds and roots. Gaining confidence, he began to send plants from beyond Port Elizabeth overseas to Kew. 'If I could go perhaps once every month it would be better. Even to get plants like *Euphorbia polygona* is not easy as it takes an hour and a half to get to the nearest plants.' A working pharmacist could only take so much time off.

Drège's plants included classics such as *Protea neriifolia* (right) and *Euphorbia cereiformis* (opposite top), although this was an unusual, distorted example sent by a friend. *Cussonia thyrsiflora*, the Cape coast cabbage (opposite centre), is endemic to the coastal region including Port Elizabeth. Drège noted that tubers of *Fockea angustifolia* (opposite bottom) were sliced and cooked with ginger to make a jam.

botany on the side 91

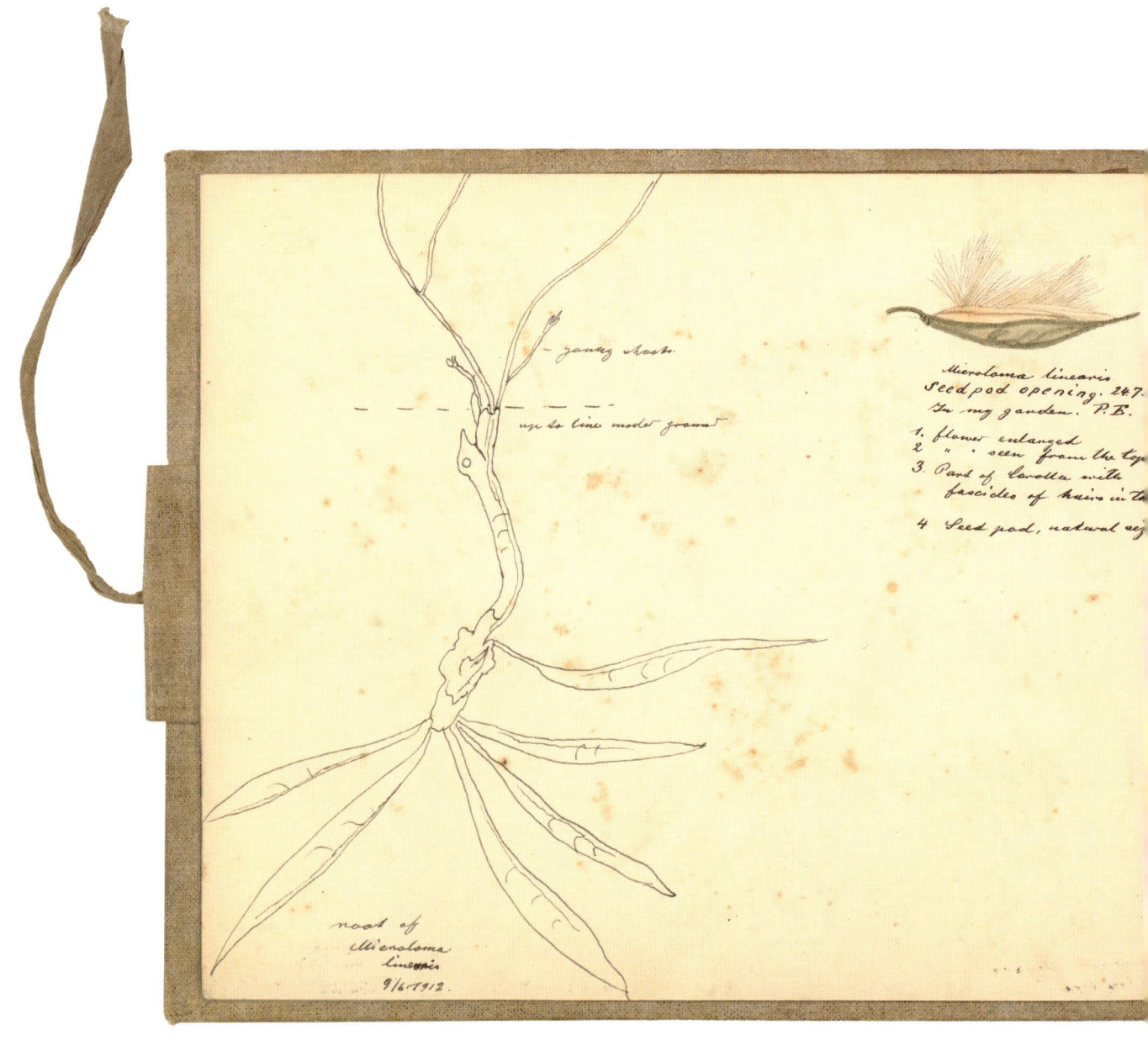

The first pages of the 'Skizzenbuch Port Elizabeth 1901' (as it was titled by hand on the cover): the sketches of '*Microloma linearis*' (*M. tenuifolium*) illustrate Drège's evolving botany. He made an initial drawing on 5 April 1901 and subsequently corrected the name. From a plant in his garden he then added details of the flower and seed pod on 24 July 1908, and finally the outline of the root and emerging shoots above soil level on 9 June 1912.

SANTIAGO CORTÉS

At times, Santiago Cortés (1854–1924) could legitimately call himself a botanist – his *Flora de Colombia* (1897) is clear testament to his claim on the discipline. But in a country with a nascent university system, his career path wound through chemistry, engineering and linguistics, as well as other fields of natural history and university administration, so botany was just one of many competing interests.

Cortés was born in Bogotá, and after working elsewhere in Colombia he returned to his native city. Soon after, he joined the newly founded Oficina de Longitudes y Fronteras, a boundary directorate, and was quickly assigned to the Comisión de Límites con Venezuela, set up to verify the boundaries between Colombia and Venezuela. This provided Cortés with a unique opportunity to travel, botanize and sketch in unfamiliar frontier regions. Not surprisingly perhaps, given his diverse background, he drew insects, shells, birds, snakes, geological formations, landscapes, waterways and maps, as well as detailed botanical specimens.

In its work, the commission followed part of the course of the Catatumbo River where it marked the boundary, which involved travelling through the surrounding jungle. On the Guajira Peninsula on the Caribbean, the most northerly promontory in South America, the commission encountered very different terrain and plants. This is partly a desert landscape, marked by immense sand dunes.

For Cortés, his exploration here, together with other travels in the Andean districts of Quindío and Tolima around Ibagué, and the province of Cundinamarca surrounding Bogotá, bulked out his herbarium and fed into the *Flora* project. Only the first volume of a projected five was ever published, however, and twenty years later a visitor from the New York Botanical Garden bought the last copy in Bogotá. The civil wars that destabilized Colombia at the end of the 19th century had frustrated many projects, including Cortés's botany.

96
Crepúsculos, espesísimo, ref
Cambios de vi
En toda esta comarca
to NE. muy fuerte de ordin
los árboles, muy marcada
que está orientado al SO. Per
turbaciones atmosféricas en
casi siempre de cambios de vi
tos del horizonte en el sent
horas. Para este cambio influ
se alternan en el día según el i
corrientes de aire frío que baja
de Sta Marta y de la Cordiller
sultante de estos vientos con el
guir su curso ordinario.
Todo cambio de viento se an
un aumento de temperatura y
co del aire, y cambios probable
(aquí, á modo de nota, la
del globo).
gran tension eléctrica
La electricidad procedente de
en forma de chispa con deton
el rayo, el trueno y el relámpa
gar en un aire enrarecido en lá
solamente produce los resplande
en las altas regiones del cielo
los semejantes producen las desc
á través de los tubos que contie
cados.
y observada en las noches de ve
por lo cual se les dá vulgarmen
verano.
Reg. pag. 98 (bis)

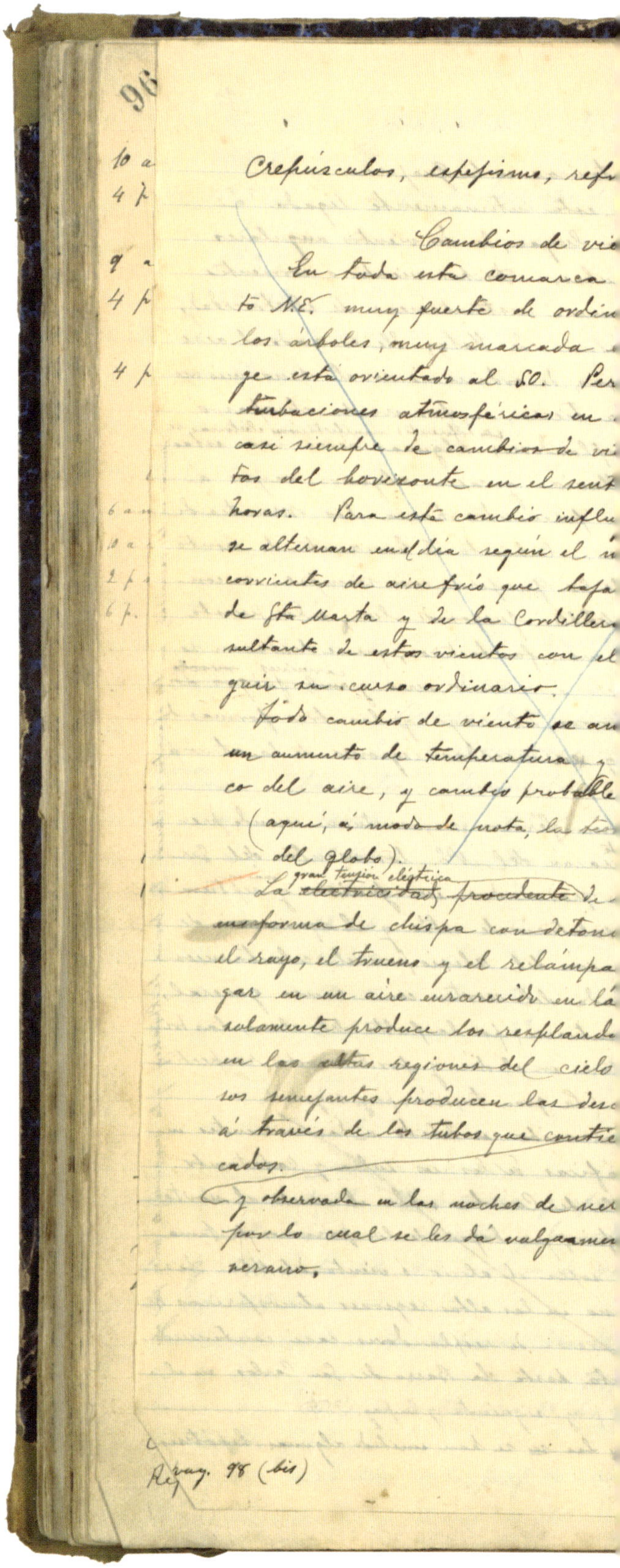

The plants here – a palm (top) and the leaf and male flower of the 'jabillo', *Hura crepitans* – are from the 'Bosques del Parhuachón', the Paraguachón forest on the border between Colombia and Venezuela.

Bosques del Parhuachón. (Geonomas y otras Palmeras).
Racimos de albaricos. Palmera de frutos, color morado bien oscuro y brillante; los racimos son bien cargados de frutos, ácidos pero no venenosos, problablemente por algún oxalato. Es semejante á la chonta pero no he visto la flor. Como la palmita es pequeña se emplea para bastones, sólidos pero de poco peso, de color de chocolate oscuro. (pag. 101).

Euforbiácea hojas de Jabillo. Hura; árbol muy grande, armado. Su jugo lácteo es sumamente venenoso, produce madera de regular calidad para carpintería en obras de aire. La base de la hoja tiene dos glándulas ó escrobículos y en la parte periférica una zona sin clorofila terminada en glándulas en cada uno de los ángulos del contorno. Las nervaduras son de verde claro; el anverso de la hoja más oscuro que el reverso. Hojas alternas.

Espiga de flores masculinas

Llevo las semillas para examinarlas en Bogotá.

Cortés was noted for his eclectic style, but also criticized for a rather muddled way of working. There is evidence of the former in this manuscript notebook dated 1900 and bearing the stamp of the Colombian/Venezuelan boundary commission, with meteorological information and panoramas of the geology and geography of the mangrove-edged Guajira Peninsula.

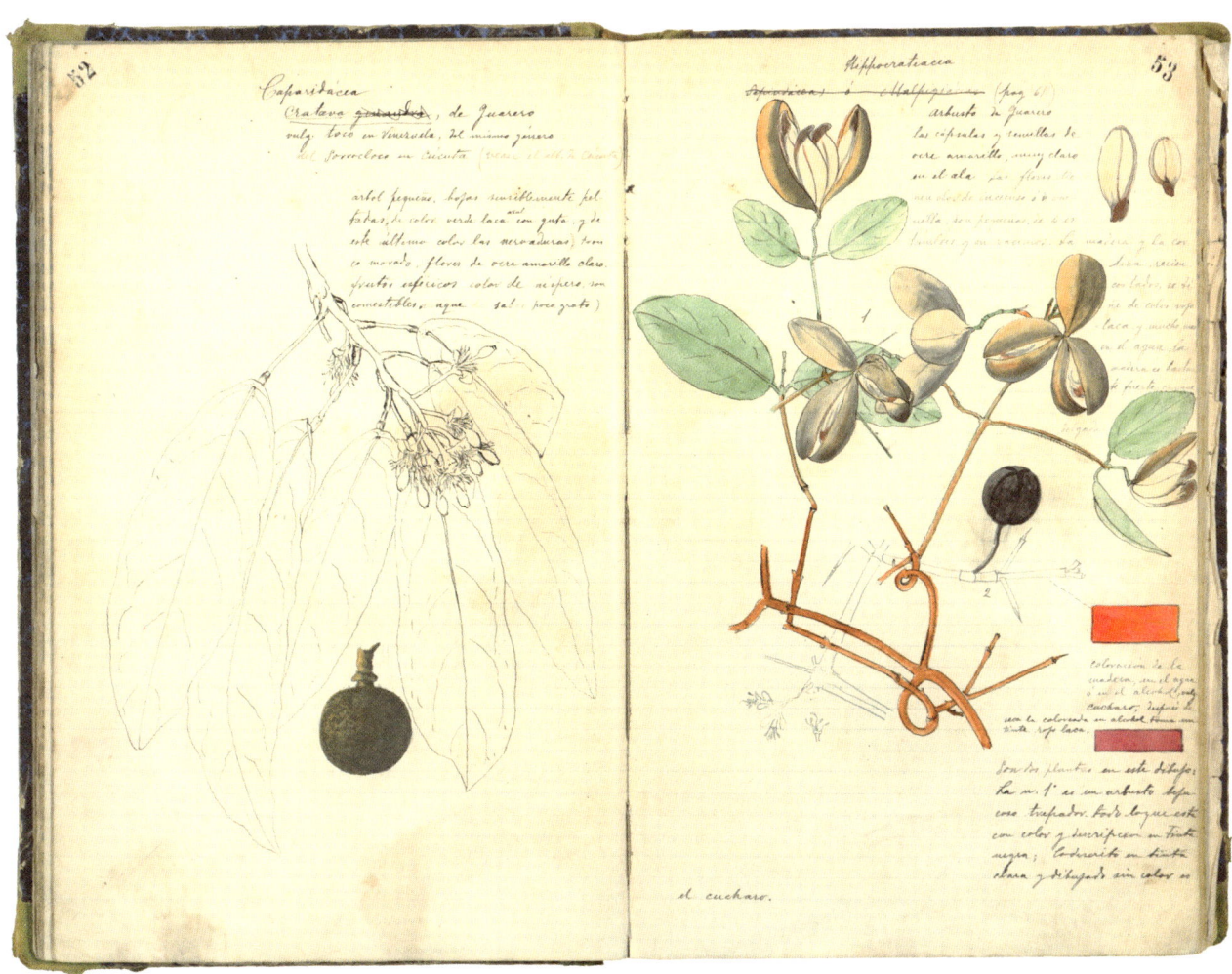

'Caparidacia' (left; possibly a *Crataeva* sp.) and 'Hippocrateacea' (right), a liana-like climbing shrub from the bush in Guarero region, again on the border of Colombia and Venezuela. Colour notes accompany the pale ink sketch.

imperial projects

The identities of many of the artists who worked on imperial projects, cataloguing indigenous plant life for the world's great empires and trading powers, have often been lost entirely. If their names are known, little else about them has lingered. Their sketches are their testament, though they had minimal if any control over the fate of their work. Among the anonymous artists are those whose works were assembled by Nicolaes Witsen to promote Dutch trading concerns in Japan, or were drawn specifically for John Cathcart to further British scientific interest in the flora of the Himalaya. Hendrik van Rheede was fascinated by the Malabar Coast, and relied on his employees in the Dutch East India Company to create a monumental record of its plants. John Reeves selected native artists to capture the plant life of Canton's nurseries and markets. The Mexican artists Juan de la Cerda and Atanasio Echeverría provided an invaluable service to the Spanish empire. William Swainson sketched for his own purposes in New Zealand, and, as an emigrant seeking to establish himself, represents a different kind of imperialist interest.

HENDRIK VAN RHEEDE

For centuries before Europe discovered the way to the spice lands and islands of Asia there had been thriving trade ports along the Malabar Coast of Kerala, India. Once the route had been charted, first the Portuguese began forcing out the original traders and then the Dutch pressed their claim. The Dutch East India Company (VOC) aggressively created a vast trading empire that required skilled administrators to run the business and private armies to defend its interests. One of its dedicated servants was Hendrik van Rheede (1636–1691).

Born of a well-connected family from Utrecht, he joined the VOC in 1656 as a soldier and fought successfully at Cochin (Kochi), where he became state officer in 1663. In 1669 he was made commander of Malabar, a position that allowed him to travel, and he wrote of his desire to see the plants of the moist broadleaf forest clothing the coastal region. This was more than mere curiosity – van Rheede was aware of the potency of local plant-based drugs and the poor condition of expensive imported medicaments. His aim was to oversee the description and illustration of the Malabar plants for the benefit of the VOC. The result would be the unsurpassed twelve-volume *Hortus Malabaricus* (1678–93), the prepatory original drawings for which are now in the British Library.

It was an imperial project par excellence, extracting indigenous knowledge for the benefit of the colonialists. Van Rheede oversaw the bulk of the work in 1674 and 1675, beginning with incomplete sketches by a travelling Carmelite priest, Father Matthew. A VOC clergyman, Johannes Casearius, helped with the Latin. Information and plant lists were collected from several Indian scholars by local Malayali people in the region of Cochin, and then from much further afield. VOC clerks and soldiers were drafted in by van Rheede as needed, and four artists were connected with the project, including Marcelis Splijnter and Antoni Jacobs Goedkint (an army ensign), who drew the material brought to them. After the vast amount of preparation in India, the book was edited, engraved and printed in Amsterdam.

Unusually the drawings for the *Hortus Malabaricus* were made on whole sheets of paper orientated horizontally rather than the typical vertical format. Playful artistic flourishes such as (opposite) the cartouche around the plant's name 'Modagam' (*Fagraea obovata*) and the European figure in full 17th-century dress sketching the 'Codda-pana' (*Corypha umbraculifera*) palm (overleaf) were not engraved for the book.

Tab.
Tab. 2.

Fig. 1.

Lat. Codda-pana
Malab. ഒ ക, ട ട ന
Karetála
Bram. करेताल
Arab. فُحَاخَا نَعْ

NICOLAES WITSEN

Burgomaster Nicolaes Witsen (1641–1717) was at the centre of Amsterdam's business world. And since Amsterdam was an international city built on vast trade networks, his role as director of the Dutch East India Company (VOC) gave him a global reach. He capitalized on this both for commerce and to fuel his passions for shipbuilding, maps and natural science. Indeed, Witsen saw no sharp divide between mercantile endeavour and knowledge acquisition, and chided contemporaries who failed to share his broad vision for a trading empire. A clear understanding of the natural resources and products of a region was essential to maintaining a competitive edge, and that understanding only came from studying its flora, fauna, geography and people.

Witsen was born into a family steeped in public service and overseas trade. He attended Leiden university and added to his education with European travel, but it was a trade embassy to Moscow in 1664–65 that opened his eyes to a different world in the east. Eurasia and its near neighbour Japan fascinated him. In 1688 he posed in a Japanese robe and in 1690 he published a remarkable map of 'Tartary' (subsequently augmented with a compendious and informative book).

To satisfy his considerable collecting habit, Witsen promoted and used a huge network of individuals, including, close to home, Maria Sibylla Merian (p. 128). Further afield, Willem de Vlamingh captained a voyage to New Holland (western Australia) in search of a lost VOC ship, and sent Witsen shells and plants. In South Africa, Witsen sponsored expeditions into the interior and ordered drawings of new plants to be copied for his paper museum. These and others (thought to number some 1,500) were assembled into the Witsen Codex. His collection also included an anonymous album of plant drawings from Japan with notes in Low Dutch at the back. This perhaps combined a growing Japanese interest in observing and recording their local plants with the foreigners' hunger for exotica in the service of science, empire and curiosity.

(Above) Crape myrtle (*Lagerstroemia indica*), labelled here 'fiacku schii qua', with a rudimentary attempt at the roots and a faintly pencilled landscape; the main stem is shown in order to indicate that this is a small tree. (Opposite) 'Omooto' (*Rohdea japonica*), the Nippon or Sacred Lily of Japan.

I Made on Location

Mooto
Plantago aquadisaca

JUAN DE LA CERDA & ATANASIO ECHEVERRÍA

In 1787 Juan de la Cerda and Atanasio Echeverría (both *fl.* 1787–1803) became the principal artists of the 'Expedición Botánica'. This exploration of New Spain in the Americas was the idea of Spaniard Martin de Sessé y Lacasta, and had the usual imperial goal of cataloguing the natural history of a vassal state. Since illustrations were considered vital, Sessé had gone to the recently founded Royal Art Academy of San Carlos in Mexico City to find promising young artists. In 1790 Sessé was joined by another botanist, Spanish-Mexican José Mariano Mociño.

From 1787 to 1799, when most of the expedition's 1,800 drawings were made, the two botanists led a series of journeys, some lasting over three years. They began in the Mexican countryside and then went further afield to Central America, Puerto Rico, Cuba, and up the Pacific Coast to Alaska. Initially they all travelled together, but from 1792, to cover more ground, a botanist and an artist (not always in the same combination) made a team. When there was no fresh material to draw while on their travels, hasty sketches were worked up and copies made.

The later adventures of the sketches of these two young Mexican artists are perhaps more remarkable than those of their creation. The sketches were first taken to Madrid from Mexico in 1803 in preparation for publication as a new 'Flora Mexicana', but Sessé's death and the Napoleonic wars intervened. Mociño was banished from Spain and followed a retreating army to Montpellier, France, in 1812 or 1813, with the drawings in a handcart. Some were copied for the great Swiss botanist Augustin de Candolle (annotations on some are in his hand) before Mociño moved to Barcelona. After he died there in 1820 the drawings were untouched for over a hundred years, surviving the Spanish Civil War of the 1930s buried in a cellar. It was a fate that Cerda and Echeverría could not have anticipated or intended for the work they had spent many years creating, but as hirelings they never had control over their unique record of the Americas.

Most sketches were unsigned, so knowing which artist was where can identify the creator. Echeverría travelled up the Pacific Coast as far as Nootka ('Notka') Island, Canada, but drew *Proboscidea althaeifolia* (above) earlier – the drawings were mixed up and Candolle introduced the error. (Opposite) The orchid '*Portaea paradoxa*' (*Cycnoches ventricosum* var. *chlorochilon*) first flowered in Europe in the 1830s.

(Overleaf) A study sheet of flower parts of various species. These details were often added later to field sketches or more finished copies.

imperial projects

Nº 168

Diaulium in
H. fol. 18

83.

Genus novum.
Curatella Americana

JOHN REEVES

It was tea that took John Reeves (1774–1856) to China. The orphaned son of a clergyman, Reeves was educated at Christ's Hospital, London. Here the Writing School prepared pupils for a life in trade and commerce. Britain's vast trading empire offered a world of opportunity, and Reeves worked his way up from the counting house of a London tea broker to become the East India Company's chief inspector of tea at Canton (Guangzhou) in 1812. This was China's single trading port, and the Company enjoyed the official monopoly on British trade.

At that time Canton was at least as large as London and equally dynamic. Foreigners were restricted to a very small part during the winter trade season and retired to Macao after the East Indiamen had sailed. The city served as a closely guarded gateway to silks, porcelain and tea, and an entrepôt for the wealth of Asia's natural history. Jesuit missionaries, who had gained access to the interior in the 17th century, were able to exploit these riches, but the dominance of British merchants in Canton afforded the potential to catch up using local agents.

Besides the plants he procured, potted and sent home, from 1817 to 1830 Reeves also sought out artists who could sketch the plants and their flowers and fruits for Joseph Banks, William Hooker and, especially, John Lindley at the Horticultural Society. Most were grown in Canton's nurseries (particularly the renowned Fa-tee nursery on the Pearl River) and market gardens, and the gardens of European and Hong merchants.

Export art was big business, so it is not surprising that Reeves employed at least four artists, whose informal names were Akut, Akam, Akew and Asung. They worked in his home, under close supervision, sketching and making sets of copies. Reeves's own collection was often made on local paper, but the drawings to be sent home were executed on imported paper. The combination of local and imported pigments, some perhaps brought in by Reeves, was striking, so too the unusual outlines in graphite pencil, a medium easily sourced from his office.

'Fruit of Cactus Triangularis. Sturges Garden'. The dragon or pitahaya fruit (*Hylocereus triangularis*) is a native of Mexico; the reliance for material on plants locally cultivated in Canton meant that the geographic origin was often obscured.

Botany and horticulture were intimately connected in the early 19th century, and there was much interest in fruits as well as the cultivated flora. These stone and other fruit have been partly annotated in two Chinese hands. The name of the peach (centre), literally 'white rice peach', refers to the way the flesh resembles cooked rice grains.

imperial projects 109

WILLIAM SWAINSON

Animal, vegetable, mineral: William Swainson (1789–1855) encompassed them all in his enthusiasm for natural history. While animals – fishes, birds, insects – occupied most of his prolific output, trees especially were the focus of his later life.

Swainson's father secured an army commission for William, and he spent 1807–15 in the Mediterranean (Italy, Malta, Greece and Sicily). By the time he retired on half-pay because of ill health in 1815, collecting and sketching were already in his blood. In 1817–18 he was in the field in Brazil, and on his return to London gained election to the Royal Society. He put his collections on display and married one of the visitors, Mary Parkes, in 1823. Swainson then became a jobbing natural history encyclopaedist and pioneered lithography in scientific illustrations, but couldn't secure the British Museum job he desired.

After Mary's death in 1835 he gradually realized their tentative plans by applying for a land grant during the aggressive early years of the New Zealand Company. Remarried, he arrived in the country in 1841, intent on becoming a colonial landowner, and established his homestead, 'Hawskhead', in the wooded Hutt Valley near Wellington. What he found delighted him: 'the vegetation is beyond all conception luxuriant. The trees are lofty ... interwoven with gigantic monstrous creepers.' His drawings became a record of nature in the process of being rapidly altered by colonialization.

Swainson's aim of becoming an official scientist to the Company came to nothing. After the Hutt war with the Māori, and the 1854 depression, he had a stint botanizing and drawing among Australian and Tasmanian trees, although William Hooker (p. 152) was sceptical of his botanical abilities. Here, and once more in New Zealand, if his botanical precision was lacking, his artistic pencil drawings captured the trees with exquisite sensitivity.

'What subjects for your pencil', wrote Hooker. 'We shall revel in magnificent scenery', Swainson replied – as the Kauri pine (*Agathis australis*; above), 'Gigantic Rata' (*Metrosideros robusta*; opposite above) and 'Silver Leaf Fern' (*Cyathea dealbata*; opposite below) bear witness.

I Made on Location

JOHN CATHCART

When he was too ill to accompany his indigenous Lepcha plant collectors any longer, John Cathcart (1802–1851) contented himself with riding out on his pony and having picnics in the jungle valleys below his house at Leebong (Lebong), a little below the hill station of Darjeeling. In the late 1840s, his final years in India, Cathcart had labourers cut a series of paths through the dense vegetation, as if landscaping a garden from the 'giant timber-trees ... clothed with climbing Palms, wild Vines, Peppers, Pothos, Hodgsonia and Ipomoea, and laden with masses of Orchids and Ferns ... cascades fringed with Ferns and Mosses ... streams, overshadowed by Tree-Ferns, Bamboos, and wild Plantains.' It was a plantsman's paradise.

Cathcart was born in Edinburgh and followed his father into the judiciary, though he worked for the Bengal Civil Service, then the preserve of the East India Company. He would probably have preferred botany to being a judge, and spent his spare before embarking for India in 1822 among plants. He continued to do the same when his health failed on several occasions in the 1830s, recovering at the Cape in South Africa and in the Scottish glens. It was among the lower Himalaya that he made his mark, not by his own pen but through as many as six unnamed artists whom he employed to sketch for him.

The 1,000 or so drawings made by Cathcart's Indian artists were of variable scientific value, perhaps sometimes awkwardly arranged to European eyes, but full of charm. The Himalayan flora fascinated plant collectors. When Joseph Hooker (p. 172) was in Darjeeling, ready to start exploring this little-known region, Cathcart asked him to teach his painters the art of perspective and the science of floral dissection, offering him the results. Cathcart died on his way home in 1851, but Hooker had Walter Hood Fitch (p. 156) create engravings for a sumptuous book, *Illustrations of Himalayan Plants* (1855).

A *Cleome* sp. (above) and *Begonia roxburghii* (opposite), and mature fruit, leaves and flowers of the Sikkim cucumber, *Cucumis sativus* var. *sikkimensis* (overleaf). None of these sketches featured in *Illustrations of Himalayan Plants*. As well as the bolder lines and colour, there are fainter, experimental sketches, especially of flower and fruit parts.

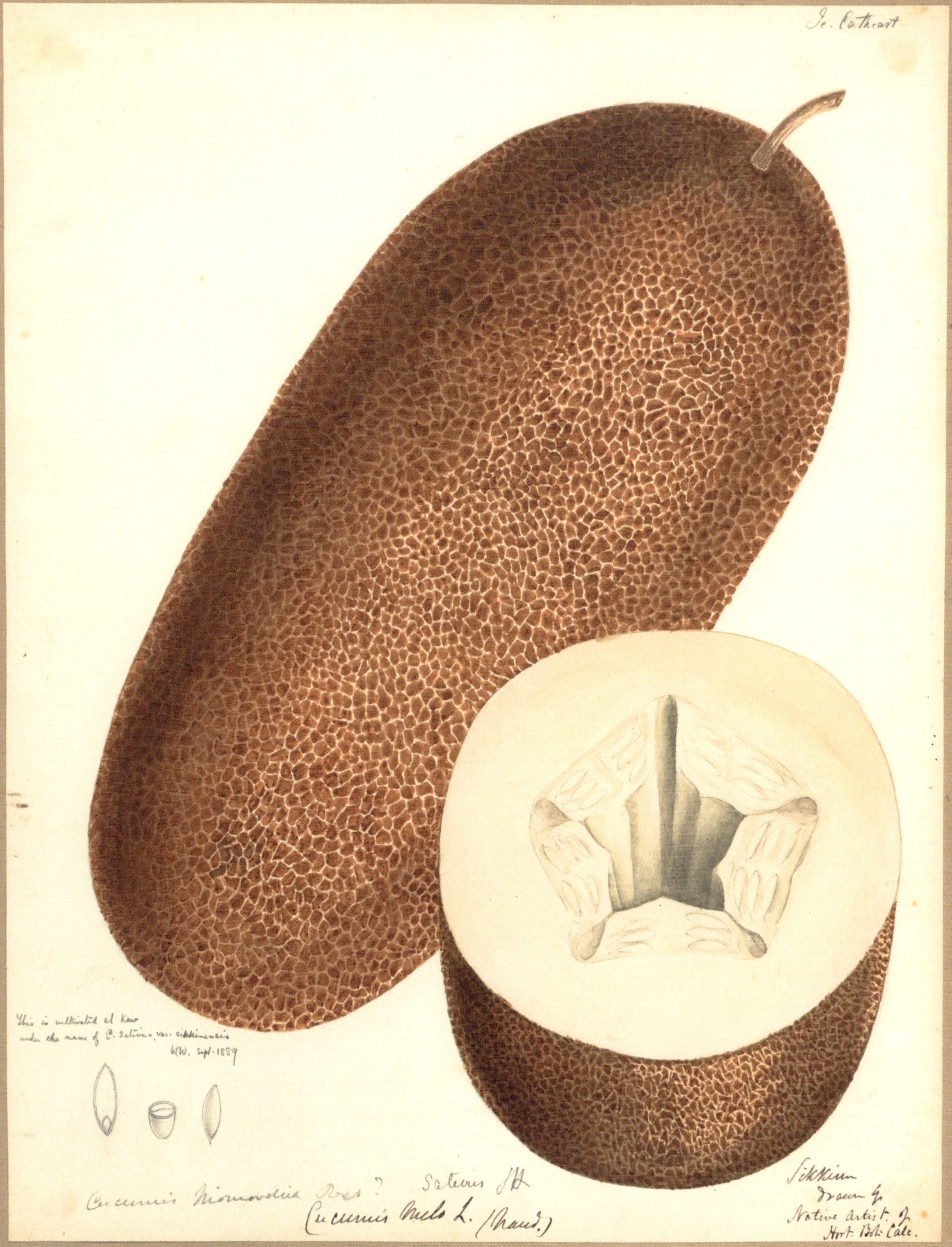

J. Cathcart

This is cultivated at Kew
under the name of C. sativus var. sikkimensis
WW. Sept 1889

Cucumis Momordica Roxb.?   sativus J.H.
Cucumis Melo L. (Naud.)

Sikkim
drawn by
Native Artist of
Hort. Bot. Calc.

II Doing Science

Think broadly, make connections, aim for an understanding of nature as a whole. This was an important principle of scientific practice in the 16th century. We are exhorted to do this again today, now that the era of specialization has begun to acknowledge its limitations and molecular biology shows the fundamental links between all life. Throughout, sketches remained important to thinking, learning and communicating knowledge of the natural world. Two exceptional men of science who had incredible breadth, but were poor sketchers, demand our attention and open this chapter with *primus inter pares*. Then we return to the 16th century to begin with earlier *naturalists*. In the late 18th century, in part in response to the rapid expansion of knowledge, distinct disciplines emerged. Plant science was increasingly served by dedicated places and people. Scientifically orientated gardens emerged from the older herbal and paradisiacal traditions, creating new careers and new networks. *From the botanical garden* looks at the sketches these locations fostered as they became prestigious places to work. In the same period, the new specialists, the *botanists*, both amateur and professional, who were concerned with scientific details and horticultural practices, carved out their roles alongside a dwindling number of the generalists.

WALTER HOOD FITCH
A sketch, with minimal colouring, of the fruit of *Telfairia occidentalis*, a West African vine grown at Kew from seeds donated by the Liverpool Botanic Gardens in 1870.

Telfairia occidentalis.

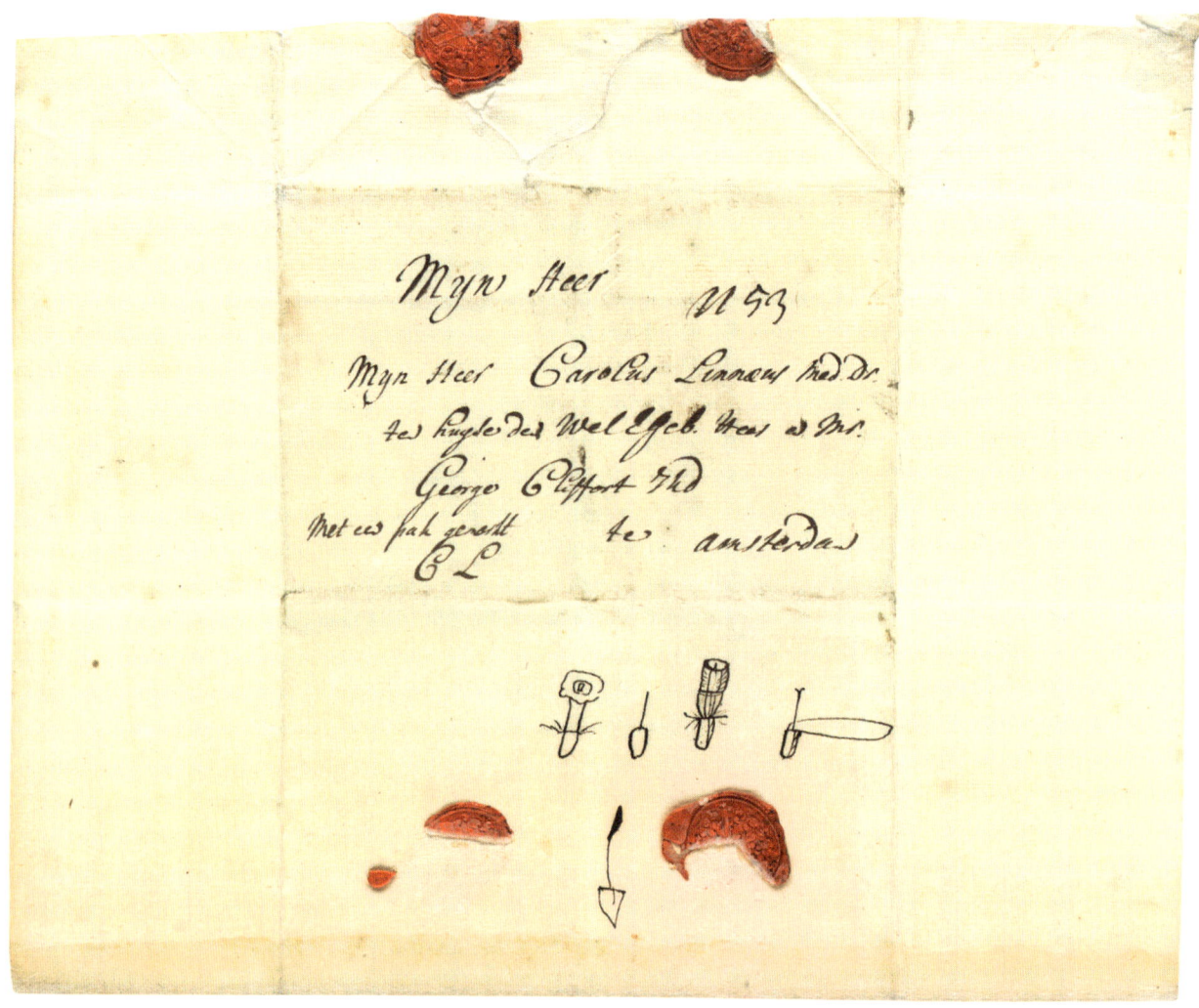

(Above) In 1735 Linnaeus was staying in Leiden with his patron George Clifford and used the address panel of a letter of 30 December from another supporter, J. F. Gronovius, to make five rudimentary sketches of the parts of a plant.

(Opposite) 'I collected all the plants, which were in flower on the coast of Patagonia at Port Desire & St. Julian', Darwin wrote to J. S. Henslow in March 1834. Attached to the pressed specimen of the orchid later named *Gavilea patagonica* was this sketch of the flower.

primus inter pares

Alongside Aristotle (384–322 BC), Carl Linnaeus and Charles Darwin are arguably the most influential naturalists of all time. Aristotle framed European natural philosophy for two millennia. His great works were subsequently illustrated by others, but nothing pictorial survives from him. Linnaeus dominated the study of the natural world for a century or more, and we still follow his insight that biological organisms can be identified by two names, their genus and their species. Thus the type specimen (the original organism first classified as a particular species) of human beings lies buried in Uppsala Cathedral. Linnaeus gave us our biological name, Homo sapiens, *and therefore he is the type. We still live in the world revealed by Darwin. He was not the first to show that biological species can change over time, but he made evolution the bedrock of biology. The ideas of both Linnaeus and Darwin are thus fundamental: they must be included, though it has to be acknowledged that unfortunately neither was a very good draughtsman.*

CARL LINNAEUS & CHARLES DARWIN

It is as easy to contrast as to compare Carl Linnaeus (1707–1778) and Charles Darwin (1809–1882). Their personalities were completely different. Linnaeus lived in a relatively loveless marriage, whereas Darwin was a devoted, if worried, family man. Linnaeus had a dark streak, with strange religious beliefs and a brooding sense of fate, whereas Darwin seems simply to have gradually lost his conventional Church of England faith and slid into what his friend, the biologist T. H. Huxley, called agnosticism. Linnaeus drew frequently, but roughly, whereas Darwin drew but reluctantly and with a delicate crudity.

Although both men saw the world clearly and distinctly, Linnaeus held that his new binomial botanical taxonomy offered unambiguous identification without need for illustrations: 'All plants are learnt in a year, at first sight, without a teacher, without pictures or descriptions, and are firmly in the memory. He who has learnt how to do this is a botanist, no one else is.' Darwin recalled of his time on HMS *Beagle*: 'Another of my occupations was collecting animals of all classes, briefly describing and roughly dissecting many of the marine ones, but from not being able to draw ... a great pile of MS. which I made during the voyage has proved almost useless.' Characteristically, he was being excessively modest.

On the other hand, both naturalists took the whole world as their subject. Linnaeus liked to see himself as a second Adam, naming all the plants and animals in the Garden of Eden. He pondered on the principles of classification and recognized that his solution for the plants, based on their sexual parts, was an artificial one, even if it brought much needed order into botany. (He also classified animals, minerals and diseases.) Darwin knew that biological classification was crucial to understanding the natural world. He devoted a whole chapter to it in his *On the Origin of Species* (1859), arguing that natural classifications must be based on evolutionary descent, and that time was an essential ingredient of the process.

naturalists

Natural history, the pursuit of naturalists, was a visual process. Its devotees concerned themselves with the description – the older meaning of the word 'history' – of the natural world. And it is their engagement with the plant section of the natural world that features here. While written accounts were vital, accurate depictions – the stuff of sketches – became increasingly important from the Renaissance onwards. Our artist-naturalists sought to capture nature in its entirety. Conrad Gesner and Fabio Colonna were keen to harmonize ancient knowledge with newer discoveries. Niccolò Gualtieri and Charles Dorat, both doctors, focused on the medicinal role of plants, where clear identification could be a life or death matter. Maria Sibylla Merian and her daughters, as well as sisters Harriet Scott and Helena Forde, and Beatrix Potter balanced themselves on the fine line between natural history as an acceptable female activity and an intrusion into a male world of professional artists.

CONRAD GESNER

When Conrad Gesner (1516–1565) died of the plague, the world lost a true polymath, one whose vision of the natural world encapsulated Renaissance natural history. Born in Zurich, Gesner was a gifted scholar who was at ease with the ancient languages. He produced a massive index to Greek, Latin and Hebrew writers that is considered the founding of modern bibliography, and he translated the Lord's Prayer into 24 languages. After his theological training he turned to medicine, studying in Bourges, Paris and Basel, and eventually became chief physician in Zurich, where he settled.

Despite the demands of his medical practice, he also pursued his love of natural history, travelling to observe flora and fauna in other parts of Europe including the south of France, venturing up to the snow line of the mountains in search of alpine species. Gesner was part of the new humanism – respectful of ancient learning but determined to appreciate the world through modern eyes. He lived to see the publication of his great *Historia animalium* (4,500 pages), but his premature death meant that the intended follow-up work, on plants, was never completed. Nevertheless, he engraved nearly 1,500 images of all the plants he knew, based on a prolific accumulation of his own plant sketches and drawings, living plants and herbaria, and books and illustrations. As well as creating images he also sought assistance from his scientific network.

In his own copiously annotated sketches, Gesner generally showed all aspects of the plant – roots, leaves, flowers and seeds – not necessarily combined into a single image of an entire plant, as the desired result could be achieved by detailed drawings of the parts. He called attention to the fact that it was the fructifying parts, the seeds and flowers, rather than the leaves, that were key to classification. His drawings demonstrated his remarkable artistic talents, his insistence on accurate representation and his vision of how the natural world could be comprehended.

(Opposite) The plant at the top of the page of drawings is *Peucedanum palustre*, or milk parsley, while lower right is cranberry (*Vaccinium oxycoccos*), which had been referred to in early reports from the eastern seaboard of the American colonies. Gesner's project to record all the world's plants was a race against time he could not win.

(Above) Attached to Gesner's drawing of black bryony (*Dioscorea communis*) is a simple woodcut of the tree mallow (*Malva arborea*). (Opposite above) *Daphne striata* and *Parnassia palustris*; (opposite below) two species of gentians: *Gentiana pneumonanthe*, 1553, and *G. ciliata*, 1564 – a wonderful example of Gesner's compilation of images; between the two he glued notes from 1552.

II Doing Science

De gentianella palustri

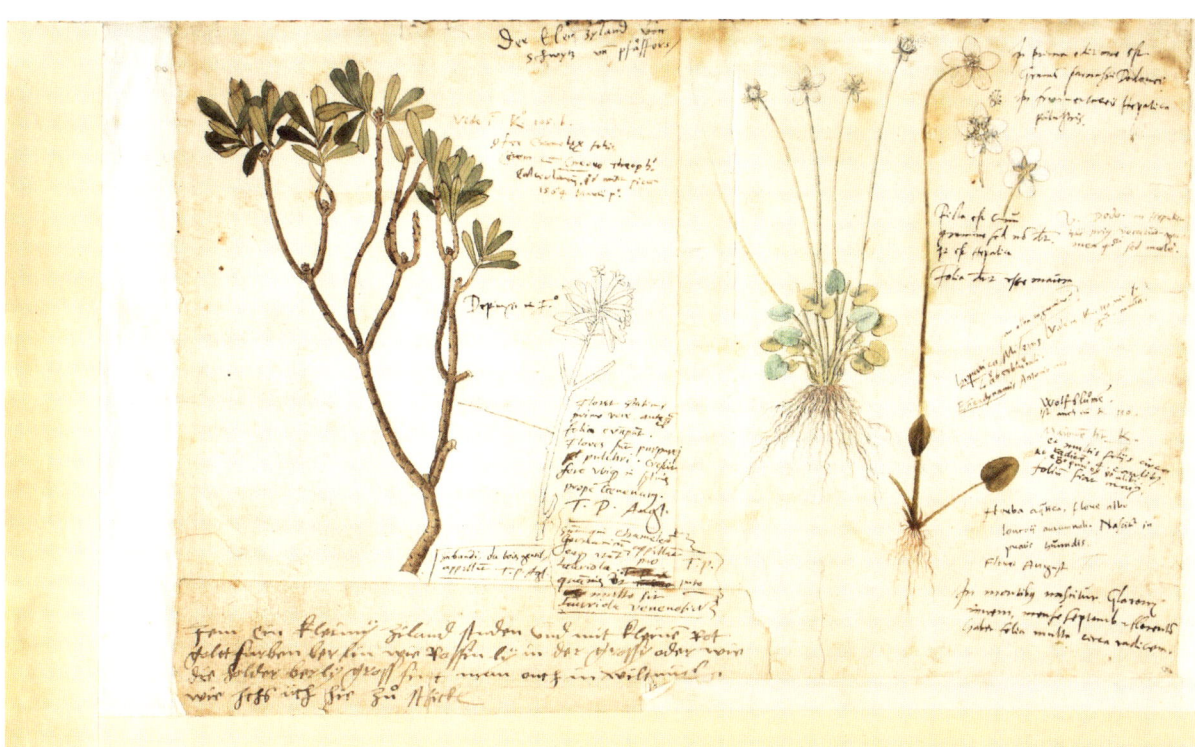

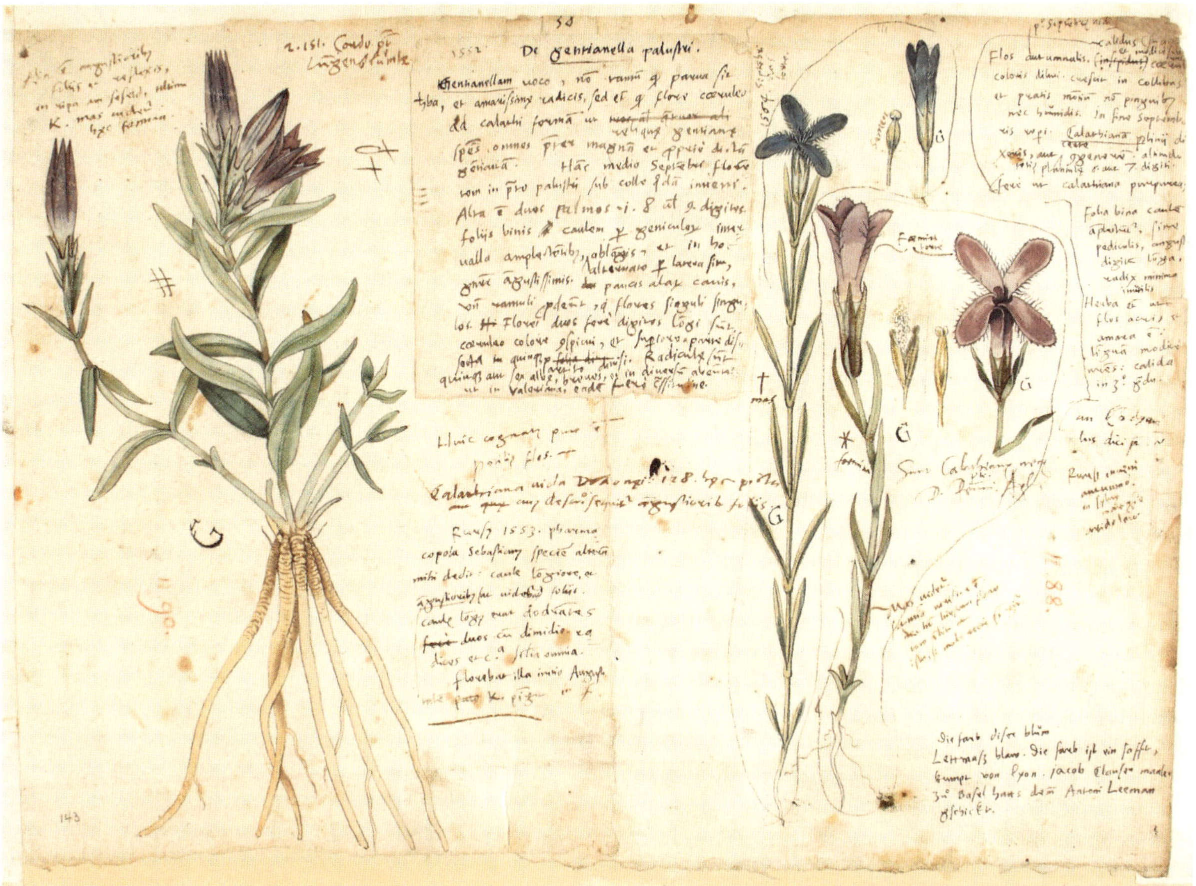

(Above left) Leaves and fruit of the common fig (*Ficus carica*), with cloves, the flower buds of *Syzygium aromaticum* bottom right. (Above right) Four conifers: a branch of larch (*Larix decidua*), long cones of Norway spruce (*Picea abies*), and cones of two pines (the larger, *Pinus pinea* and the smaller, *Pinus cembra*), both of which provide edible seeds that Gesner also drew. (Opposite) Chinese cinnamon (*Cinnamomum aromaticum*): Gesner added numerous annotations to his immense collection of drawings, providing him with a rich store of knowledge for his projected master work on plants.

II Doing Science

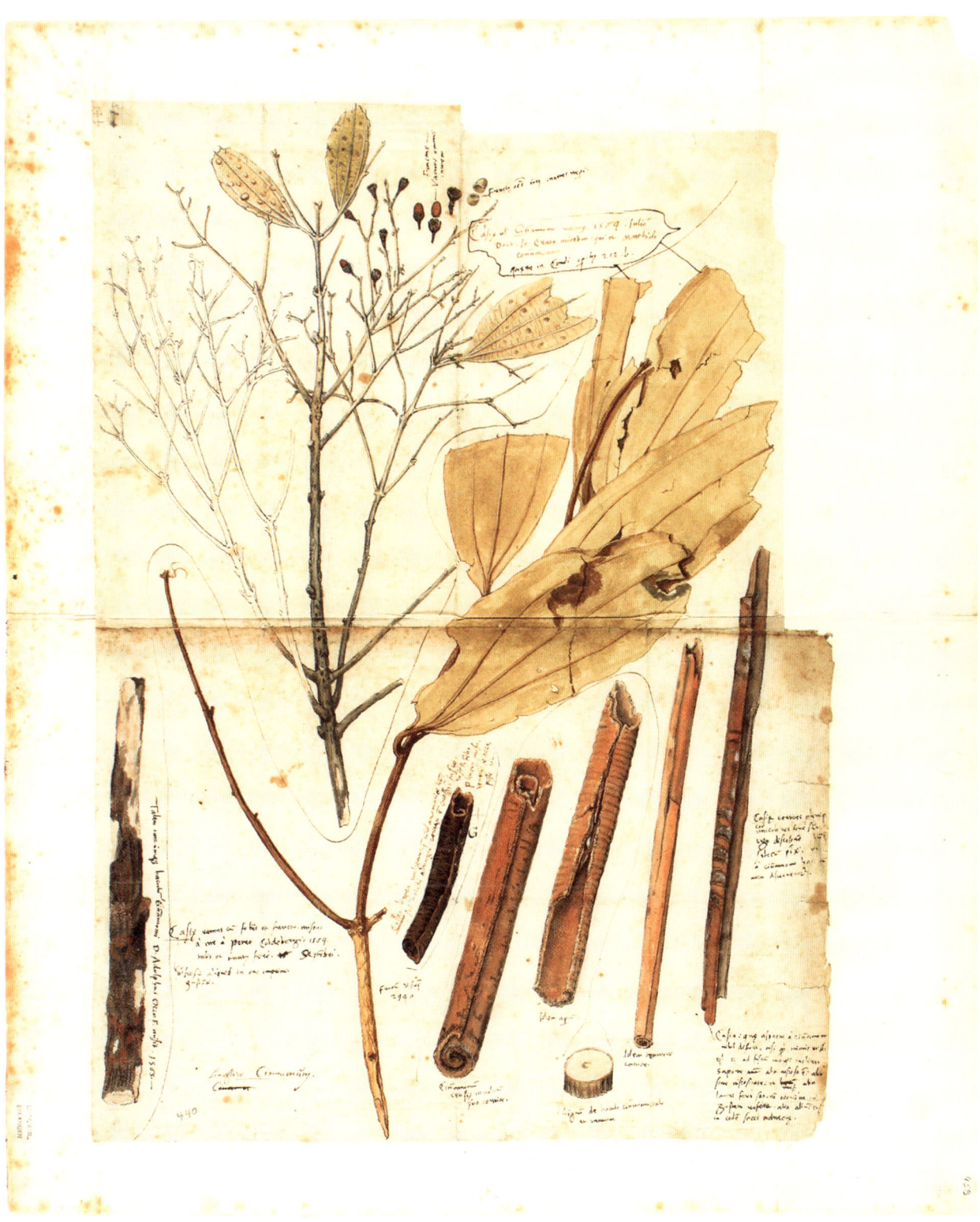

Scrophularia maior.

FABIO COLONNA

During his collecting career, the English bibliophile and biblical scholar Richard Ellys (1688–1742) added two volumes of a botanical manuscript, *Icones ipsis plantis*, to his burgeoning library, now at Blickling Hall, Norfolk. Probably bound in the early 1700s, the sheets were the work of Fabio Colonna (1567–1640), and form a collection of astonishingly beautiful composite images of plants. Colonna combined nature printing – a complex method involving printing directly from a freshly cut specimen – with his added ink and watercolour sketches to highlight parts of the plant difficult to reproduce by printing. The sketches focused on roots and stems; small, delicate leaves; flowers and flower parts; fruits and seeds. These were coloured in a simple, repeated palette of greens and reds, with some pink, blue and yellow.

Born in Naples to an established family, Colonna seemed destined for a career as a jurist before his epilepsy intervened. Such was the perceived authority of the ancient medical authors that Colonna decided to apply his skill in Greek and Latin to identify precisely the plants once used against this disease, knowledge he considered lost. He began with a comprehensive study of the native herbs of the Neapolitan region. His ambitious project combined textual analysis with the new emphasis on *autopsea* – seeing for oneself the objects in the living world.

Colonna extended his studies to include other aspects of natural history, such as conchology, and expanded the range of his plant hunting after his health improved. He had tried unsuccessfully to become Director of the Vatican Botanical Garden, but did enter the exclusive Lincean Academy in 1612. He published on plants in *Phytobasanos* (1592) and *Ekphrasis* (1606, 1616), envisaging that their accurate copperplate illustrations would allow the reader to verify his text.

So where do the *Icones* fit in? These were most likely the sheets Colonna prepared from specimens collected on his expeditions. They are thus a kind of field notebook, complete with notes on location, and form a record of both his botanizing as well as his later more detailed investigation of the parts of the plants for classification. Once held in loose folders, allowing easy rearrangement for scientific purposes, after his death they were always liable to be jumbled, but at least they survived.

'Scrophularia maior' (*S. nodosa*), or the great figwort, was commonly used against scrofula – tuberculosis of the neck glands. The nature-printed leaves are joined by the inked sketch of the square stem, with the lumpy root drawn above. The smaller leaves are printed and coloured, blending into the drawn flowering parts.

naturalists 127

MARIA SIBYLLA MERIAN, JOHANNA HELENA HEROLT & DOROTHEA MARIA GSELL

Maria Sibylla Merian (1647–1717) was already adept at picturing the natural world when she moved to Nuremberg in 1670 with her husband Johann Graff. Here, the young mother taught her skills to her 'company of maidens', daughters of the city's professional and mercantile elite. Later it would be her own daughters, Johanna Helena (1668–1723/30) and Dorothea Maria (1678–1743), who formed the 'company'.

Merian grew up in Frankfurt, in a household dominated by draughtsmanship, engraving and publishing. Both her father, Matthäus Merian, and step-father, Jacob Marrel, ran busy workshops. She served an unofficial apprenticeship under Marrel, learning partly by copying prints by acknowledged artists such as French flower painter Nicolas Robert. There was less family precedent for her fascination with insects. Merian collected caterpillars and observed the plants they fed on. Bringing these 'worms' and their food home, she watched and recorded their ensuing life cycles.

Besides her teaching, Merian also began to publish. In 1675, 1677 and 1680 her flower books, *Florum*, appeared as sets of twelve engravings; the *Neues Blumenbuch* (1680) brought all 36 together. Pictured in them were some of the most popular flowers of the 17th century, including the bulbs from the east that now enlivened northern Europe's gardens. Merian intended that these would be pattern books for decorative arts such as embroidery or 'needle painting', as well as for drawing, painting and engraving.

Her growing series of insect metamorphoses overlapped with the flower painting. On fine parchment in watercolour, Merian had amassed a collection of life-sized paintings, which formed the basis, when bound, of her 'study book'. This was a working document, part natural history, part collection of master illustrations. In her *Raupenbuchs* (1679, 1683 and 1717) the insects moved centre stage, posed on the plants on which they fed. She continued her insect studies after she left her husband and moved with the children to Frankfurt and then Waltha Castle in 1685. Here the Labadist religious community benefited from the patronage of Cornelis van Sommelsdijk, governor of Surinam, and the castle housed his collection of South American flora and fauna. What Merian saw here and later in Amsterdam inspired her to venture to Surinam in 1699, where she and Dorothea spent 21 months.

In Surinam, both women sketched from life, sometimes using black chalk to outline larger drawings painted in watercolour on vellum. These portable masters were then rolled up and taken home, along with specimens for study and sale. Merian published the magnificent *Metamorphosis Insectorum Surinamensium* in 1705. She was already renowned, but this book took her fame to a new level, even if she still struggled financially.

While Maria was the lead artist, her daughters worked with her, on occasion on the same sheets. Some were studies, others copies made by transfer printing, coloured for sale. The younger women also forged their own careers. With so much unsigned, it is difficult to attribute exactly who did what, but increasingly attributions are being made. What is clear is that many compositions were effectively a collaborative 'collage' of studies taken from master drawings. Johanna (married to Jakob Herolt in 1692) began her own commissions before leaving with her husband for Surinam in 1711. She continued to supply material from South America, where she probably died. After ten years of marriage, Dorothea was widowed in 1711. She cared for Merian after she'd had a stroke (1714) and following her mother's death married as second time, to Georg Gsell, and left for St Petersburg in 1717, where Peter the Great had already purchased Merian's work. Dorothea taught at the Academy of Sciences along with Gsell, and painted flowers and birds for the Tsar's cabinet.

Merian recycled her practice drawings (the faint black chalk guidelines are visible) for her early books. This narcissus sketch appeared in the third of the *Florum* sets, with the butterfly and caterpillar but not the wasps.

(Above) Formerly thought to be watercolour and bodycolour work by Merian, the nasturtiums and insects are now attributed to Dorothea. They are part of an album of Merian's work that once belonged to the phenomenal British collector Sir Hans Sloane, exactly the sort of client the women wished to cultivate. (Right) *Dracunculus vulgaris*, with its 'collage' yellow butterfly by Johanna. (Opposite) Papaya (*Carica papaya*) with a Noctuid moth on the unripe fruit, from Merian's Surinam period. She could already have been familiar with members of this family of moths as they are found also in Europe, but papayas need the tropical conditions of their original home in Central America.

NICCOLÒ GUALTIERI

Famed for his interest in shells and the *Index testarum conchyliorum* (1742), Niccolò Gualtieri (1688–1744) was also fascinated by plants. Born in Florence, he studied medicine in Pisa before returning home to serve as physician to the wife of the 6th Duke of Tuscany and then the 7th Duke. Gualtieri was both cultured and learned, combining his skills in natural history with poetry and draughtsmanship. He established a typical collection of *naturalia*, or curiosities, such as shells, fossils, animals of land and sea, minerals, plants, woods and resins.

Both Florence (1545) and Pisa (1544) already had long-established botanical gardens thanks to the patronage of the Medicis. The gardens had originally concentrated on the 'simples' – plants used for medicine – but the arrival of a flow of unfamiliar plants through greatly expanded trade and exploration brought new aesthetics in design as well as new species. Gualtieri was charged by the head of the garden in Florence, Pier Antonio Micheli, with improving it by adding material from Pisa. In 1716, along with Micheli, Gualtieri was one of four founder members of the Società Botanica Fiorentina, the Botanical Society of Florence, the first of its kind in Europe. It was in these years that Gualtieri made his simple plant sketches – bold images painted in a restricted colour palette with occasional floral details. They were annotated according to the classification system of Frenchman Joseph Pitton de Tournefort, which had become popular. In this way, Gualtieri was demonstrating his contemporary botanical knowledge.

With the death of the 7th Duke in 1737, Gualtieri's star waned and he returned to the University of Pisa. In 1742, just two years before he died, he had the plant drawings bound. By this time the paper on which many of the drawings were made had seen much wear, as if they had been used for reference purposes over the years since their creation.

Gualtieri's plant sketches share a similar flattened appearance and were perhaps drawn from pressed specimens. (Opposite) *Bunias erucago*, known in Italy as casellore, is used in various ways in regional cookery. (Above) At the end of his bound volume Gualtieri included several pages of marine algae. (Overleaf) Gualtieri's bold renditions of various arum leaves.

HARRIET SCOTT & HELENA FORDE

Natural history ran deep in the Scott family. Alexander Scott (1800–1883) first ventured to New South Wales, Australia, in 1827. Here he would indulge a love for butterflies and moths inherited from his father, a doctor, botanist and East India Company bureaucrat in Bombay (Mumbai). Before he married her in 1846, Harriet Calcott (*c.* 1802/3–1866) gave birth to two daughters, Harriet (1830–1907) and Helena (1832–1910), in Sydney. She cultivated their early love of plants with morning walks to the botanic gardens, and all the Scotts, it seemed, could draw.

When the girls were teenagers, the family home on Ash Island in the Hunter River estuary near Hexham was a meeting place for like-minded family, local and visiting natural historians, artists and explorers. Conrad Martens (p. 250), an old friend from Sydney days, came and sketched, glad of the work during the depression of the 1840s. Harriet and Helena were not formally trained in natural history, but imbibed it at their father's side, first in Sydney and then with greater independence during the Ash Island years.

The young women kept comprehensive botanical records, plant lists, dried and mounted specimens, drawings and plant notes. The botany in their drawings was supplemented by the developmental stages of the local lepidoptera and the intimate relationships with the plants that sustained them, reminiscent of the Merian women almost two hundred years earlier (p. 128). The entomological results were published in the acclaimed *Australian Lepidoptera and Their Transformations* (1864).

What had been an amateur pleasure became tinged with sorrow after financial and personal difficulties transformed their lives. First their mother's death and then Alexander's bankruptcy in 1866 forced the sale of their beloved Ash Island home and a move for Harriet and her father to Sydney. Helena joined them later that year; she had married another practical artist, the draughtsman and surveyor Edward Forde in 1864. Subsequently, the Fordes travelled to the Darling River with their sketchbooks, he on official business for the Department of Harbour and River Navigation, she with a view to producing a flora of the region. Within a year Forde was dead of fever and Helena found herself a young widow.

While these immensely talented women were proud to have their names on *Australian Lepidoptera*, they were nervous and ashamed to ask for money for their exquisite zoological and botanical illustrations. Women of their social position were uncomfortable in business, but their earlier correspondence network and personal connections came to their aid as contacts provided commissions for serious natural history illustration. Decorative work came their way too. Both sisters produced botanical-themed Christmas cards in 1879 and 1880, thought to be the first in Australia. Harriet drew for a railway guide, but marriage gave her security, while Helena continued to support herself by her art. She tried teaching and continued to develop her relationship with the Australian Museum, where much of the Scott family collections found a home, for a modest price. In Helena's obituary, tribute was paid to the sisters as the 'Last of the Artist-Naturalists'.

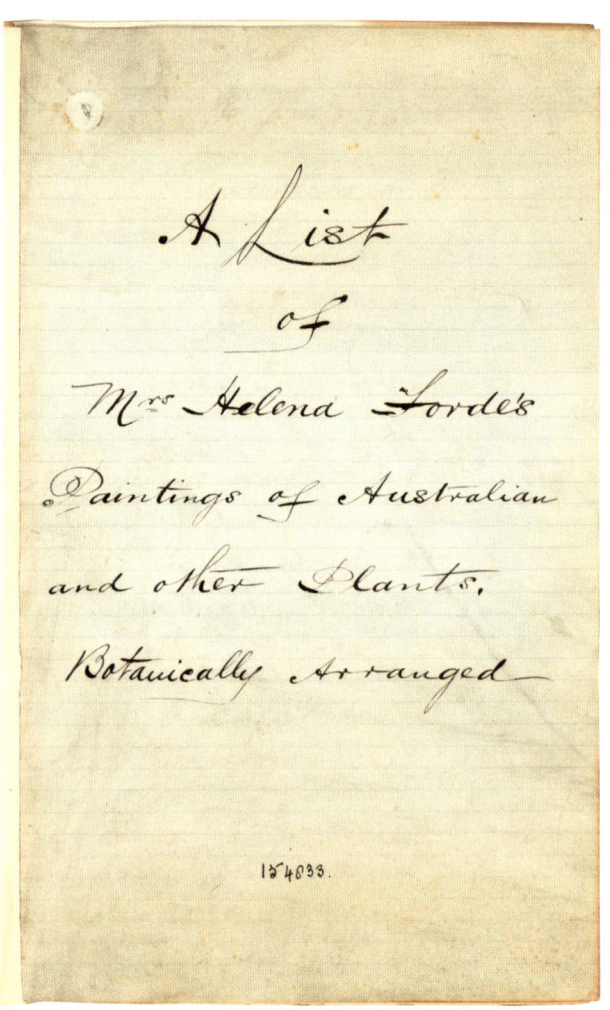

Helena Forde created an album of her botanical work dating from at least 1851 to 1896. Often a preliminary sketch was turned over and a delicately coloured drawing created on the other side.

Alexander Scott used Conrad Martens's unfinished sketch of Dawes Point, Sydney, as background for the sawfly and its larvae feeding on *Corymbia citriodora*. It was developed by one of his daughters into a 'beautiful and accurate drawing' for publication in 1859.

(Above) Harriet Scott's sketch of the climber Moreton Bay bignonia (*Pandorea jasminoides*). (Opposite) Harriet sketched *Blandfordia nobilis*, known as Christmas Bells or gadigalbudyari (in the local Aboriginal dialect) at home, but the plant had been collected at Lake Macquarie, south of the Hunter River.

(Page 140) Helena's sketches of *Acacia longifolia* (above), for which she had asked for help in naming, and '*Pithecolobium pruinosum*' (*Pararchidendron pruinosum*), a genus with a single species, but closely related to Acacia.

(Page 141) On the Darling River expedition, Edward Forde sketched the limestone cliffs on the Murray River below Blanchetown (above). (Below) Helena's sketch of the 'Valley of the Palms' at Dapto (now a suburb of Wollongong). *Livistona australis*, the cabbage palm, grows in great stands and is native to the east coast of Australia.

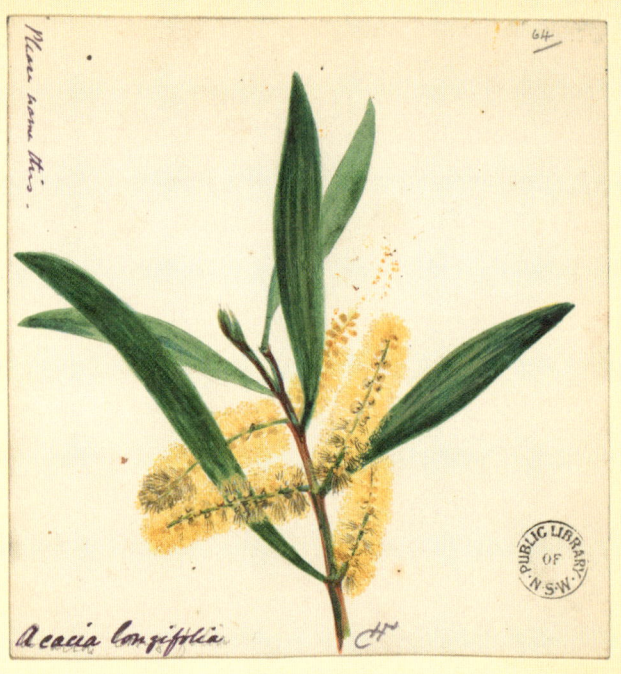

Please name this.
64
Acacia longifolia
PUBLIC LIBRARY OF N.S.W.

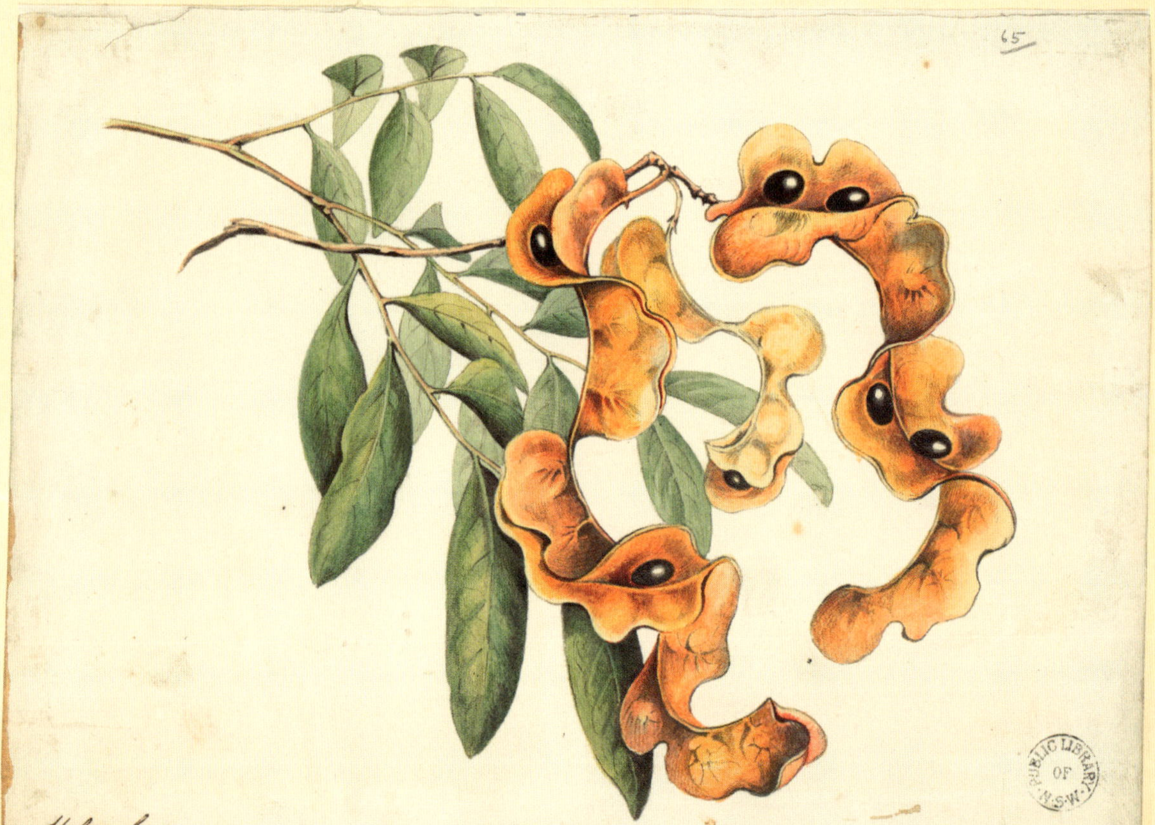
65
Helena Scott
Ash Island
Pithecolobium
pruinosum
PUBLIC LIBRARY OF N.S.W.

CHARLES DORAT

Today, Charles Dorat (*fl.* 1850s–1860s) might be called a naturalist with an inclination for ethnobotany. This doctor living in El Salvador was equally at home riding through the wooded landscapes of the coastal interior or up the Izalco volcano as he was corresponding with colleagues in Britain and North America. His letters were eagerly anticipated: they came with carefully prepared botanical specimens, seeds, samples of indigenous drugs and drawings. Dorat was an inveterate sketcher, both in his journal and in detailed pencil, pen and ink and watercolour drawings of plants, insects, snakes and scenes of local life, made on the spot. He also recorded the plant names, collecting equipment and practices of the indigenous ethnic groups who inhabited the Pacific side of El Salvador and Guatemala. Some of this region was known as the 'Balsam Coast', from the renowned if misleadingly named 'Balsam of Peru' that was harvested and processed from *Myroxylon pereirae* trees. To prevent 'biopiracy', the local people were keen to keep their knowledge of how they managed the trees secret – it was their inheritance and livelihood.

Dorat's botanical correspondents included Joseph Carson, professor of *materia medica* and therapeutics at the University of Pennsylvania, and Daniel Hanbury of the London pharmaceutical company Allen & Hanburys (though he was an active partner only for two years). Hanbury's enthusiasm was for medical botany. Plants were vital sources of new drugs in the 19th century (as they remain today), and it was crucial that the correct plant was being used. Dorat was essential for Carson and Hanbury if they could not travel themselves.

Dorat was eager for such connections. He found himself caught up in uncertain times as the more liberal El Salvador and conservative Guatemala went to war. He turned to Carson in 1860 to try to generate interest in his publishing projects – a comprehensive social, political and natural history of the Central American states and a more focused medical flora. Despite the uniqueness of his work, this came to nothing, but at least his sketches remain.

Dorat collected in the Cedros region among forest trees. He sketched the plants and also recorded local medicinal uses. 'Conchalagua No. 1' and '2' (right and left) are species of *Schkuhria*, one a sudorific (sweat inducing), the other used for syphilis, skin diseases and as a diuretic. The 'suntule' root (*Cyperus articulatus*; top) is an 'astringent'.

naturalists

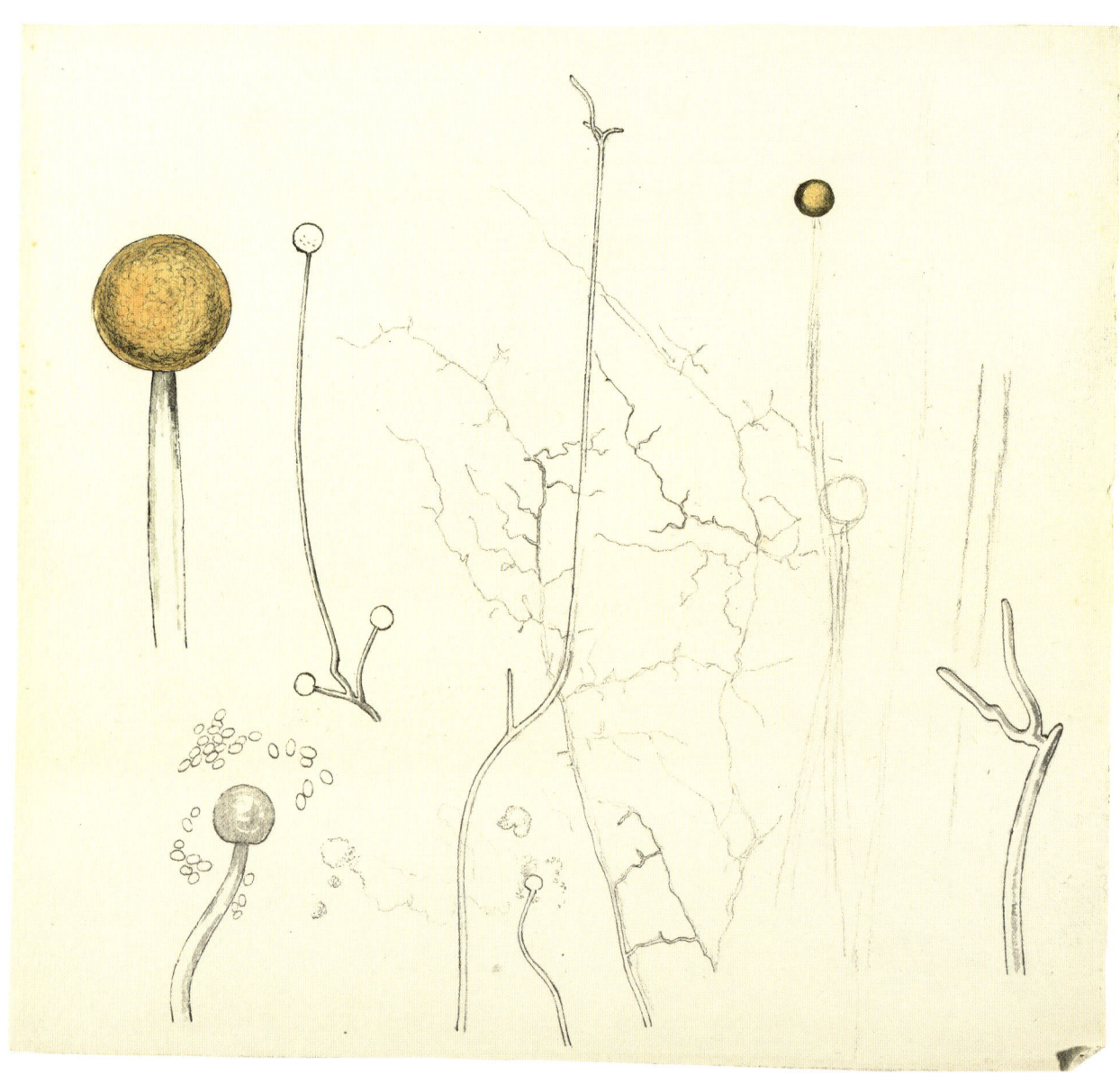

(Above) *Mucor* sp. – Potter has captured the branching hyphae and the resulting mycelium as these organisms grew. (Opposite) Fruiting bodes of *Flammulina velutipes*, which Potter knew as *Agaricus velutipes* and which, as she proudly reported, 'I have grown twice and Mr Massee has also grown according to my direction at Kew'.

BEATRIX POTTER

It didn't seem to matter whether it was tempting publishers with designs for Christmas cards or engaging in scientific debate about fungi, Victorian society demanded that, as a young woman, Beatrix Potter (1866–1943) must have a male intermediary. Little wonder that her independent purchase of Hill Top in the Lake District in northwestern England in 1905 brought her so much pleasure. It meant increasing liberation. As Mrs William Heelis, Beatrix became a champion Herdwick sheep breeder and a champion for the region she loved.

By 1905 Potter had already created many of her famous and cherished characters, whose stories we still read to our children and whose images we use to decorate their bedrooms – Peter Rabbit wallpaper went on sale that year. Potter's illustrations are so evocative because she set the animal protagonists in intensely observed settings. This was the result of her obsession with engaging with the natural world through sketching, drawing and, later, photography. Plant forms delighted her, fossils intrigued; she scrutinized small subjects with microscopes and was fearless in handling insects and amphibians. The Natural History Museum, close to the Potters' London home, became a favourite haunt.

In the 1890s, Potter's interest in collecting and drawing the fruiting bodies of fungi developed into a serious passion, often pursued on holidays in Scotland. She was enthused by Charles McIntosh, a renowned amateur mycologist from Inver near Dunkeld. He helped her identify specimens and critiqued her drawings, in which she learnt to include cross sections to better depict stems and gills. She also became intrigued by lichens, though did not correctly appreciate their symbiont nature. 'Uncle Harry' (the chemist Sir Henry Enfield Roscoe) helped her to obtain a student ticket for Kew Gardens, a fraught business for an amateur woman naturalist. The culmination of her mycology phase was a paper read on her behalf at the Linnean Society by George Massee of Kew in 1897. This was never published, and Potter moved on, as science had too, with professionalization and specialization increasingly sidelining curious naturalists, even if they could sketch with infinite grace.

from the botanical garden

The first botanical gardens appeared in Italy in the 16th century for medicinal purposes. Their evolving functions as plant repositories and places of investigation, science and education involved artists and botanists in special relationships. Sometimes it was the botanists who drew. William Jackson Hooker and Nicholas Brown mark important moments in sketching from the garden. Alternatively, artists could be employed by the botanists. Francis Bauer represents the golden age of botanical art, Walter Hood Fitch the 19th-century revolution in lithography and Mary Grierson the continued importance of art in botany in the 20th century, even after the advent of photography. The last three were associated with Kew, an exemplary botanical garden. The role of John Tyley, about whom we unfortunately know little, at the botanic garden on the other side of the world in St Vincent, is equally intriguing and fascinating.

FRANCIS (FRANZ) BAUER

There were three artistically gifted boys in the Bauer family. Joseph (1756–1830) emulated their father, Lucas, as court painter to the Prince of Liechtenstein; Francis and Ferdinand (p. 246) painted the natural world. Lucas Bauer died in 1762, but his artistic influence lived on because the boys' mother, Therese, shaped their prodigious talents by having them copy his works. She also found them mentors, men who could propel the fatherless boys forward. In 1788 Francis (1758–1840) began travelling through Europe with Joseph von Jacquin, the son of his Viennese employer, the botanist Nikolaus von Jacquin. The tour included the London collections of Joseph Banks, who offered Bauer a job as draughtsman at Kew for £300 a year. He accepted.

Bauer is regarded as Kew's first resident botanical artist, although Banks paid his salary and at the time the gardens were still the domain of the royal family. He remained there until his death, his salary converted into an annuity after Banks died. As 'Botanick painter to His Majesty', Bauer's tasks included recording new plants arriving in the gardens and providing art lessons for various royal ladies.

Banks was keen to have a publication that celebrated Kew's novelties, too many of which were appearing in print elsewhere. Accordingly, Bauer drew for the short-lived periodical *Delineations of exotick plants cultivated in the Royal gardens at Kew* (1796–1803), but he also had ample time to devote to other projects. Some were for Banks, whose practical concern with diseases of apples and cereals became a long-running interest for Bauer. He also drew orchids for John Lindley, who was closely involved with the Horticultural Society's gardens, ferns for William Hooker (p. 152) and the genus *Rafflesia* for botanist Robert Brown of the British Museum. Bauer's precision preparatory sketches and drawings were achieved with the aid of microscopes; he used sixteen during his career. His techniques included outlining in pencil, using a fine brush to form the shape, and then completing the image with a main body of watercolour.

Bauer took the depiction of plant dissections to a new level with his drawings of pollen. He was fascinated with floral mechanisms and fructification, and illustrated these beautifully in his work on orchids. Elected to the Linnean (1804) and Royal (1821) societies, Bauer was so much more than a leading flower painter in this golden age of botanical art – he was at the heart of the growing significance of the new botanical gardens.

The organism *Puccinia graminis* causes stem rust on cereal crops and can devastate a harvest. It has a complicated lifecycle, involving different species of plant hosts, although this was unknown at the time Bauer sketched the appearance of the various stages.

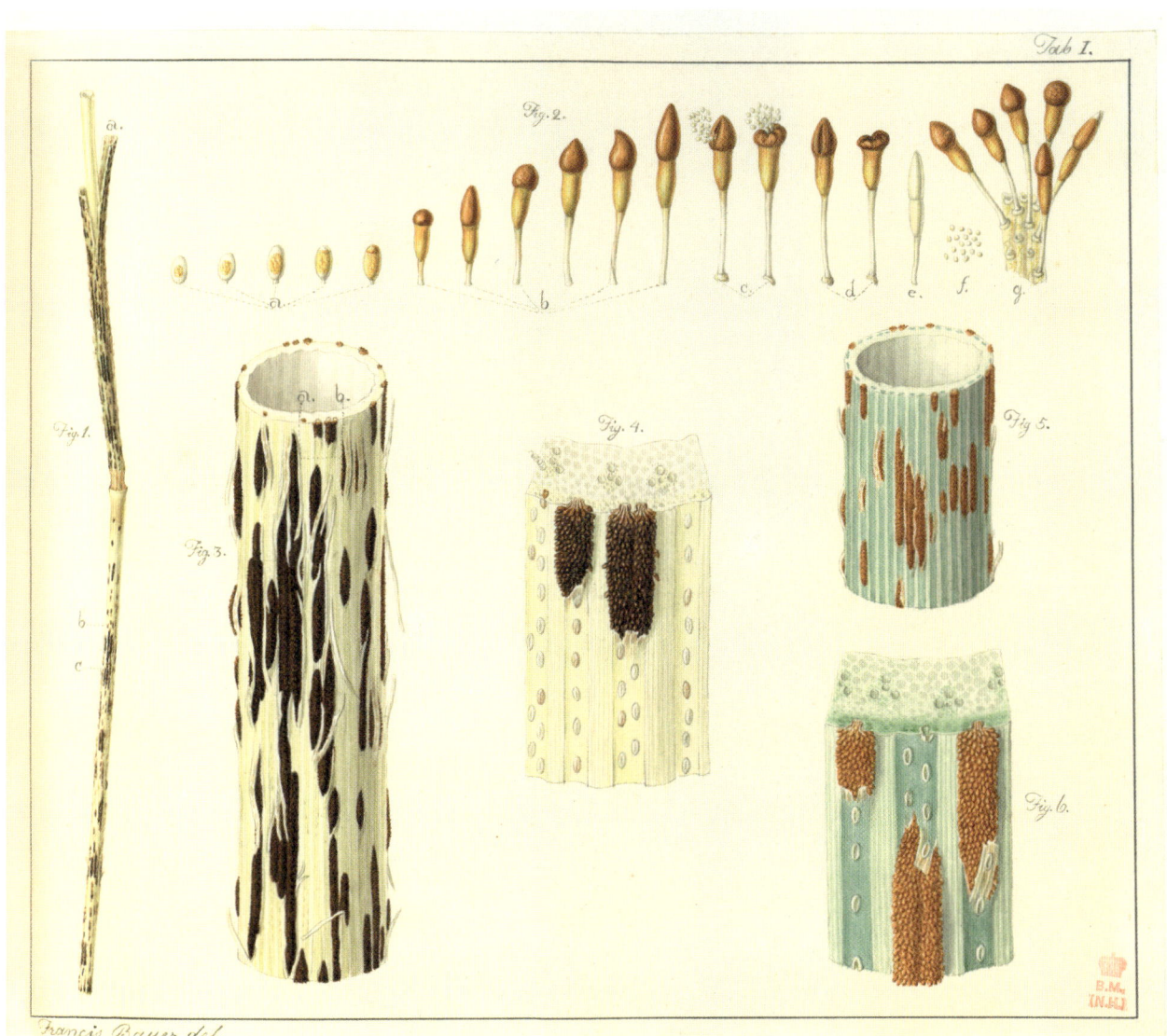

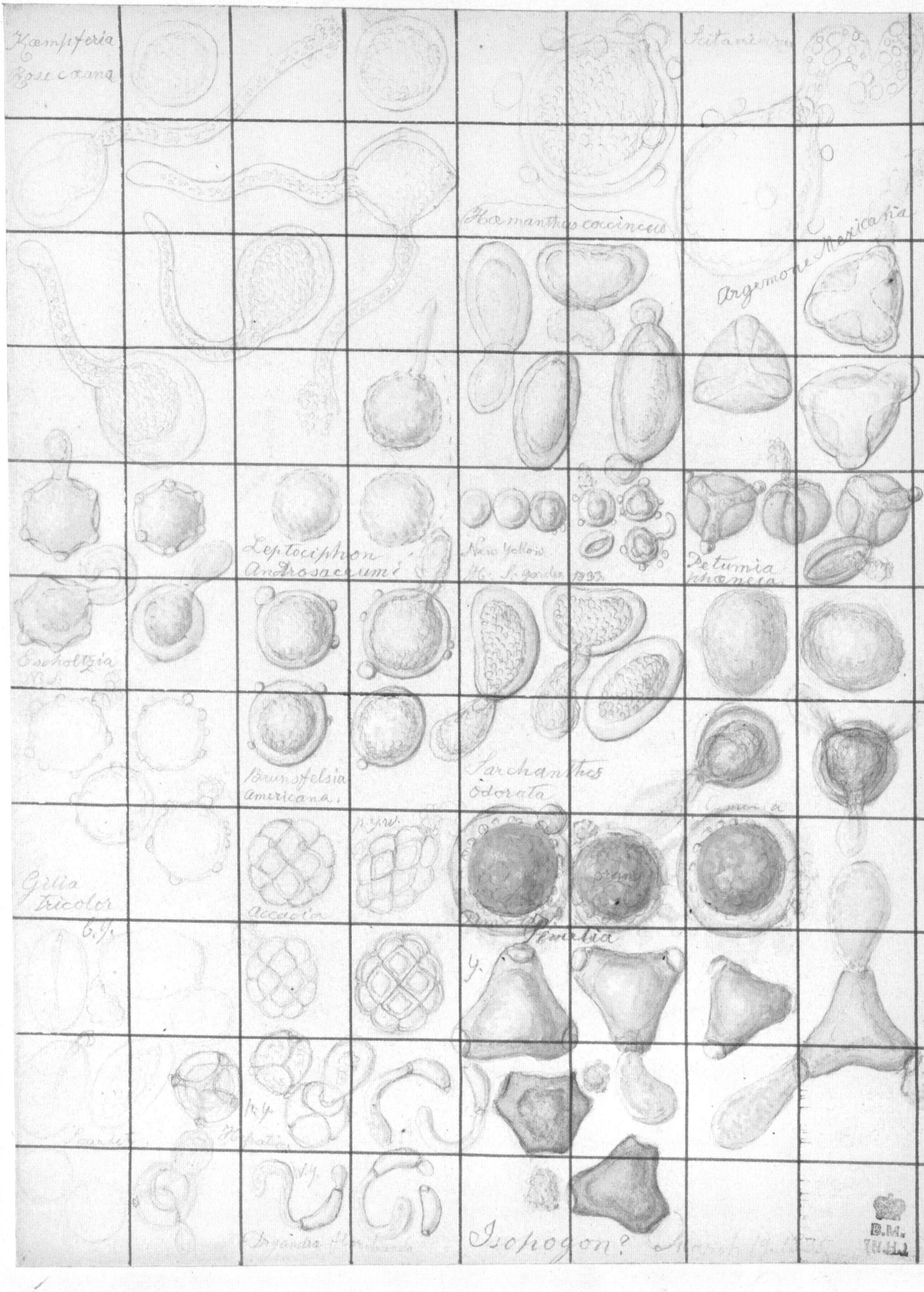

Kaempferia Roseceana						Titania	
				Haemanthus coccineus			Argemone Mexicana
Eschscholtzia		Leptosiphon Androsaceum		New Yellow		Detumia	
		Brunsfelsia americana		Tarchanthes odorata			
Gilia tricolor		Accacia					
				Isopogon?			

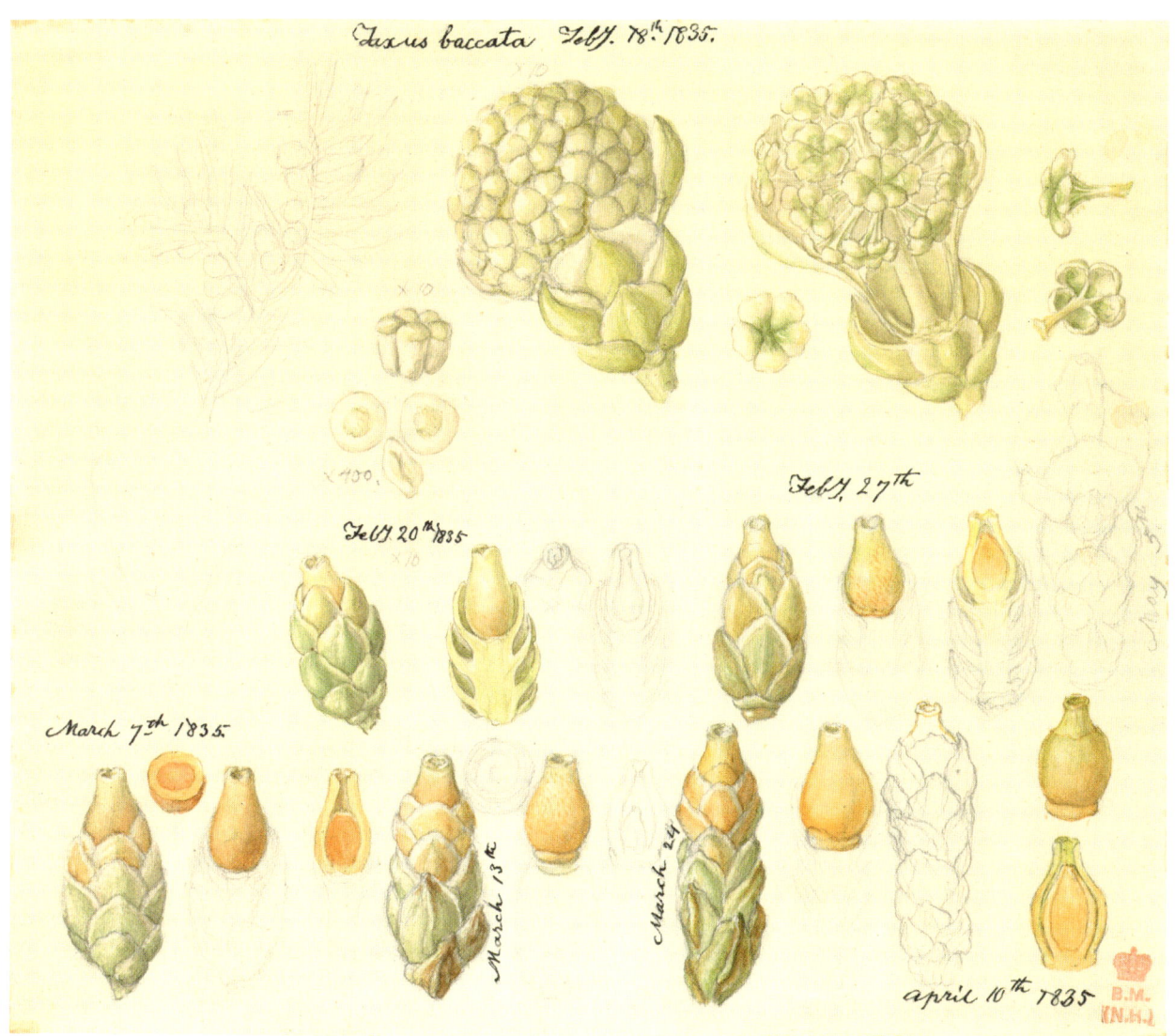

(Opposite) Drawn on squared paper to give a sense of proportion, Bauer's illustrations of pollen cells (some germinating) of at least fifteen different species of plants unintentionally create a fascinating abstract effect. Pencil notes give a date of 1833 and indicate that the Chiswick gardens of the Horticultural Society were the source of some. (Above) Bauer recorded the development of the seeds of yew (*Taxus baccata*) at Kew in a series of dated sketches of 1835.

from the botanical garden 149

John Tyley. del.

Itea Cyrilla W
Cyrilla racemiflora Linn

JOHN TYLEY

Subaltern artists on the margins of society can be shadowy figures, especially when they are people of colour. John Tyley (*fl.* 1790s–1800s) is one such. He is known for both his association with Alexander Anderson (*c.* 1748–1811), superintendent of the St Vincent Botanic Gardens, Kingstown, and his delightful watercolour sketches of the plants of the Caribbean islands.

Anderson was born in Scotland and had some training in medicine in Edinburgh and botany at the Chelsea Physic Garden before leaving for New York in 1774 to join his brother. After an eventful journey, involving his capture by the French at sea and ransom, he found himself on the island of St Lucia. Working in the garrison hospital he was at last able to indulge his botanical interests in the company of Dr George Young. Here he found a febrifuge, a local species of cinchona – *C. floribunda* (*Exostema sanctae-luciae*).

In 1785 Anderson was appointed as the second superintendent of the gardens at Kingstown on St Vincent, having been recommended by Young, and the ubiquitous Joseph Banks. Once in charge, Anderson fulfilled the original idea for the garden. He botanized widely in the Caribbean and Guyana in South America, collecting plants with medicinal, commercial and edible potential. The seedlings and cuttings were intended to enhance the flora of the island, helping to make it more self-sufficient as well as diversifying production away from the reliance on sugar monoculture. He also received the first breadfruit plants from Bligh's second voyage to the Pacific. Anderson was a proto-environmentalist who wanted to preserve the native flora. Informed of the value of plants, especially trees after the discovery of oxygen in the 1770s, he clashed with the Caribs and the slave-holding planters, who wanted to clear the land for agriculture.

John Tyley was an Antiguan, described by Anderson's nephew in 1798 as a 'young mulatto' living with his uncle and serving as his draughtsman. Banks had wanted Anderson to gather the plant lore of the indigenous Caribs and blacks, so perhaps Tyley was able to provide assistance. Anderson left his manuscripts unpublished at his death, including the *Hortus St Vincentii*; he also prepared extensive plant lists of the garden's plants. Tyley's careful watercolours could have been associated with any of these projects.

Among Tyley's drawings of plants are *Cyrilla racemiflora* (opposite) and 'Jar plum' (*Syzygium cumini*), the Java plum or jambolan of East and Southeast Asia (above). The Java plum had medicinal uses in its home territories, which may have attracted Anderson's attention.

WILLIAM JACKSON HOOKER

William Jackson Hooker (1785–1865) oversaw the transformation of the Royal Botanic Gardens, Kew, into a global scientific resource. He was 57 before he became Director in 1841 and brought with him his formidable expertise in botany, as well as a vision of how a modern botanical garden might function. He saw it as a place of public instruction, a tool of empire that acted as an entrepôt for economically significant plants and their products, and a repository of plant science which botanists could visit and communicate their knowledge to one another.

At 21 an inheritance gave him some financial security, and he spent several years in Halesworth, Suffolk, managing a brewery, but was able to pursue his love of plants. He was elected to the Linnean Society in 1806 and travelled to Iceland for Sir Joseph Banks (his specimens were lost at sea). An early interest in cryptogams, plants reproducing by spores rather than seeds, was stimulated by illustrating them for Dawson Turner, who later became his father-in-law. Hooker also wrote about liverworts, mosses, ferns, seaweeds and lichens, part of his ongoing fascination with plant structure.

Banks recast Hooker as a full-time botanist when he helped him gain the chair in botany at the University of Glasgow in 1820. Hooker expanded the botanical garden, took students botanizing in the Highlands and wrote a botanical textbook, because none existed. As well as discovering plants, Hooker discovered the artist Walter Hood Fitch (p. 156). They came to Kew together, forming a new synergy between botanist, artist and botanical garden. Hooker was already the editor (1827–65) and illustrator of *Curtis's Botanical Magazine* and he brought this important publication to Kew, effectively institutionalizing it there.

His fine botanical library and vast herbarium, both established using his own money, eventually swelled the Kew collections. Here he also instigated a new Museum of Economic Botany for plant products. Hooker's permanent legacy was to place Kew at the centre of all things botanical, a model for gardens throughout the expanding British empire.

(Above) The initial sketch, dried leaf and final colour plate drawing of *Heteropterys chrysophylla*. (Opposite) 'Perhaps there is not a more unsatisfactory figure in all the Fifty-four volumes of the Botanical Magazine than that of this singular plant', Hooker wrote of an earlier illustration of the skunk cabbage, hence his preparatory sketch for a new one.

Color may be fuller & brighter especially of the leaves.
W. J. H.

Bot. Mag. t. 3184

3184.

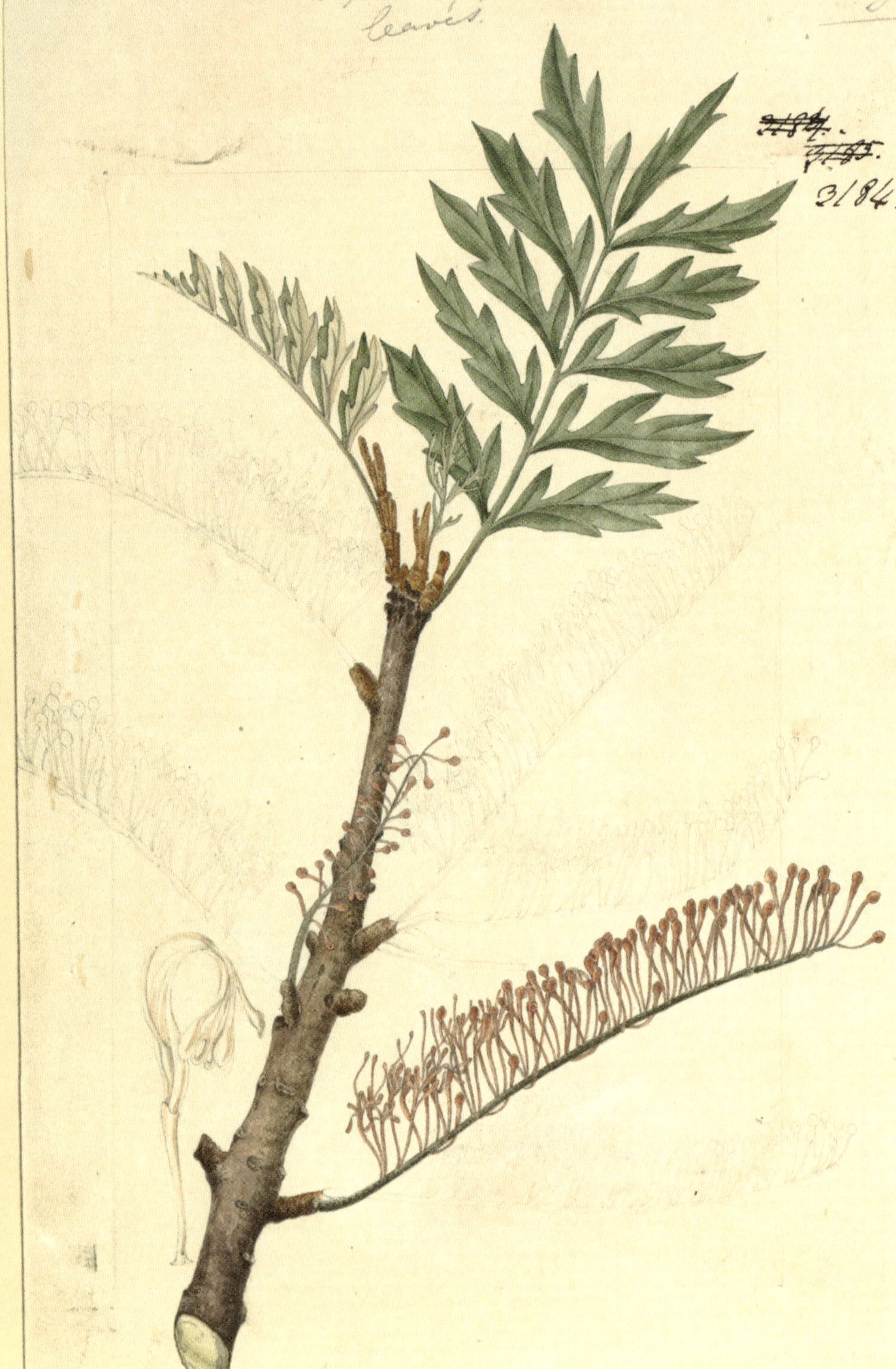

Grevillea robusta

H.101-23
Bot. Mag. Original presented by R. Hort. Soc. 25·1·23

(Opposite) Hooker annotated this sketch of flowers and leaves of the tree *Grevillea robusta* 'colour may be fuller and brighter especially of the leaves', and it appeared thus enhanced in *Curtis's Botanical Magazine*. It was probably created by the prolific plant collector and explorer Allan Cunningham, a regular correspondent of Hooker. (Above) An example of the 'submerged algae' that fascinated Hooker, from his album of sketches.

WALTER HOOD FITCH

Artist Walter Hood Fitch (1817–1892) was born in Lanark, Scotland, and trained in drawing and lithography in Glasgow. He was plucked from an apprenticeship and perhaps obscurity as a textile pattern-maker by William Hooker (p. 152), then professor of botany at the University of Glasgow, who appreciated Fitch's speed and accuracy. Hooker hired him as his personal artist and took him to Kew when he was appointed Director there in 1841. Together, the two men shaped the artistic output of the botanic garden.

Fitch developed a special style and pioneered the use of lithography in botanical illustration. He often drew from dried plants, and had a gift for rehydrating the stuff of the herbarium. In 1859 he went to Madrid to revive and illustrate 80-year-old plants. He specialized in the general rather than the specific, rarely including any patches of yellowing or insect holes and conveying instead the essence of his plant, which was perfect for botanical description. He also prepared the drawings of others from the field (for instance Joseph Hooker's, p. 172) for publication, always combining what he had in front of him with his considerable botanical knowledge. As well as practising his art, Fitch also authored instructional pieces on botanical drawing for *Gardeners' Chronicle*, a popular Victorian magazine.

Increasingly sought after to illustrate the publications of other botanists, including the plates from the Grant and Speke expedition (p. 22), he resigned from Kew in 1860 to become a freelance artist. He continued to work for *Curtis's Botanical Magazine* until 1878 – indeed Victorian issues of *Curtis's* would have looked very different without Fitch. By then he had created almost 3,000 plant illustrations for the magazine, and his nephew John Nugent Fitch (1840–1927) continued the family tradition.

Fitch later insisted that the Hookers had insufficiently appreciated him, although Joseph Hooker did secure him a civil pension in 1880. It was deserved, for Fitch's output is astonishing. His published images amount to almost 12,000, an average of nearly five a week throughout his working life, and many unpublished ones remained as part of the collections at Kew.

(Right) Even serious botanists are not above value judgments: Joseph Hooker described the South African *Bowiea volubilis* as possessing little beauty, but Fitch certainly caught its 'curiosity'. (Opposite) '*Scolopendrium krebsii*' (*Blechnum punctulatum* var. *krebsii*), with instructions to copy the colours and make the crown of this African fern less dense.

Scolopendrium Krebsii = Lomaria punctulata.

(Opposite) *Pistia stratiotes*, an aquatic plant known as water lettuce. (Above) *Tacca leontopetaloides* is an amazing flower that arises from a starchy tuber. Fitch's specimen was grown from a Madagascan tuber given to Kew by Mary Anne Stebbing's father, W. W. Saunders.

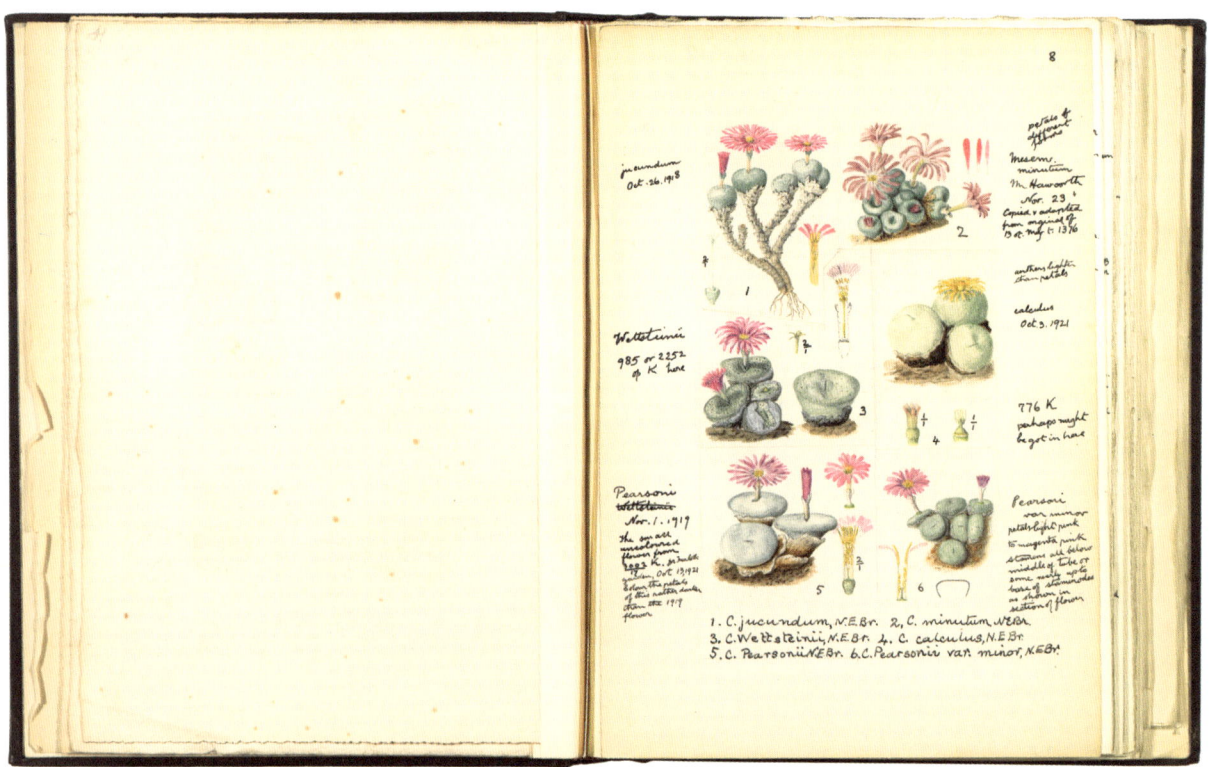

Brown recorded subtle differences in the same plant over a series of growing seasons, and as they developed in different growing conditions.

NICHOLAS BROWN

Although he lived into the era of professional botany, and became a botanist himself, Nicholas Brown (1849–1934) is a transitional figure. He had no formal education beyond grammar school, but a passion for botany seemed to be in his blood. He trained on the job, as curator in the private museum of William Wilson Saunders (father of Mary Anne Stebbing; p. 180) in Reigate. Saunders, a great enthusiast, also edited a journal, *Refugium Botanicum* (1869–73). This introduced Brown to both eminent botanists and families of plants – orchids, aroids and bromeliads – for which he developed a lifelong interest.

In 1873 Saunders was bankrupted, and Brown found work in the Kew herbarium. He became Assistant Keeper in 1909 and stayed on after retirement, a total of 61 years. He never sought personal advancement and quietly got on with the job he loved best: botanical systematics – the classification of plants. For several years he methodically described plants new to Britain for both *The Gardener's Year Book* and *Kew Bulletin*. He took on the difficult groups and could be territorial about plants he brought order to, such as the genus *Euphorbia*, Asclepiadaceae (including shrubs, woody vines and succulents) and Mesembryanthema (including the iceplants and other succulents).

Much of his career was devoted to taxa from tropical and South Africa, although he never actually travelled there. Instead, botanists from South Africa would regularly come to Kew to consult with him, an illustration of how important botanical gardens are as repositories of both plants and people. Brown made drawings for the twelfth volume of John T. Boswell Syme's *English Botany* (1886) and its four-volume Supplement (1892), but his art was otherwise placed in the service of his dedicated pursuit of systematics. His approach is perfectly captured in his albums of succulents, which contain examples showing how his more refined work was elaborated from initial sketches (see opposite below). All illustrate how botanical draughtsmanship aided the process of taxonomic science in the botanical garden.

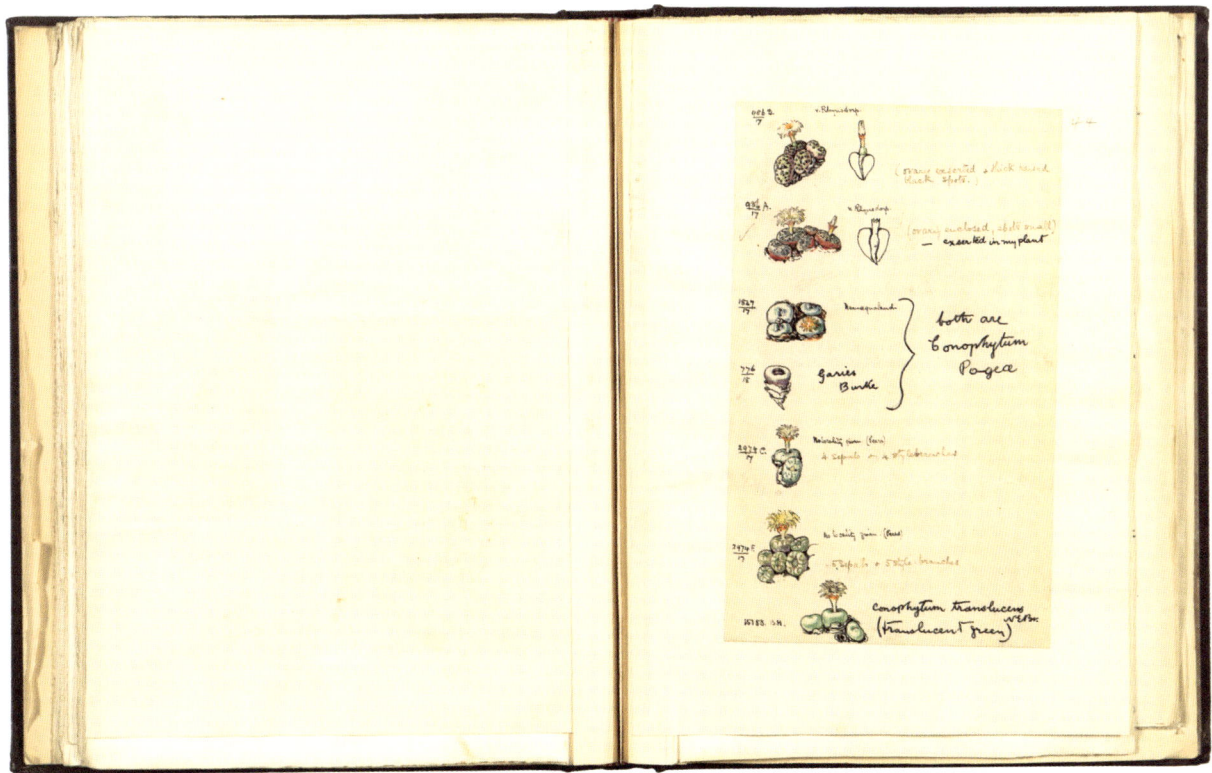

Many of the plants Brown's work helped to understand are in the *Conophytum* genus from the Succulent Karoo semi-desert regions of Namibia and South Africa.

from the botanical garden

MARY GRIERSON

'It never entered my head that one day I would find myself on the way to Hawaii.' Ever modest, Mary Grierson (1912–2012) was faintly surprised that her latent talent for botanical art drove the second half of her life. During the Second World War she had worked in aerial reconnaissance, analysing photographs. Her attention to detail, so evident in her art later, was put to good use, and she continued in this kind of employment after the war.

Always keen on wildflowers, she was once so delighted with a group of Pasque flowers that she picked one to take home to paint. This was around 1957, when her employers, Hunting Aerosurveys, sent her on a pen and ink drawing course at the Field Studies Centre, Flatford Mill, where John Constable (p. 198) had painted his famous landscapes. There she appreciated John Nash's tuition and developed a private portfolio of botanical sketches. She happened to show these to one of the interview panel at Kew Gardens in 1960 when she applied for a job as exhibitions officer. The position she was offered was that of staff artist in the herbarium.

Grierson became renowned for her skill in depicting botanical details, often from dried specimens, though she also worked intently through the course of a long day to capture a living plant. Precision was married to the acknowledged beauty of her compositions. Little wonder that from her base at Kew she gained outside commissions, including decorative work for postage stamps. She was a keen needlewoman, and the bold sweeping lines of her sketches were eminently transferable to embroidery designs.

Kew provided contacts with other botanical gardens, and this was the basis for her visits to Hawaii in the 1970s to paint at the Pacific Tropical Botanical Garden, Kauai (now the National Tropical Botanical Garden). Although familiar with the tropical plants in Kew's glasshouses, the exuberance of the island's flora, its profusion and colour, almost overwhelmed her. She relished memories of her sense of shock and wonder. These qualities, apparent in her sketches, are as powerful as the formal accuracy and beauty of the finished work.

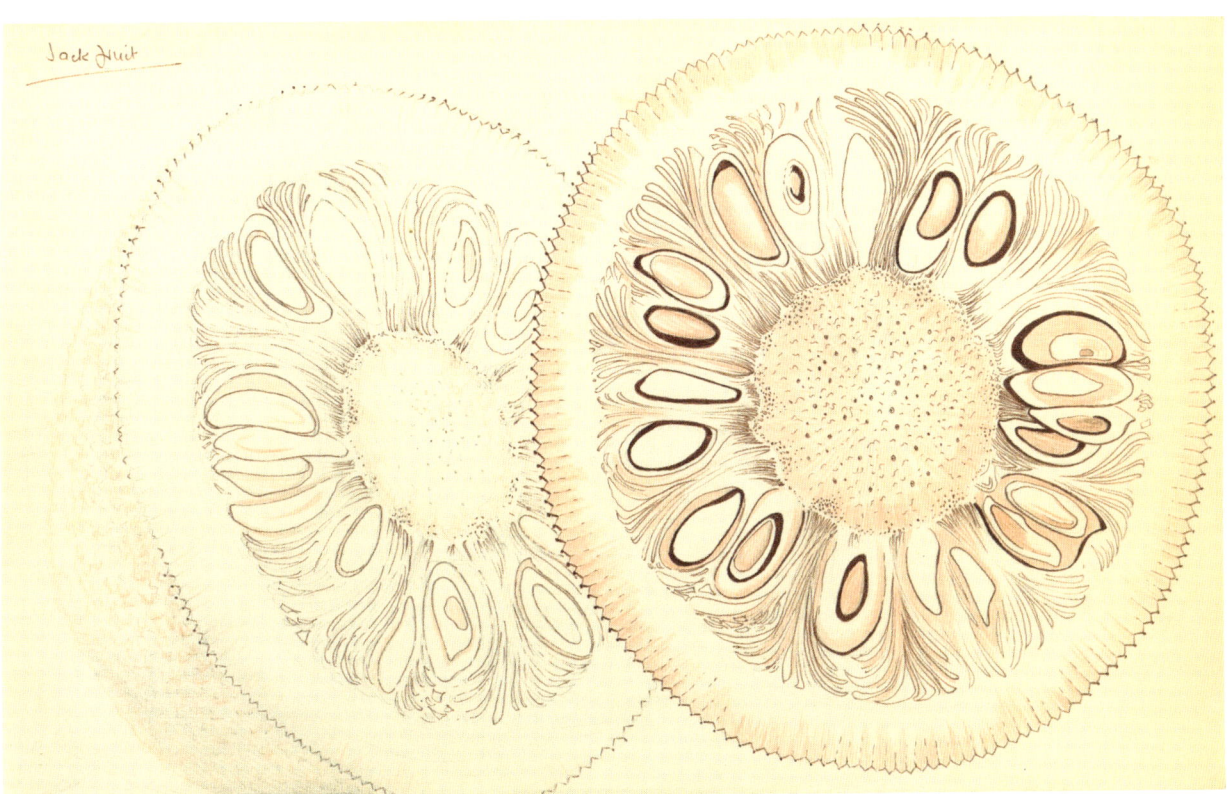

Grierson recorded plant forms in confident, clear lines: '*Sadleria cyatheoides* fern fronds' (opposite) and 'Jack fruit' (above) were from her Hawaiian adventures. A series of 'Spirals in nature' featured 'Lianas – Spirals in the Forest – Nepal' (page 164). (Page 165) Sweet chestnut (*Castanea sativa*) was drawn on brown wrapping paper.

LIANAS — SPIRALS IN FOREST — NEPAL.

botanists

Plants were once just part of the general, wider studies of naturalists. The drive to specialization and the creation of distinct disciplines in the late 18th century carved out botany and its practitioners – the botanists – as distinct entities. Where botanists worked and sketched illustrates how botany functioned as a science. University botany departments were the home of John Stevens Henslow and Arthur Harry Church. William Griffith, Joseph Dalton Hooker and Otto Stapf switched between the field and botanic garden. Charles Maries reminds us of the importance to botany of private gardens, practical gardening and horticulture. Mary Anne Stebbing was one of the first female members of the Linnean Society in the early 20th century, and represents the enduring importance of the amateur as botany professionalized.

JOHN STEVENS HENSLOW

When Charles Darwin (p. 118) was an undergraduate at Cambridge, he was known as 'the man who walks with Henslow'. Henslow fostered Darwin's love of the natural world, and a modern interpretation might have it that it was 'Henslow, who walked with Darwin'. Nevertheless, John Stevens Henslow (1796–1861) was an important scientific figure in his own time, and is a natural transition between the naturalist and the botanist.

Intrigued by geology, Henslow's first post at Cambridge was as professor of mineralogy. He eagerly gave it up after three years when the chair in botany, held for more than half a century by Thomas Martyn, at last fell vacant. Under Martyn, botany at Cambridge was described as 'moribund in the summer and dead in winter'. Henslow, an effective lecturer, dedicated teacher and ardent reformer, changed all that. He revived the Botanic Garden in Cambridge and worked to make natural sciences a serious academic subject within the university.

Henslow was interested primarily in plant distribution, structure and function; he believed that systematic botany (the classification of plants) was subservient to these more fundamental aspects of plant science. His lectures were illustrated by a series of famous charts he created, and his artistic talents are revealed in his drawing of *Dieffenbachia seguine*, which also demonstrates his fascination with inflorescences, seed formation and plant reproduction. A typical 'herbarium-type' drawing, it was published in *The Botanist*, a short-lived journal that aimed to 'convey both moral and intellectual gratification' to its readers. Today it would be regarded as outreach, as would Henslow's talks on botany and horticulture offered to his rural parishioners at Hitcham in Suffolk, for Henslow combined his university botany with practice as an Anglican clergyman. One of Henslow's sons became a botanist and one of his daughters a professional botanical artist, while another daughter married Joseph Hooker (p. 172).

Henslow drew this specimen of '*Dieffenbachia Seguinum*' (*Dieffenbachia seguine*), known as dumb cane, from a plant flowering in the hothouse of the Botanic Garden at Cambridge University in 1839. Native to the American tropics, its acrid juice was allegedly used as a punishment by slave owners.

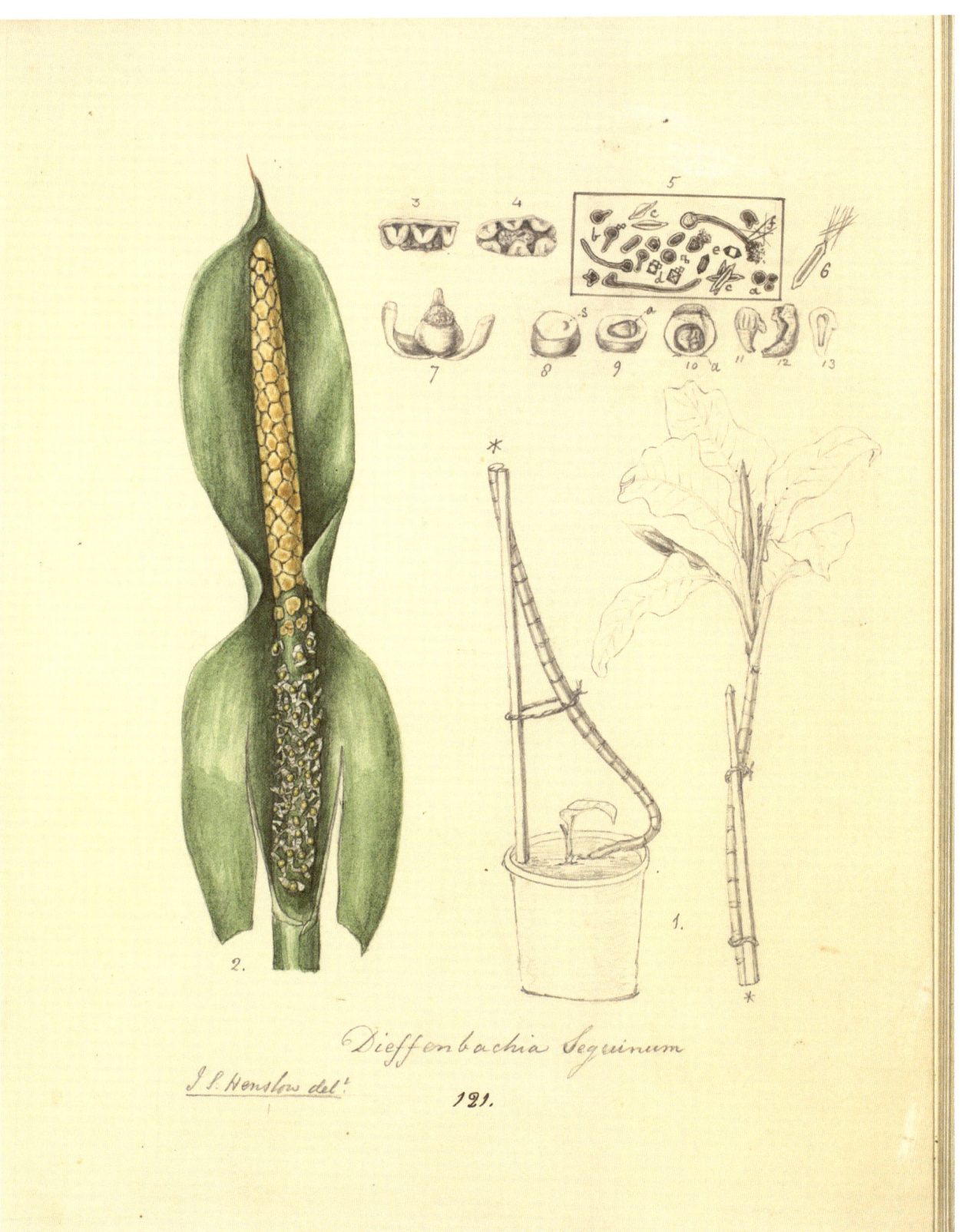

Dieffenbachia Seguinum

J S Henslow delt

121.

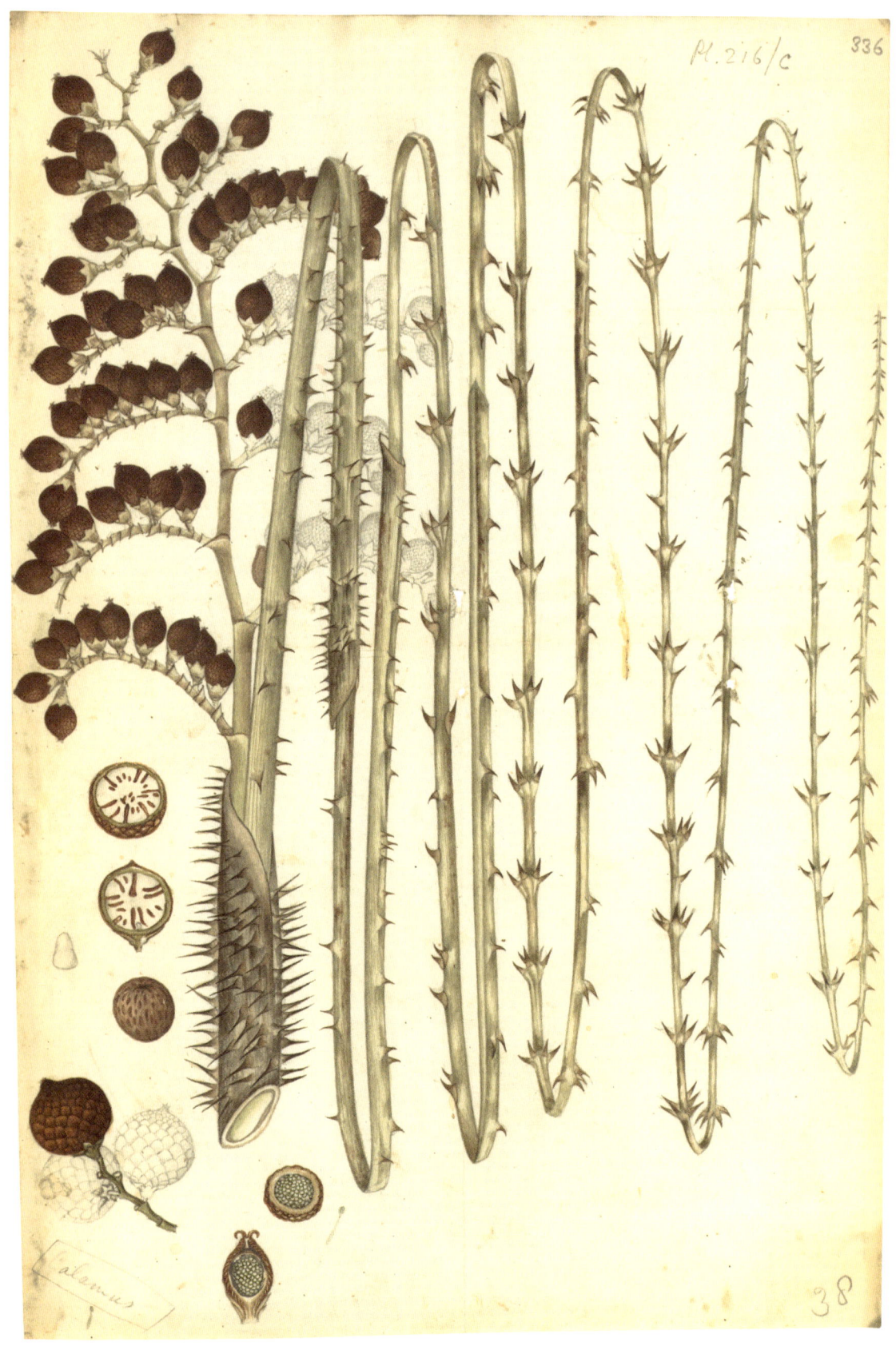

WILLIAM GRIFFITH

In 1842, William Griffith (1810–1846) officially became a botanist. He was appointed acting superintendent of the botanical garden and professor of botany at the Medical College in Calcutta (Kolkata), taking over temporarily from Nathaniel Wallich, who was on sick leave. It was the high point of Griffith's short life and he set to work controversially overhauling the planting of the garden. Much of the Indian subcontinent was the domain of the East India Company, and botany was a commercial and an imperial enterprise. It was also a developing science, and those working in exotic locations often risked their health for their passion and potential discoveries. Some were content to accumulate novel introductions; Griffith, however, was determined to develop what was known as 'philosophical botany'.

He joined the East India Company as an assistant surgeon in 1832, and already during his medical education had enjoyed his first foray into botanical illustration, drawing for Wallich's celebrated *Plantae Asiaticae rariores* (1830–32). Wallich secured Griffith's involvement in an exciting expedition to Assam in 1835 to search for indigenous tea plants in this little explored region, but the two fell out. Griffith, supported by his friend the geologist John M'Clelland, complained that Wallich resisted his independent collecting and wanted to claim anything new for himself. Joseph Hooker would describe these men as 'the three most ill-tempered fellows in all India'.

Griffith's time in Assam set the tone for his career. As medical officer on various deputations, he explored most of the mountainous fringes of the expanding British empire in India, travelling down through today's Myanmar to Yangon (then Rangoon) and across the Hindu Kush into Afghanistan. His letters, including ones to the leading naturalists of the day, are replete with vivid descriptions. He energetically made dissections of plants with a microscope, puzzled over the laying down of woody tissues and pondered the meaning of the geographical distributions of species. He made quick, picturesque sketches of landscapes and detailed botanical drawings of his plants.

His aim was to write a new scientific flora of India, but he published little before his sudden death, not long after his time in charge of the botanical garden ended. He had willed his 9,000 specimens and 20 folio volumes of notes, half of which were sketches, to the East India Company, who paid for some of this mass of information to make it into print.

(Opposite) Fruit and spiny parts of the climbing palm rattan, *Calamus wightii*, beautifully compressed by Griffith into a single page. (Above) Detailed notes on the flower parts of *Cryptolepis dubia*.

(Overleaf) Griffith's notes and drawings, some just on scraps of paper – here on what he thought was a new species of 'Asclepiadae' – were difficult to order and publish.

1731 1 Flower viewed vertically
2 Corona Staminea
3 Outer view of Anther
4 Inner Do
5.6 Pollinic 2 glands
7. Stigma and part of ovaric. Pollinic in situ
8 Corona staminea: Anthers dehisced transversely. Pollinia in situ

JOSEPH DALTON HOOKER

Many botanists sketched, but Joseph Dalton Hooker (1817–1911) is perhaps the most accomplished artist. He inherited his artistic talent from his father, William Hooker (p. 152), along with his passion for botany and his post as Director at Kew. He initially trained in medicine and his first expedition was as assistant surgeon (and naturalist) on HMS *Erebus* (1839–43), but botany was his abiding love. The *Erebus* explored the Great Ice Barrier (the Ross Ice Shelf) of Antarctica, as well as New Zealand and the islands of the South Pacific. Hooker discovered many plants previously unknown to European science, and his six large volumes on the flora of the Antarctic, New Zealand and Tasmania established his reputation.

His notebooks from the expedition, as well as from his famous trip to the Himalaya (1847–51), demonstrate his artistic skills, as much in close-ups of individual plants as in landscapes and scenes including the people he encountered. Walter Hood Fitch (p. 156) prepared the plates from his drawings for the subsequent publication on rhododendrons, the first part appearing, under his father's supervision, while he was still in Asia. It was Hooker's work on rhododendrons that introduced these popular plants to British gardens, and his *Himalayan Journals* (1854) is a classic of Victorian plant exploration and its adventures, including his incarceration when he was accused of espionage.

After Hooker succeeded his father as Director at Kew in 1865, he turned the gardens into a centre for the collection of botanical material and its transmission to all parts of the British empire. He continued working tirelessly throughout his long life, publishing volumes of flora with introductory essays setting out his more general botanical principles and inevitably enriched with beautiful plates, often made from his own drawings. He excelled as a systematic botanist and as a researcher of the geographical distribution of plants, the subject of much of his correspondence with his lifelong friend Charles Darwin. He was privy to Darwin's ideas on evolution long before the publication of *On the Origin of Species* (1859), and he publicly supported Darwin thereafter.

Despite his closeness to Darwin, who never held a scientific post, Hooker was ever anxious to sideline the lesser dabblers and enthusiasts who peopled botany, and to establish its practice as the preserve of professional scientists.

(Above) Hooker's watercolour sketch of the Sikkim larch, *Larix griffithii* (first discovered by and named for William Griffith, p. 168), captures not only the form of the pendulous branches but also their movement in the wind on a mountainside at Lachung, Sikkim. (Opposite) A Himalayan landscape framed by a tree covered with epiphytes. Hooker was living his dream of 'acquiring a knowledge of exotic botany'.

(Overleaf) Hooker included a tremendous amount of detail in his field sketches, including the shape (in the bottom right corner page 174) of the tree rhododendron *R. grande*, and the characteristic leaves of *R. falconeri* (page 175), which are huge, at 'eighteen inches', as he reported, and covered with fine brown hairs, or indumentum, underneath.

II Doing Science

little of them being very cheap in this part of the country, or any
but very cheap grades, for the natives who can command no supply.
I am sending two astonishing hats for you used by the Lepchas, made
neatly of Bamboo & plaited over leaves, the brims are more than
6 feet across. I am also getting a Lepcha Umbrella made which
consists of a singularly constructed hood worn over the head
thus:
The Palms now number 9 species, Phoenix 1,
Caryota 1, Calamus 5 & 2 other genera I cannot
name by Kunth. I have museum specimens
of all, but they are great troubles. I have also
two specimens skeletons of the Cycas, one with
roots but too large I fear to send. I only got them this morning from
a place about 10 miles off, where I first found it & where only I
have seen it: in a fearfully hot narrow valley, blocked up at both
ends with Mts: the Ficus elastica grows in it & Pinus longifolia,
Shorea robusta, Careya arborea, long Saccharum, aroms, Pothos, & such like
heat loving plants. There are 8 Bamboos here, Campbell has got
me specimens of all, & I have dried the leaves & preserved sticks for the
Museum, both long pieces & short. The latter you had better split & shew
their thickness, placing the section beside the stick. I have preserved the
leaves of all, but they scarcely offer any specific differences. I can only get the
flowers of 4, which belong to two genera at least. Tobacco here is found
here, but I have not been able to get any yet. It is only to-day that I
have found out that there are two distinct Bananas here, one
grows from 4 – 6500 ft; the other below that limit: the male flowers
are totally different, & the seed also; of cult.d var.s there are several
hill vars, but not from the denser thicker wild stock. They all afford
of which no use is made. The Iris are now in seed, I have got
little sheaves of 8 kinds for you, they are very pretty, as are some of the
other Cerealia, Panica – Enormous Cucumbers are much eaten, but
them I cannot do more than sketch hurriedly, they are of the same
species as in the plains. Aleurite. The wild species are numerous &
generally poisonous of course. "a vegetable must be very bad to be
acknowledged poisonous by these people who may come under Saunders
definition of the genus Homo, "an omnivorous thiopod who eats all he
can get." Fern tops (not rodier pitth) Solanum leaves, vites &c. Urticeae (such
that they save the spring hail under glass, or make soup of the nettles) Byletia &

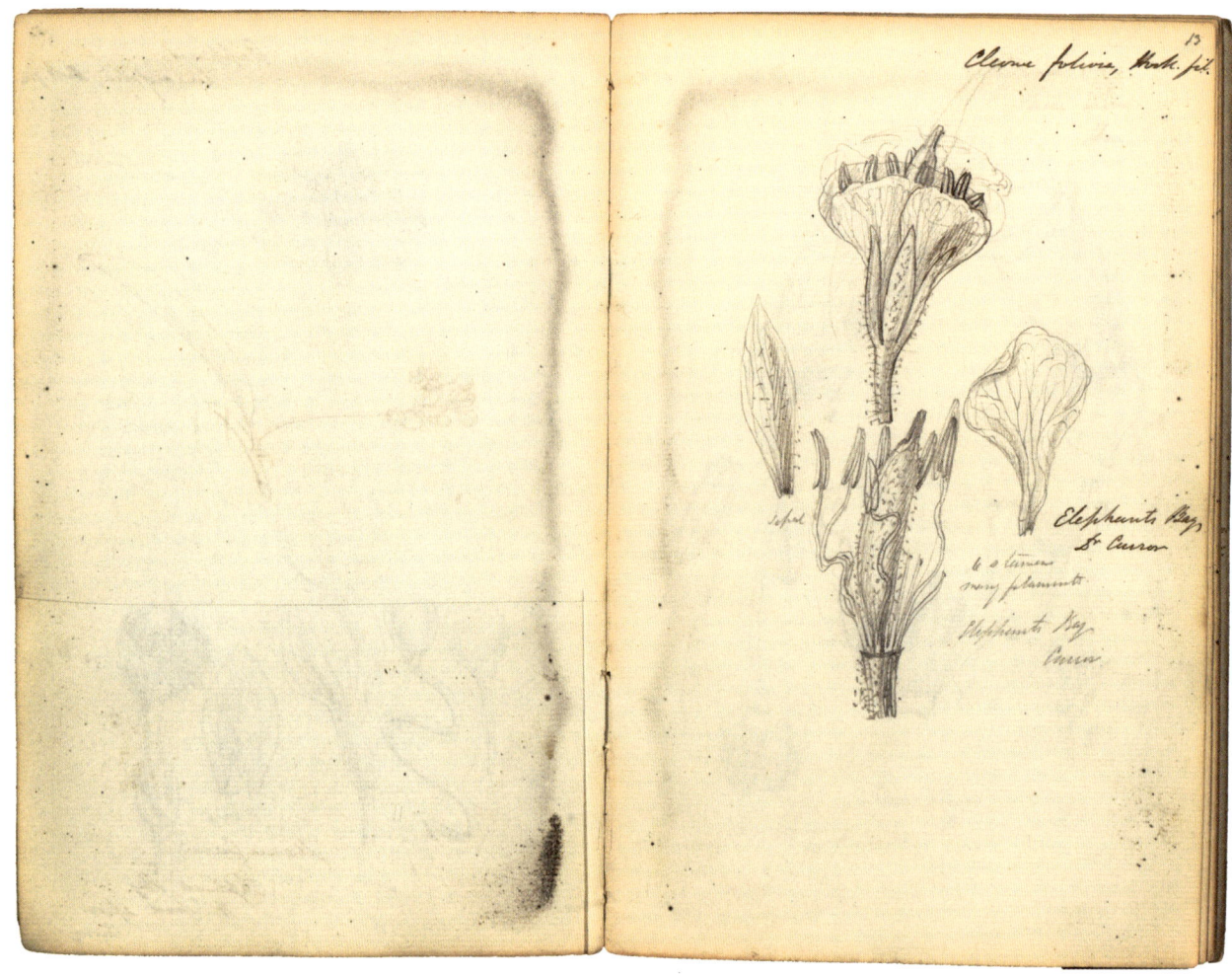

(Previous pages) Field sketches of the whole fruit and leaves (above) and seeds (below) of the Himalayan vine *Hodgsonia macrocarpa*, a member of the Cucurbitaceae family. Across a letter to his father (30 August 1848) Hooker sketched the form of the fruit and seeds. He commented on how it was raining constantly in Darjeeling, and he had ordered a Lepcha umbrella to keep himself dry. Whatever happened to him next, once the letter was safe in England his discovery of this plant would be official.

(Above) *Cleome foliosa* flowers from Hooker's notebook of around 1845. He was working with his father at Kew on the collection of plants made by Theodore Vogel, who had died while serving as botanist on the Royal Navy's River Niger expedition of 1841. (Opposite) In a finished plate drawing all parts of a plant, whatever their sequence of development, were shown in a perfect and therefore artificial state. In a sketch it was different – here Hooker noted that the whip-like spadix of this cobra-lily, *Arisaema propinquum*, was 'too withered to draw'.

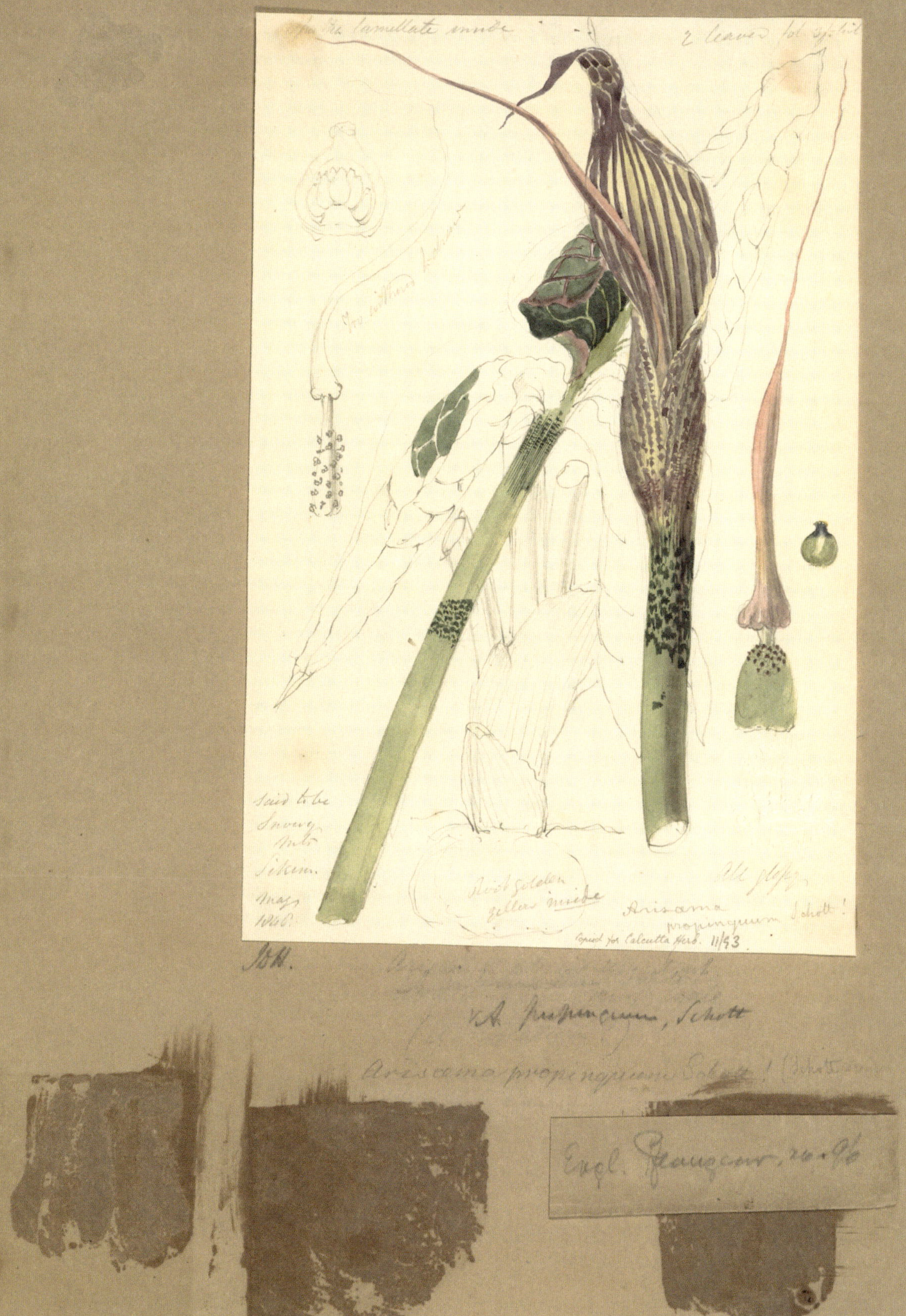

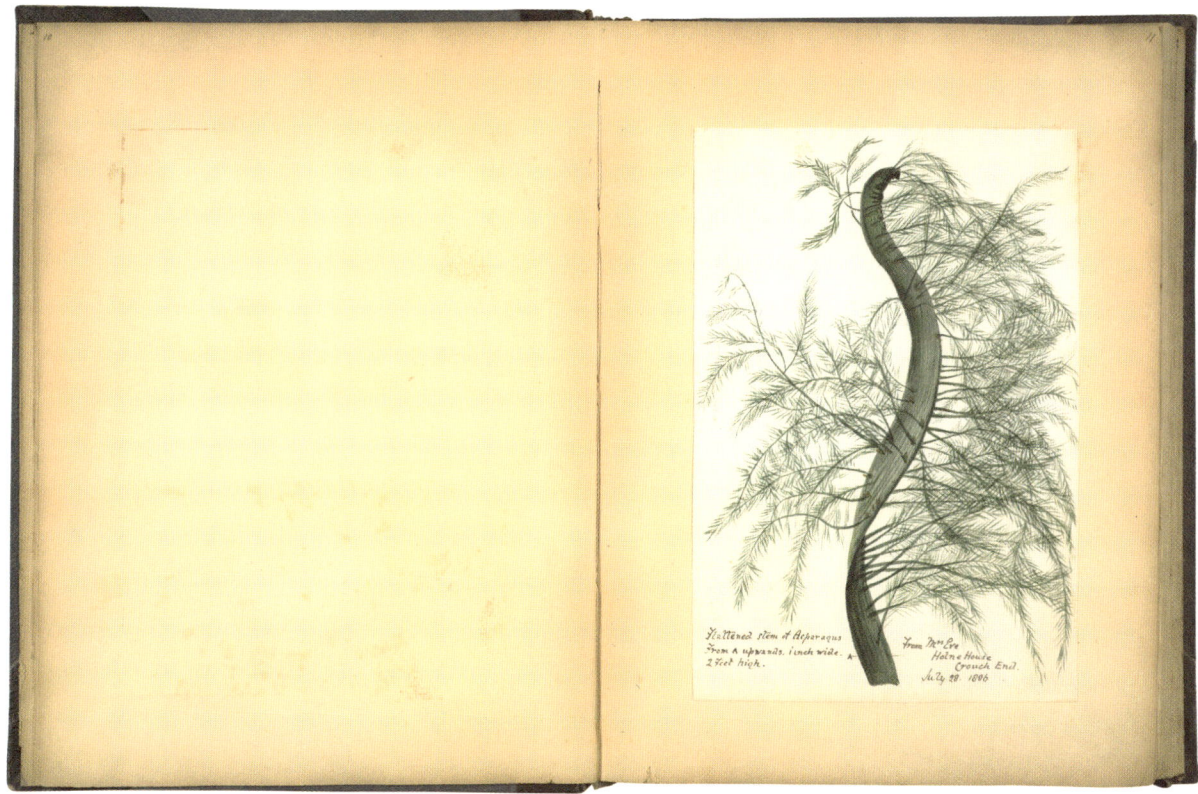

MARY ANNE STEBBING

If it hadn't been for a house fire in Tunbridge Wells in 1881, Mary Anne Stebbing (1845–1927) would probably be much better known. A substantial part of her sketches and drawings of British flowering plants, images she was amassing for publication, was reduced to ashes.

Mary Anne was the youngest daughter of William Wilson Saunders, insurance underwriter by day and avid entomologist and botanist in his spare time (with his own private museum, see p. 161). Saunders was instrumental in founding the Holmesdale Natural History Club, Reigate. Here Mary Anne met her future husband, the Reverend Thomas R. R. Stebbing. He likened the Saunders family to a 'very nest of naturalists', and Mary Anne's wedding gift to him was a lovingly inscribed volume of orchid watercolours.

The Stebbings moved to Torquay in 1868. The couple were keenly involved with the Torquay Natural History Society; such clubs, with their excursions, meetings, libraries and collections, epitomized the growing fascination with natural history during the 19th century. In 1877 they moved to Tunbridge Wells, closer to London's high-powered scientific museums, societies and clubs. In 1905 Mary Anne followed Thomas (and her father) in being elected as a Fellow of Linnean Society (FLS). She was among the first group of women to achieve this distinction, attending meetings regularly until the outbreak of the First World War.

After the destructive fire in 1881, Stebbing enlarged her botanical scope. Unlike her earlier flower paintings, her album of 'Curious fruit and flowers' displayed a more scientific bent, delineating developmental anomalies, or teratologies. From her careful annotations it's possible to build up a sense of her collecting material, even checking the vegetable delivery in the kitchen for oddities. Mary also shared her late father's fascination with fungi. With the help of Annie Lorrain Smith, FLS, she identified those drawn by her sister-in-law Anne (p. 272), bridging the developing professional and amateur worlds of botany. She also diligently illustrated Thomas's work on crustacea. The Stebbings had no children and they spent their golden wedding anniversary working together, dissecting and drawing a prawn.

Stebbing recorded the effects of fungal pathogens on *Knautia arvensis* (opposite above left) and possibly insects on *Daucus carota* seeds (opposite above right), though the red flowers are fairly common; (opposite below) abnormalities of an ox-eye daisy. (Above) 'Flattened stem of Asparagus'.

(Overleaf) From friends' gardens she drew 'a pea from a mummy from Egypt?' and *Fuchsia* 'Daniel Lambert'.

botanists 181

58

From a pea, from a
Mummy from Egypt-?
Stem very thickened.
growth clustered.
Flowers in pairs-
3 pairs of leaflets on each leaf.
Leaf sometimes dividing.
Leaflets not always opposite.
Leaflets & bracts crimson at base.
Growth very vigorous.
Sown 5 April 1902. Seedlings
appeared 15 April 1902. Now
it is 5 feet high. Mary Watlin
July 8. 1902.

Grown at Mrs Meyers.
Chesterfield House-

Daniel Lambert
M.a.S. 10.9.80   Broad Path

CHARLES MARIES

The mango is the national fruit of India and the Philippines, and the national tree of Bangladesh. Little wonder, then, that Charles Maries (1851–1902), who spent almost twenty years of his short life in India, was drawn to mangoes. He hunted, studied, bred and described them, pursuing his botany as a mango horticulturalist. And, of course, he also drew them.

Maries was introduced to botany at grammar school by George Henslow, son of John Stevens Henslow (p. 166). He then worked with his brother Richard as a nurseryman in Lancashire before joining the long-established nursery of James Veitch and Sons, in Chelsea, London. Veitch was sufficiently impressed with Maries to send him on a plant-hunting expedition to Japan and China in 1877–79. Maries was extremely successful, sending back several hundred new species of plants for British gardens.

In 1880 he secured the post of chief gardener to the Maharaja of Darbangha, in the state of Bihar in northeastern India, who had constructed a new palace. Maries laid out the gardens with a combination of tropical and European plants. He also further developed his interests in economic botany, attempting (unsuccessfully) to process the fibres of the Rhea plant (*Boehmeria nivea*). During his ten years there he continued his plant collecting, including orchids. Darbangha was also a centre of mango production, and it was here that Maries began work on a book about the fruit.

Maries moved in 1890 to become superintendent of another garden, in the hot, dry climate of Gwalior, seat of the Maharaja of Gwalior, one of the richest men in India. He finally finished drafting and illustrating the mango book, but his London publisher was unable to attract enough subscribers for publication. After his death, his drawings were sought after by the US Department of Agriculture, who wished to develop a mango industry and needed an easy visual means for identifying the right horticultural varieties.

(Above) Wild mangoes from the jungles of Kangra, Himachal Pradesh, India, with colour notes. These are small fruit – Maries noted the weights varying from 1 oz to 4 oz (28 to 113 g), very different from the cultivated varieties such as 'Bombay' (opposite).

OTTO STAPF

Although Otto Stapf (1857–1933) became a stalwart of three quintessentially British institutions – the Royal Botanic Gardens at Kew, the Royal Horticultural Society and the Royal Society – he was born in Austria and did not arrive in Britain until he was 33 years old. By then, his abiding scientific interests – in grasses, systematic botany and the flora of Southwest Asia, particularly what was then Persia (Iran) – were already established. In 1889 he sent his work on the *Ephedra* genus, a shrub long used for the stimulating properties of its leaves, to Joseph Hooker, along with a note saying that he was unhappy with his position in Vienna. Hooker's successor at Kew, Sir William Thiselton-Dyer, offered him the post of assistant for India in 1890; Stapf stayed for the rest of his career, ending as Keeper of the Herbarium.

Stapf's work at Kew required him to expand his geographical scope, although grasses remained his principal focus. He published an important work on the flora of Mount Kinabalu in Borneo, and assisted Joseph Hooker (p. 172) with the grasses for his *Flora of British India*, as well as writing on the grasses of Africa. In later life he made a contribution to the study of the early history of wheat, especially the genus *Triticum*, for which his knowledge of the ancient botanical literature (in the original languages) was invaluable. After his

retirement from Kew his botanical learning reached a wider general audience when he edited the Royal Horticultural Society's *Botanical Magazine*, where his articles educated the gardening public.

Stapf was familiar with the botanical collections of the 1882 expedition of Jakob Polak in Persia, and his own chance to travel there came in 1885. It was a high point in his botanical life. He recorded his adventures in a cloth-bound sketchbook, creating linked panoramas of the landscape, as well as details of buildings and individual plants. Working in pencil and watercolour, he captured the challenging environment to which the plants had adapted.

Stapf experimented with his colours, and his pages were often packed medleys, here yellow- and pink-flowered *Dionysia* and *Viola*, and *Coprinus* and other fungi, but he was also interested in landscapes and buildings.

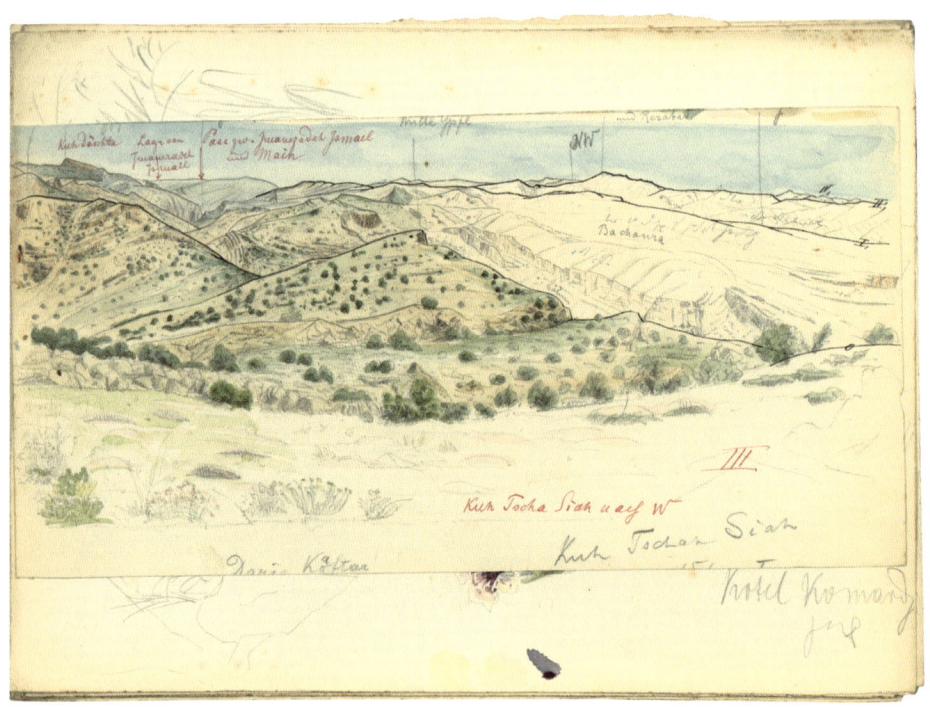

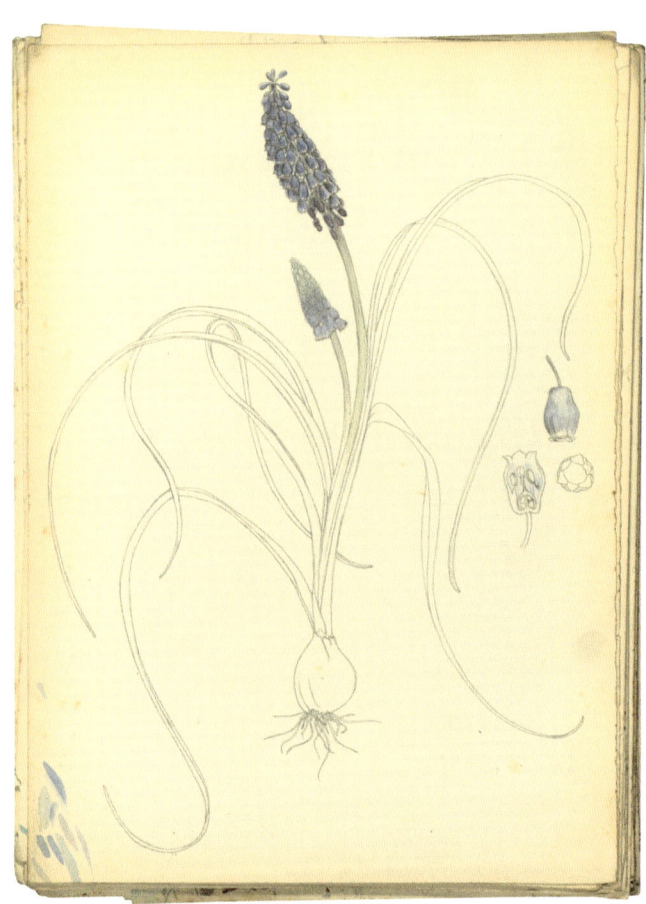

(Above) An annotated panorama of the 'Kuh Tschah Siah' in the Fars province of Iran. (Right) Possibly a sketch of the grape hyacinth that Stapf collected on 2 June 1885 near Shiraz, also in the Fars province. (Opposite) Detail of the flora of a canyon in the gypsum outcrops.

Schlucht in den Gypsbergen bei Daläki.

ARTHUR HARRY CHURCH

Arthur Harry Church (1865–1937) spent his whole botanical career at Oxford University, but despite his dedicated brilliance, he never quite penetrated the inner circles of the university or the wider botanical community. From an ordinary background, Church had studied at University College, Aberystwyth, before, aged 26, he became an undergraduate at Oxford. He received the recognition of being elected to the Fellowship of the Royal Society, but retired from Oxford as simply a lecturer in botany in 1930.

Nor were his many publications likely to make a dramatic impact. He intensely disliked having his novel ideas edited, so much of his work was privately published, at his own expense, in *Oxford Botanical Memoirs*. And since he could not afford to illustrate these densely written studies with his own exquisite colour drawings, their reach was further limited. He once told a student that it would take an hour to read properly three pages of his writings. He was, however, able to use his artistic talents in his lectures, drawing rapidly on the chalkboard as he talked. In all his art, he mastered both colour and form, as is strikingly and beautifully displayed in his visual explications of flower structure. Some of these he used for *Types of Floral Mechanism* (1908).

Church's botanical interests were impressively wide: plant evolution, algae, seaweeds, fungi, angiosperms, conifers, flower structure, and leaf-and-stem arrangements ('phyllotaxis'). After his wife and a daughter died in quick succession, Church sank into a deep depression; his recuperation was aided by research for his innovative review of the 'plant life' around Oxford, which required long country walks. For this, he also perfected another skill: botanical photography.

Hypericum calycinum, 1905 (above), and *Nymphaea rubra*, Indian red water lily, 1907 (opposite). Church planned to feature the '100 best flowers' in four volumes arranged by seasons; only one appeared. These startling images could have been created by an Art Nouveau artist rather than a botanist.

III Making Art

Making Art is a privileged look into private worlds – a storehouse of colour, shape and texture that artists created, and to which they could return when wanting to conjure a rose in full bloom, or recall the veining of a leaf or the peeling of bark. We are fascinated by how artists work, and some of the sketches allow us a unique window into the rarefied world of the very best specialist botanical artists, while others reveal the studies and preoccupations of those concerned with the accurate depiction of the natural world and its flora in the high and decorative arts. Making art is also about the difficulties artists faced in supporting themselves and furthering their careers. A greatness of vision is displayed in *nature in art*. The practical realities of reliance on others are examined in *patrons' dependents*. From near perfect plate drawings to the most preliminary sketches, *in print* explores the preparatory work of illustrators. The sketches in *jobbing* tell of those for whom botanical art was only one element in their careers, or who worked uncertainly as various kinds of artists-for-hire. All tried to make a living by making art.

ALFRED RIOCREUX
Only the bottom half of this sketch of *Pelargonium diadematum* was used as a plate for *Herbier général de l'amateur*, the faint pencil line above it marking the part included.

Pelargonium. Garden var. hybrids of Cucullatum formosissimum

nature in art

One of the fundamental challenges of bringing nature into art is finding the balance between the realistic depiction of plants and the artist's aesthetic vision. Sketches are experimental spaces, where thought processes are explored and elements destined to be used in finished compositions can be tried out. Leonardo da Vinci and Albrecht Dürer are masters of the Renaissance, who brought precise depictions of nature into sublime art. Yoshikawa Kokei and Charles Rennie Mackintosh exemplify the portrayal of plants in the decorative arts. John Constable in his elevation of the commonplace, Samuel Palmer in his search for an almost mystical ideal and John Ruskin in a lifelong quest for the unity of truth and beauty sketched plants as part of their individual ways of representing nature in art.

LEONARDO DA VINCI

That Leonardo da Vinci (1452–1519) was a genius we know not just from his finished works, but also from the approximately 5,000 pages of his notebooks and sketches that were his private laboratory. Here, in the crowded images and annotations, his urgent desire to capture and understand nature takes shape. A plant was not just a specimen on a page, as typically depicted in a contemporary herbal (with which he was, however, familiar), but a living entity. It was connected to and influenced by the ground its roots penetrated. Leonardo's vision was one of nature unified. Human anatomy, plant life, birds in flight, swirling water set in a geologically informed landscape, all were studies in form and energy as well as the things themselves. In the inanimate world, his interest in functionality led to his inventions of mechanisms and machines. He reputedly carried a notebook with him, to which he would at times retreat, leaving commissioned work unfinished. In his career-long sketching habit he used black and red chalk, red chalk on red prepared paper, pen and ink, metal point and combinations of these media.

Leonardo was born illegitimate in a small village near Vinci, Tuscany, and initially lived with his grandfather before joining his father in Florence (*c.* 1464/9), becoming apprenticed to the artist Andrea del Verrocchio. As his renown grew, he worked for the most powerful patrons of the time, moving on, as their fortunes fluctuated, between Milan (1481–99, 1506–13), Florence (1500–06/7) and Rome (1513–16). He died in France, where he was in the service of Francis I.

In his earlier paintings and altarpieces, Leonardo's plants were more traditionally mannered, but this changed. Some of his sketches of flowers and plants can be found incorporated into finished works, such as a Star of Bethlehem (*Ornithogalum umbellatum*) in his lost painting *Leda and the Swan* (known from copies). There is no purely botanical manuscript by him, but across the corpus of his works a commitment to a knowledge of plants, gardens and garden architecture is apparent. This is always infused by the twin motivations of portraying nature and gaining a botanical understanding of plant life. Hints from his drawings made between about 1508 and 1510 suggest he may have planned a botanical treatise, but it's not certain. Concern with senescence dominated Leonardo's final years, movingly embodied in his deluge drawings and those revealing the intricate beauty of aged trees.

A perfect example of a *disegno*, a drawing or design, by Leonardo. He rarely worked on one theme at a time – here *Viola* plants sit alongside small diagrams relating to a lead roof covering, along with streams of notes.

ALBRECHT DÜRER

'For, verily, art is embedded in nature: whoever can draw her out, has her.' So wrote Albrecht Dürer (1471–1528), whose commitment to depicting the truth of nature united all his work, whether in representing the mundane plants of the wayside or the love of mother and child in his portrayals of Mary and the infant Jesus. Indeed, he took such traditional themes as the holy family and placed them with great originality in the acutely observed world of his day. His compositions, both paintings and prints, were replete with the plants and animals that he sketched in his studies. Art in nature drove his theoretical as well as his practical exploration of the techniques of proportion and perspective. In this way, Dürer helped to bring the ideas of the Italian Renaissance over the Alps to his home in Nuremberg.

It was intended that Dürer would follow his father as a goldsmith, but his immense artistic talent intervened. His plan of studying with Martin Schongauer ended when the older artist died before Dürer reached the Upper Rhineland in the early 1490s during his post-apprenticeship travels, or Wanderjahre. Having spent a year in Venice to escape the plague in Nuremberg, Dürer returned home in 1495 and opened his print workshop. Commercial success with the *Apocalypse* series established his reputation; it also brought him lucrative commissions that allowed him to travel. He drew constantly, sharpening his powers of observation and creating a rich resource of potential material to be incorporated into complex compositions. If his nature studies were in the tradition of 'specimen books' of the medieval painter's workshop, Dürer's work was so much better, more alive. Ironically, his famed rhinoceros (1515), as well as some other animals, was not drawn from life.

The Great Piece of Turf (1503) was once thought to have been drawn outside, at a stopping point on a journey. Part study, part finished composition, it is more painterly than his quicker pen and ink, charcoal or chalk sketches. And it is remarkably 'tidy' and free of such things as leaf litter, so is likely to have been created in the studio. Famous studies of plants by Dürer include the iris and lilies of Christian iconography, and exotics such as the dragon tree, but the turf plants are unusually ordinary.

Dürer's work was much imitated soon after his death, and many plant studies are now attributed both to his studio and to those who paid their homage to the master by emulating his style and faking his monogram.

(Above) Study of a spruce tree. (Opposite) *The Great Piece of Turf*. Dürer painted the mundane grasses and flowers of the wayside, life-size, in watercolour and opaque; his aim, which he achieved, was to render nature perfectly.

III Making Art

Oil studies of water lilies (*Nuphar lutea*). Constable used these aquatic plants to indicate slow-moving water in his Stour valley paintings – an allegory for a more sedate pace of life as the rapid progress of industrialization encroached on the rhythms of the rural world.

JOHN CONSTABLE

Despite the esteem that John Constable (1776–1837) is held in today, his career was hardly smooth. He always wanted to be an artist, but his attempts to win acceptance from the Royal Academy (the premier British association of artists) met with repeated failure. He had been exhibiting at the Academy's annual show for years, yet the RA's president told him he had been merely lucky. He was in his 30s before he sold an uncommissioned picture to someone who was not a friend or acquaintance. The commissions were for portraits of people or country houses, or copies of other paintings; he did all well, but the genre that always fired his imagination was landscape.

Those landscapes were mostly of the Stour valley in what is now called 'Constable country', the area around East Bergholt, a town on the Essex–Suffolk border where he was born and grew up. He returned there regularly even after his career demanded he live in London. His most famous paintings, the 'Stour valley six-footers', were of scenes from his childhood, carefully observed as a mature artist. He was an inveterate sketcher, and many of his landscapes were composed in his studio using the detailed drawings as elements of the finished work. As he pointed out, light changes rapidly in real time, so he used his imagination to create the lasting image.

Constable is also remembered for his paintings of Salisbury Cathedral. The Bishop was an early patron, and his nephew and private chaplain, John Fisher, became a close friend. Fisher officiated at the wedding of Constable and Maria Bicknell, after a fraught courtship of seven years. Their happy marriage lasted twelve years and produced seven children before Maria died of tuberculosis in 1828.

During his lifetime, Constable was accused of producing 'unfinished' pictures, by which was generally meant that he used paint too thickly. Though the French were enthusiastic about his work, he said he would rather die poor in England than rich abroad. He often painted flowers and could have made flower painting, a Continental speciality, into a distinguished British genre. Instead, he loved the English landscape, the clouds, light, farm workers and harvest time, and excelled in the transformation of the commonplace, perhaps one definition of great art.

YOSHIKAWA KOKEI

Should artists strive to draw true to life, representing nature as it appears to the eye, or should their feelings and spirit infuse the finished work, making an abstraction of nature? What is the best source, the vagaries of memory and the imagination or the veracity of direct observation? These perennial questions were posed in Japan by Maruyama Ōkyo (1733–1795), who founded his own school of naturalistically inspired art.

Maruyama may have produced traditional pieces, scrolls and screens, but they were informed by meticulous detail. He was renowned for keeping a sketchpad with him, in which he practised *shaseiga*, drawing plants, insects, animals and birds from life. These studies were reference points for finished work, distinct from a reliance on memory or looking at other works of art. He was influenced by Japanese traditions, the 'bird-and-flower' genre of Yuan and Ming dynasty China, and the arrival of western, scientific illustrations of natural history subjects, including European botanical prints. These foreign images entered through the tightly controlled trading port of Nagasaki during the closed years of the shogunate.

The *Maruyama-Shijo* (or Kyoto) school may have been the inspiration for Yoshikawa Kokei or Kodo (*fl.* 1820s–1850s). Sadly, we know little of Yoshikawa in the west beyond the stunning series of sketchbooks in which he recorded his 'drawings from life' in ink and watercolour. Drawn over a 30-year period, from 1822 to 1855, all but one are arranged by the seasons. Poetry was the earliest expression of the beauty and transitoriness of the four seasons, and artists incorporated and illustrated the written word. During the Edo period, when Yoshikawa was making his sketches, seasonal flowers had become an important means of signifying notions of change, a fundamental concept of Buddhism.

Yoshikawa's sketches feature animals, insects, even a few drawings of people, but are overwhelmingly concerned with plants. (Opposite) A stem of a fig tree and caterpillars on a different plant. (Above) Peonies.

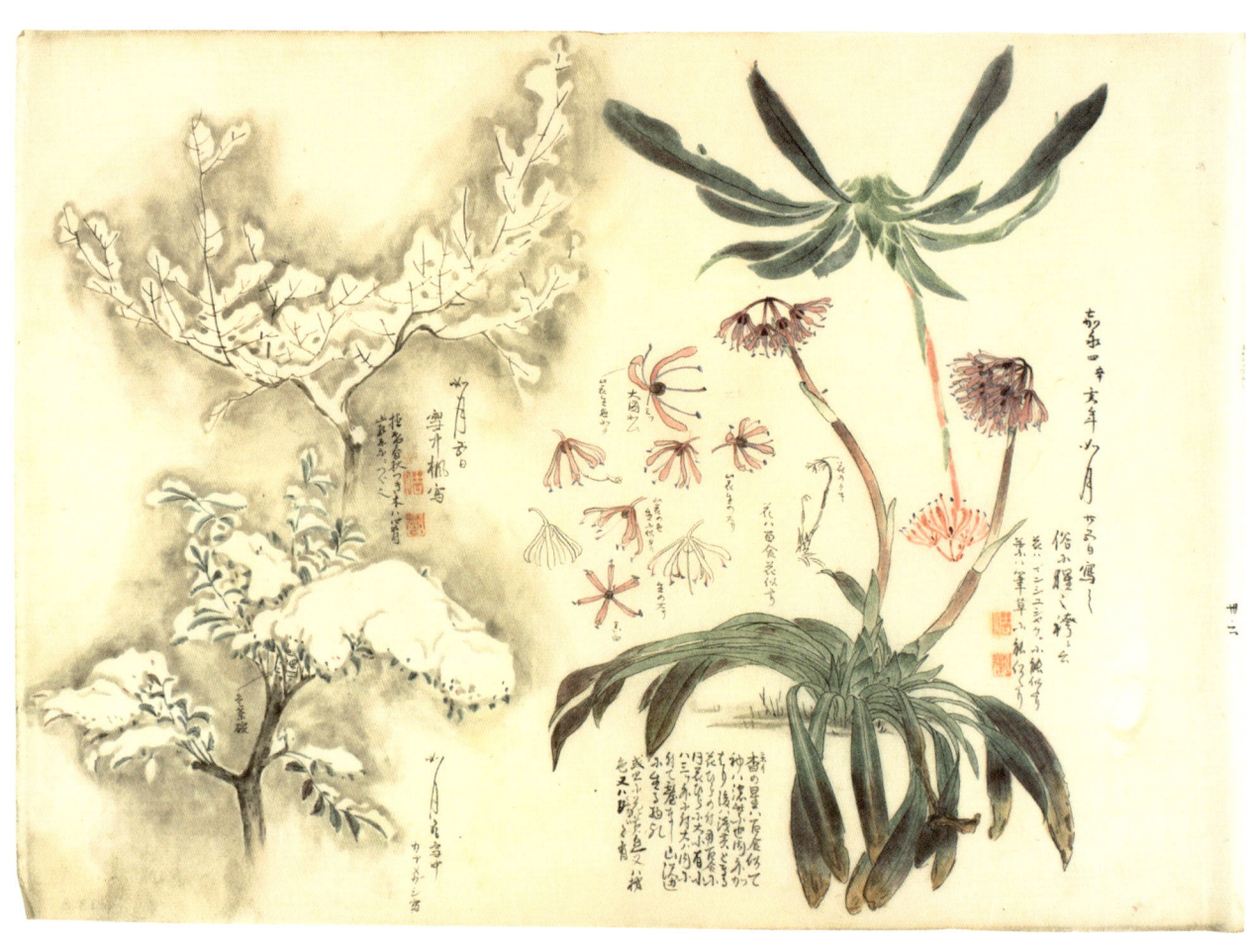

(Above) Bare stems of a maple (*Acer* sp.) and, below it, the evergreen *Photinia glabra* covered in snow; on the right are studies of another evergreen, *Heloniopsis orientalis*. Yoshikawa's intense scrutiny of flowers and leaves is also evident in the sketch of 'Torikabuto' or aconite (opposite), which is highly poisonous but also used as a medicine, as the notes mention.

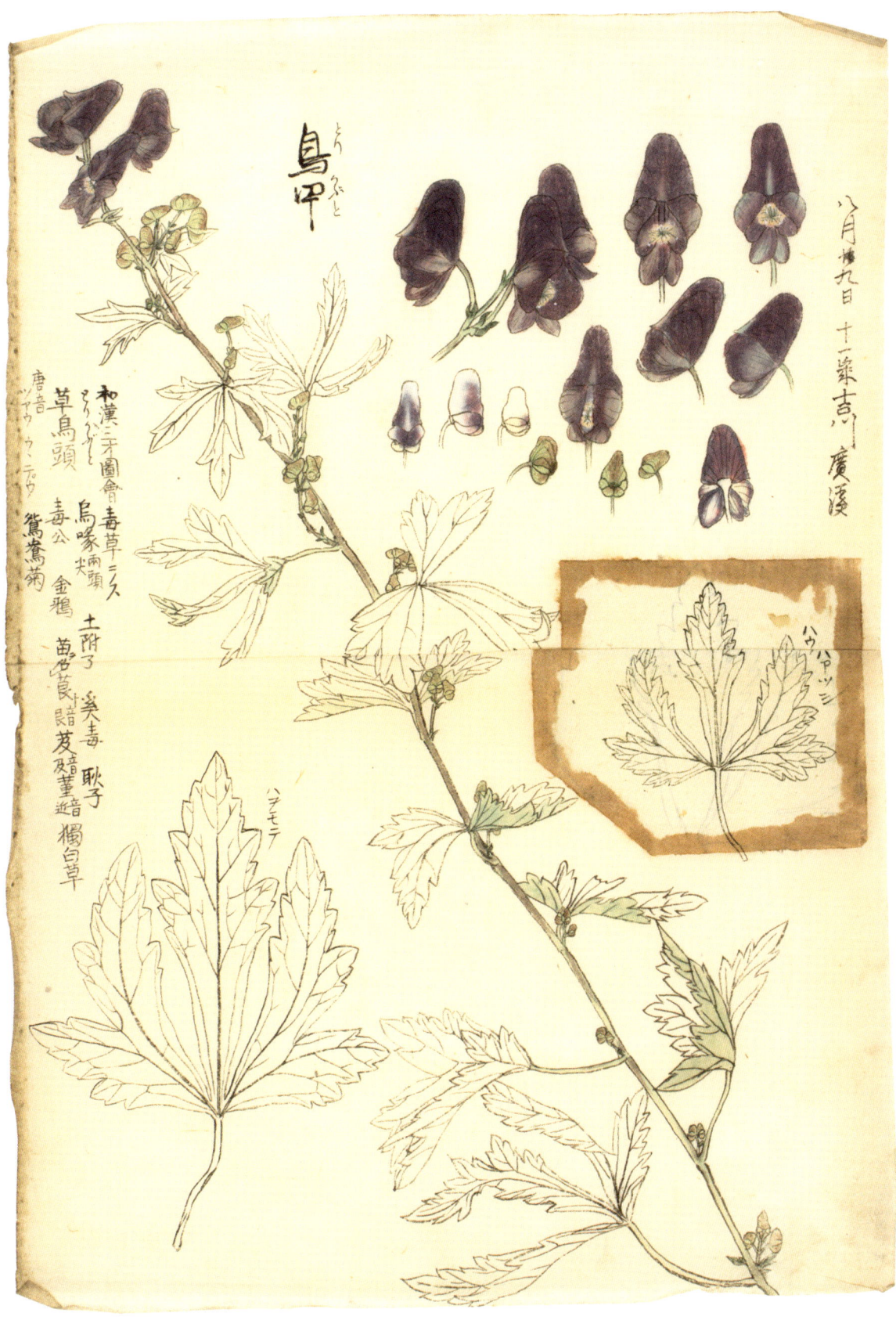

SAMUEL PALMER

Like many artists, Samuel Palmer (1805–1881) held on to his sketchbooks. However, Palmer's son burnt most of them after writing his father's biography. Only two survived the conflagration; fortunately, one is from 1824 and 1825, the beginning of a period of Palmer's most creative and original artistic endeavours. He met the dying William Blake in 1824, and although Palmer shared little of the radical political and social sympathies of that great visionary, Blake's art inspired him. Many years later, Palmer too would illustrate John Milton's poems.

Palmer was born in London and lived there for much of his life, but the countryside provided his greatest stimulus. He went often to Dulwich, then a village south of London, and lived for several years in Shoreham, in rural Kent. Here, the surrounding area became his 'valley of vision'. His sketchbook documents themes that he incorporated into a series of astonishing paintings in the late 1820s, his haunting self-portrait among them, which helped to revitalize English Romanticism. The sketchbook also includes a few poems, and musings about art and the imagination. 'Nature', he wrote, 'is not at all the standard of art, but art is the standard of nature.' He was insistent that he did not want to be a naturalist, but to convey through his art his own vision of reality. The sun and moon, domestic animals, rural folk, church steeples and trees and leaves, all fascinated him.

By the early 1830s, this intense artistic vision had begun to fade. He returned to London, married and took his new wife to Italy for two years. He briefly used oils, but watercolour was always his favourite medium. His reputation is higher now than it ever was in his lifetime, and the sketchbook of 1824–25 is a precious record of a crucial time in the artist's development.

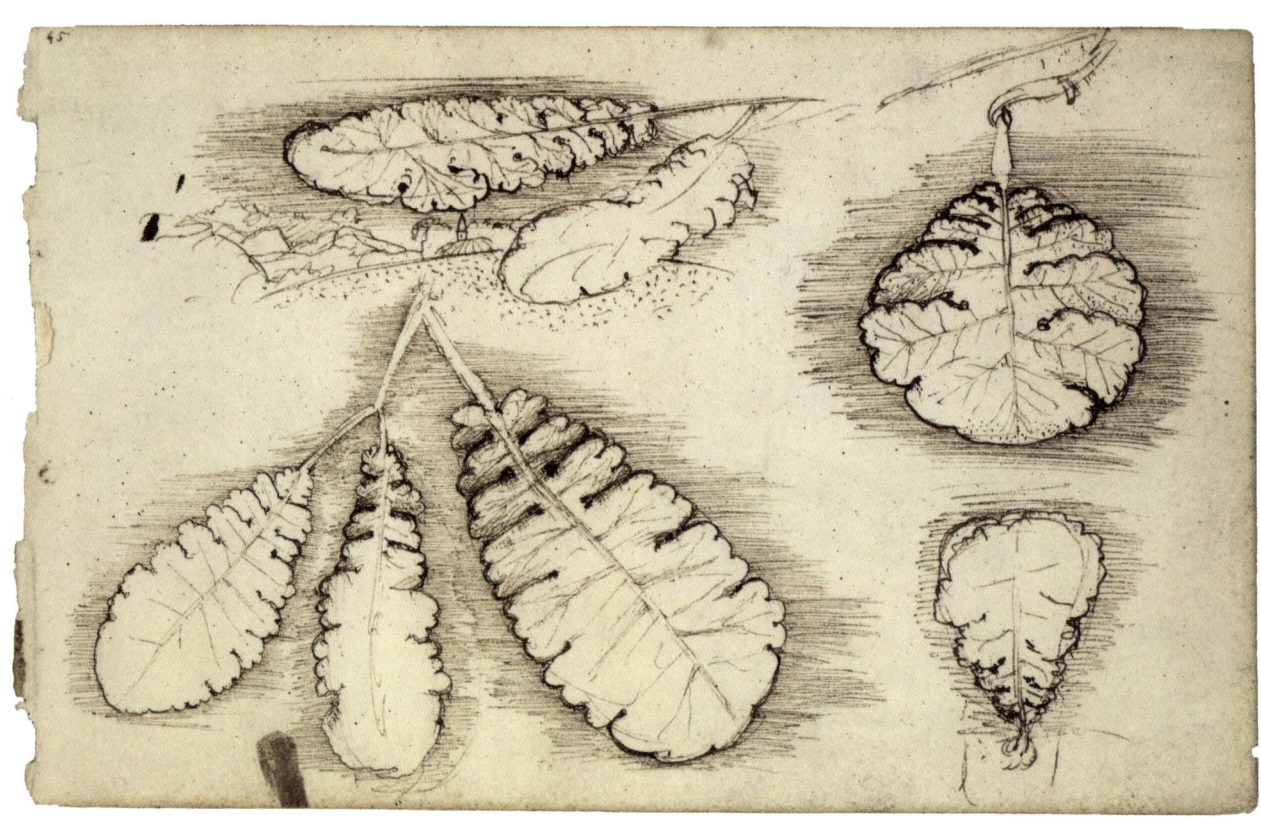

(Above) Studies of kale leaves, although they could also be oak, with a tiny landscape near the top left. (Opposite) Palmer's fascination with trees, especially oak and beech, is evident in this landscape sketch and the finer details at 90 degrees, both delicately and boldly figured in India ink.

JOHN RUSKIN

Art critics generally look and then write. John Ruskin (1819–1900) looked, criticized and wrote prolifically, but he also drew, with great skill and from an early age. His diaries and notebooks throughout his life included annotated botanical sketches which he drew on his travels in the Alps and Mediterranean and even copied from works of art. He never quite escaped his cloying parents – his mother moved to Oxford when Ruskin was an undergraduate, the better to keep an eye on her only child. His psyche was further scarred when he spat blood while there, so his education was interrupted by a tour of the warm climates of Italy, with his parents.

Ruskin painted successfully, and also taught painting. He was the first Slade Professor of Art at Oxford University, where he illustrated his lectures on botanical themes with his huge studies, watercolours and sepia washes. In many ways he drew because that was how best to look. Of flowers he wrote 'It is difficult to give the accuracy of ... their beauty without drawing them.' His botanical descriptions are prose poems, and he clearly loved plants, especially flowers, but not, unfortunately, botanists. His own botanical book, *Proserpina* (1875–86), was a strange amalgam. Illustrated in part from his sketches, he preferred its 'pretty mysteries' and personification of plants to the 'so-called science of botany'. Ruskin was a shrewd geological observer, too, but geologists also fell foul of his beliefs. He saw science as part of the materialism that he decried in economics and society. His was a vision of a lost world, one he believed could be recreated, which also tied in with his role in the Gothic Revival in British architecture.

Beyond his own artistic output, Ruskin wanted to educate the world to appreciate beauty (and truth, since, like the poet John Keats, he equated the two), which he found in accurate representations of nature. In the five volumes of *Modern Painters* (1843–60) he championed J. M. W. Turner, Samuel Palmer (briefly) and then the Pre-Raphaelites. If personal relationships with several members of this Brotherhood were strained, he shared their Victorian aesthetic and moral use of floral emblems.

(Above) Probably the perennial cornflower (*Centaurea montana*); in *Proserpina* Ruskin refused to call such plants weeds, but felt they were also 'scarcely' flowers, so settled on the term 'unluminous' to describe these waysiders of the English landscape. (Opposite) 'Ling' or heather (*Calluna vulgaris*), typical of the smaller studies Ruskin used at the School of Drawing he opened in 1871 at Oxford.

CHARLES RENNIE MACKINTOSH

Sketching, though seemingly innocuous, can occasionally get you into trouble. Early in 1915 Charles Rennie Mackintosh (1868–1928) architect, designer, decorative artist and creator of inspired botanical sketches, was accused of being a German spy. The First World War had stranded Mackintosh and his wife Margaret Macdonald (1864–1933) in Walberswick, a village on the Suffolk coast of England. They were holidaying there when hostilities broke out and, unable to continue on to France as intended, they stayed put.

Mackintosh was recovering from drink, depression and lean years as an architect in his native Glasgow. The sketching had been most helpful – it was a recuperative pleasure, though plans for developing the sketches were vague and never realized. With fears of invasion rife, his habit of working outdoors, involving long solitary walks to find the plants he wished to draw from life, led to accusations of espionage. The phase which had produced over forty compelling pencil and watercolour sketches of flowers came to an end.

No stranger to sketching plants, Mackintosh had long captured their form in precise detail and translated it into stylized representations in his stunning interior designs. He had worked as architectural draughtsman for Honeyman and Keppie from 1889, becoming a partner in 1901 (until 1913). Over an extended period (1883–94) he also attended the Glasgow School of Art, and it was fitting that it was his design for a new building for the school that was chosen in 1896. His organically inspired interiors included designs with Margaret for the Willow Tearooms run by Catherine (Kate) Cranston in Glasgow, which opened in 1903. Later, while in London from 1915, it was swirling fabric designs that provided both some money and an outlet for his continued engagement with the living plant world.

Many of the plant drawings were in his general sketchbooks, where, often in a record of his travels, a flower might sit next to an architectural detail. There is one dedicated botanical sketchbook covering a year from 1894 to 1895. The clear line drawings are regarded as private musings. Yet for someone who wrote that 'Art is the Flower, Life is the Green Leaf', there was never likely to be a complete separation between the pleasure gained from a sketch's creation and its potential for public display.

Pencil studies from 1895 of snapdragon (*Antirrhinum majus*; above) and aconite (*Aconitum napellus*; opposite) explore the structures of flowers and show Mackintosh's flair for pattern and linearity.

(Overleaf) 'Crab-apple Chiddingstone', 1910, and 'Alder catkins Walberswick', 1914. The plants are familiar, the palette in watercolour is simple, while the powerful lines are reminiscent of the restraint of Japanese art.

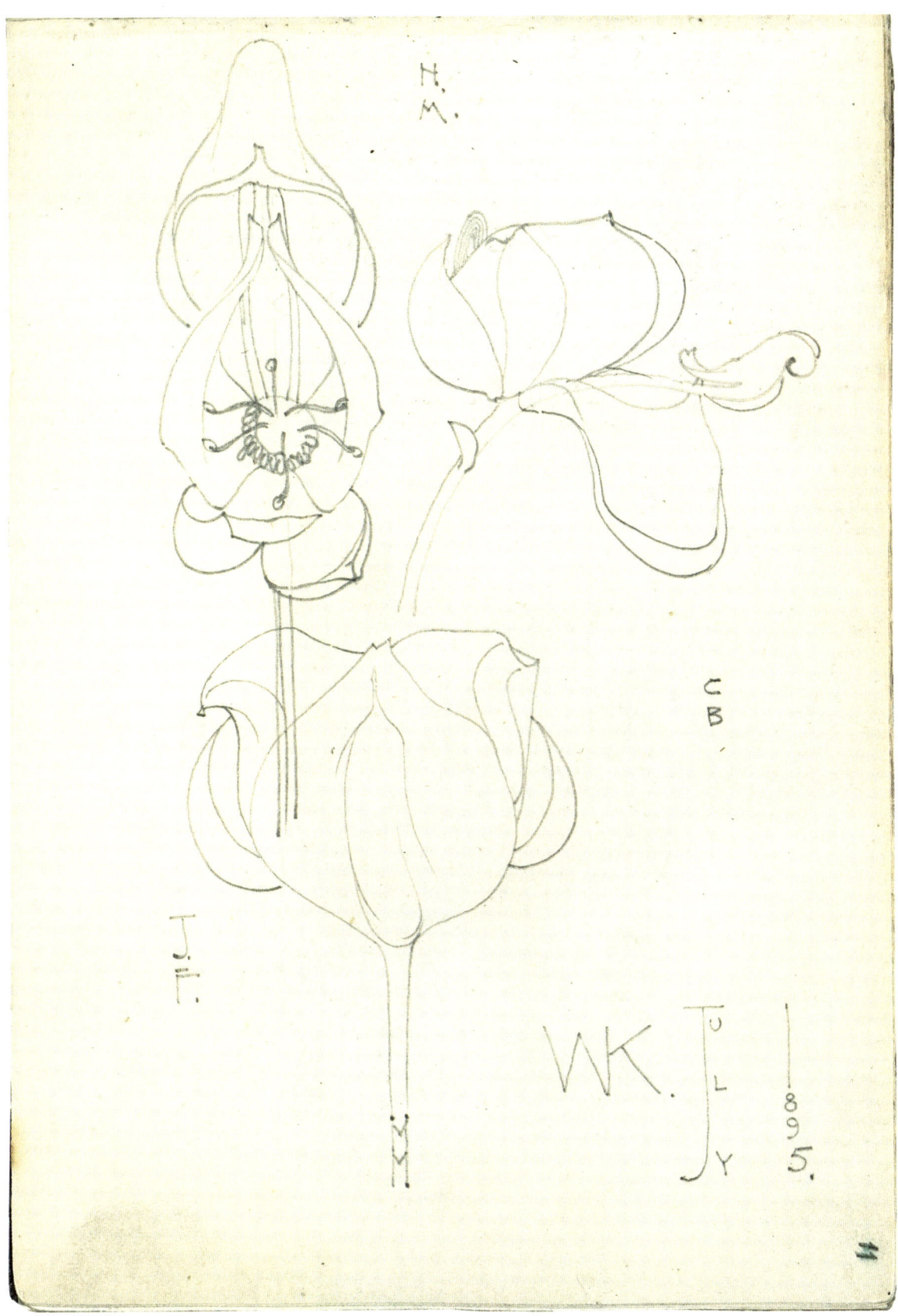

nature in art 211

patrons' dependents

Artists have long been reliant on patronage. Its bestowal was a way of announcing the benefactor's success, be it social, economic or political. Patronage was essential and much welcomed, but could also be fraught with risk, and constrain as well as set free an artist's talents. Sebastian Schedel benefited from the patronage of the church, and Shafi' 'Abbási from rulers of empire and merchants. Georg Dionysius Ehret had many patrons, but among them men of learning and the aristocracy were significant. Pierre-Joseph Redouté was talented enough to survive the end of the French monarchy and the rise and fall of Napoleon. Their sketches are a behind the scenes record of these relationships.

SEBASTIAN SCHEDEL

The distance between Eichstätt and Nuremberg in Germany is just over 70 km (*c.* 44 miles). A rider on horseback could make the journey in a day, but a horse-drawn wagon would take two. For a period in the early 17th century, the Bishop of Eichstätt, Johann Conrad von Gemmingen, apparently sent each week 'One or two boxes full of fresh flowers' from his garden along this route to the apothecary Basilius Besler in Nuremberg 'to be sketched'. Both the flower garden – ornamental flowers were the Bishop's passion – and the book, *Hortus Eystettensis*, eventually produced under Besler's supervision, were remarkable achievements.

The production of the *Hortus Eystettensis* (one of the great early *florilegia*) relied on the Bishop's patronage, and, after his death, on that of his much less interested successor. In Nuremberg, Besler acted as agent, albeit a botanically literate, artistically astute and business-minded one, arranging for artists to work on the weekly delivery from Eichstätt. These artists created a series of preliminary studies and then drawings, from which the plates for printing were engraved. Colourists transformed the monochrome prints into the beautifully painted versions of the de luxe edition. Among the wealthy literati there was a passion for 'contrafetten', images of objects, especially transient ones like flowers, which were more highly regarded than the real thing.

One of the artists at the beginning of this chain who can be confidently identified was Sebastian Schedel (1570–1628). He had spent some time earlier on a tour of neighbouring countries, supporting himself by his art, but at the time of the boxed deliveries he worked as an ensign and then from 1608 as steward for the butchers' guild in Nuremberg. Art appears to have been his true love. The Bishop's desire to pay homage to God by capturing the rapidly expanding 'book of nature' as new plants flowed into Europe provided Schedel with a means to this end.

On various qualities of paper and subsequently bound together as Schedel's 'Kalendarium' are a series of plant studies by him. Naturalistic sketches from life sit alongside more stylized interpretations of flowers. It is as if he were looking both at the real floral world (possibly, as has been suggested, also in the gardens of Eichstätt) and simultaneously working towards a required, mannered mode of depiction, characteristic of the *Hortus*. Schedel left the butchers' guild in 1616 under a cloud, and relied on his art to make a living thereafter.

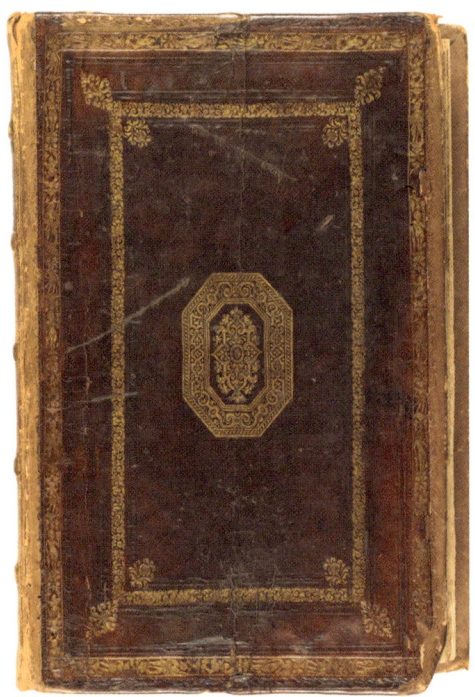

(Above) Schedel's leather-bound 'Kalendarium' is organized by month of flowering, with the multicoloured maize head (*Zea mays*; opposite) appearing in October.

(Overleaf) It was important in the studies to capture the colour as well as the form of the flowers (the rose on the right is showing a mutation), for these would be used later by the colourists. Subsequent additions, pressed flowers and floral details on pasted cards indicate it was perhaps a work in progress until Schedel's death.

III Making Art

Cyclamen
Serotinum.

Centifolia.

173.

(Above) '*Sigillum salmonis*' or Solomon's seal (*Polygonatum* sp.). (Opposite) '*Stramonium Vel. Datura Turccarum*', the 'thorn apple' renamed *Datura stramonium* by Linnaeus. This and a couple of other species of *Datura* begin to be recorded from the mid-16th century in herbals, and gradually became a widespread and poisonous weed in Europe.

SHAFI' 'ABBÁSÍ

Isfahan became the magnificent centre of the Safavid empire (1501–1722) when Shah 'Abbas I made it his capital in 1598. Near an oasis on the Iranian plateau, it was not only a beautiful city but also a thriving mercantile centre. In its heyday, a succession of merchants, clerics, envoys and craftsmen from Europe, Russia and India came there bringing goods and gifts, including paintings, prints and illustrated books. Exposure to these encouraged eclectic artistic styles to emerge under the patronage of the Safavid court. One leading artist was Muhammad Shafi' also known as Muhammad Shafi' 'Abbásí or simply Shafi' 'Abbásí, a title that recognized his connection with the court. Following in his father's footsteps, he flourished from 1628 to the 1660s.

Shafi' 'Abbásí finessed the 'bird-and-flower' genre, and employed it to great effect in the decorative arts such as lacquer-work book covers as well as paintings. The plants of 'bird-and-flower' work combined Mughal depictions with European floral compositions, while maintaining the fluid lines of the older traditions. Some fine examples of this subject matter and technique were quick, single-page ink sketches, which were then often made into albums. Such sketches advertised the artist's talents to potential patrons beyond the court. They also served as designs for textiles, a very lucrative part of Persian trade that the Shahs were keen to promote. Some of the sheets in the album featured here were pounced, the design being transferred to another surface by pricking its outline.

There is some suggestion that Shafi' 'Abbásí left Isfahan towards the end of his life and moved to the Mughal court at Agra, changing patrons as Safavid power waned, but the information is fragmentary.

(Opposite) A clump of violets drawn in ink and watercolour and pounced to transfer the design. The inscription gives a date of Monday 5 Muharram 1054 AH or AD 5 April 1642.
(Above) 'Rosebushes, bees and a dragonfly': striations and cross-hatching indicate that European engravings were used as a source.

patrons' dependents

(Above) A sketch of *Gloriosa superba*, known to Ehret as '*Methonica Malabarorum*' or '*Lilium Zeylanicum Superbum*' referring to the Malabar Coast, India, or Dutch Ceylon. (Opposite) A work sheet from an album: 'Rare Fruits and Seeds Collected and Drawn by G. D. Ehret 1748'. Additional details as seen here could transform plant portraits into scientific illustrations. Included are two species of jasmine, passion fruit 'Granadilla' and 'the True Seed of the Jesuit Bark' (*Cinchona* sp.), which came via Peter Collinson, intermediary for William Bartram's father and Mark Catesby's patron.

GEORG DIONYSIUS EHRET

The patrons of Georg Dionysius Ehret (1708–1770) were a veritable 'who's who' of the world of 18th-century plantsmen. Through their benefaction, and as a result of his own talent and determination, this German-born journeyman-gardener would become one of the leading artists of the 'golden age' of botanical art.

Like many artists, Ehret first learnt from his father. Subsequent formal schooling was cut short by his father's death, and Ehret became a reluctant gardener, apprenticed to his uncle. He was eager to leave the garden for the drawing studio, and his break came in the late 1720s in Regensburg when the apothecary Johann Wilhem Weinmann commissioned 1,000 drawings for a fixed fee. Ehret soon discovered that such arrangements could be difficult. After a year, Weinmann paid him less than he was due, and the two parted company.

Among Ehret's most significant patrons was the Nuremberg doctor Christoph Jacob Trew. They corresponded first and then met in 1733. Trew commissioned Ehret to picture exotic plants on the fine quality paper he provided, advancing the artist's career and at the same time becoming a lifelong friend. He also encouraged Ehret the botanist by teaching him to appreciate plant 'characters', the floral and fruiting parts used for classification. Ehret overcame his initial aesthetic reluctance and included them in his drawings.

Trew's correspondents welcomed Ehret, and he painted in the gardens of this distinguished group of men in Switzerland, France, England and Holland. In Paris over the winter of 1734–35, Ehret learnt to paint on vellum, using opaque paints. This became his preferred medium for completed drawings. He also devised the signature he used on his finished work; sketches and studies remained unsigned. In 1735 he arrived at the garden of George Clifford in the Dutch republic at the same time as Carl Linnaeus (p. 118). Great art met zeal for systematization and Ehret made his famous drawing of Linnaeus's sexual system of plant classification.

In 1736 Ehret settled in England and expanded his patronage network. He illustrated books and papers for Sir Hans Sloane, with his vast collection, Philip Miller, who was in charge of the Chelsea Physic Garden, and Joseph Banks. But dissecting a plant for a scientific publication took much time and paid less than a plant portrait for a titled dilettante. A frustrating year as a gardener at the Oxford Botanic Garden (1750–51) reinforced his desire for a regular income, which he found finally as a painting teacher and plant artist for the nobility.

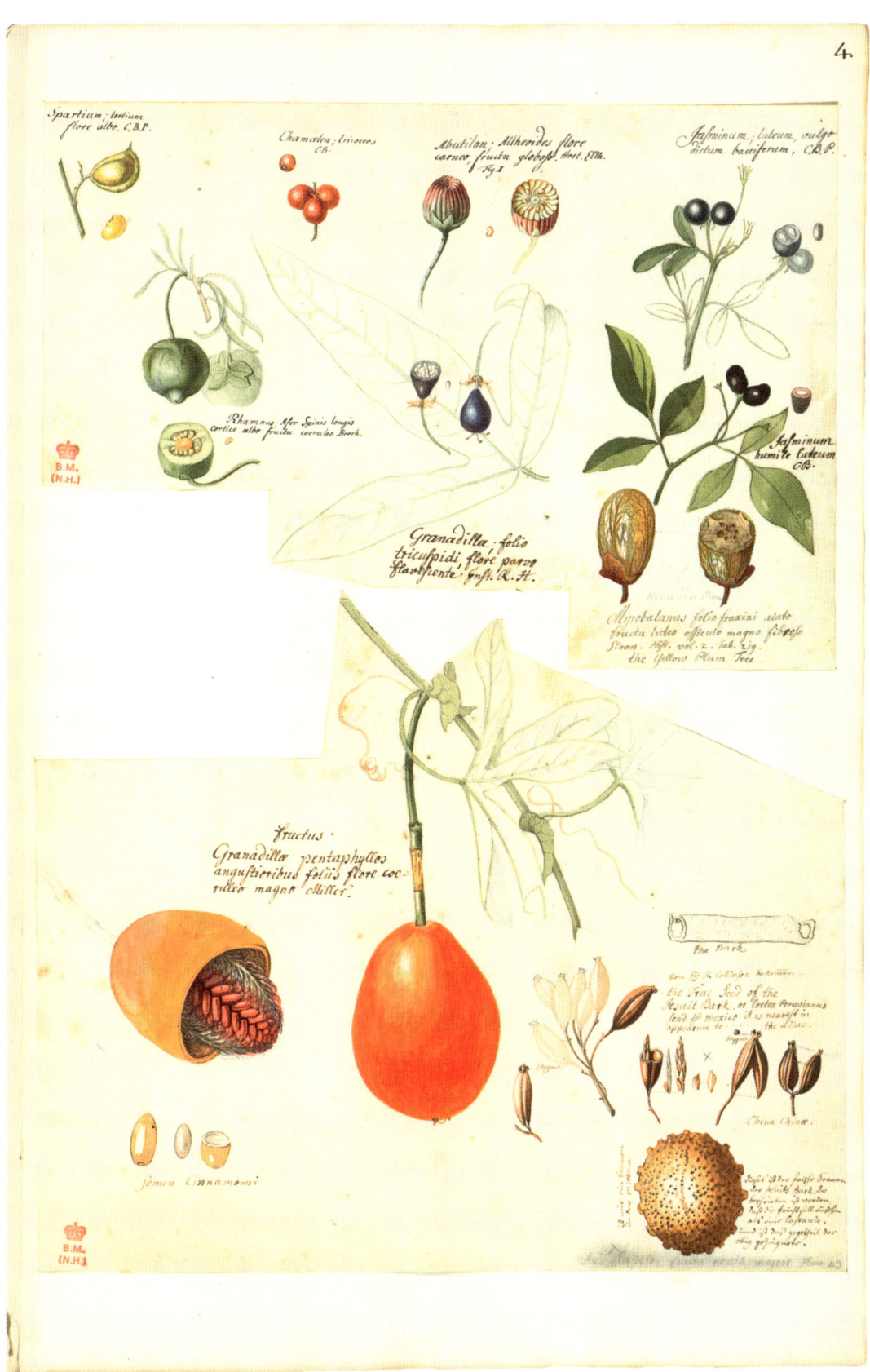

patrons' dependents 221

P. J. Redouté pinx.

n.º 9. Q. rubra ~~canadensis~~
         Q. caroliniana

PIERRE-JOSEPH REDOUTÉ

Anyone connected with the French court had reason to be nervous during the years of the Revolution and Terror. If Pierre-Joseph Redouté (1759–1840), the 'Raphael of flowers', had suffered through his connection with his royal patron, Marie Antoinette, the world of botanical art would be very much poorer.

After leaving home in Belgium aged thirteen, Redouté spent ten years as an itinerant artist in the Low Countries. He began concentrating on plant portraits, inspired by the elaborate Dutch flower compositions he had seen. In 1782 he joined his older brother Antoine-Ferdinand in Paris, helping him to paint theatre scenery and spending his free time painting in the Jardin du Roi and making engravings of plant portraits. This brought him to the attention of the artist Gerard van Spaendonck and botanist Charles-Louis L'Héritier, and his career as a botanical illustrator as well as flower painter began under the latter's instruction.

In 1786 came the appointment as draughtsman to Marie Antoinette's *cabinet*. The following year Redouté travelled to Kew to draw the exotic plants. More importantly he met the engraver Francesco Bartolozzi and learnt about his stipple engraving, a technique that Redouté would bring near to perfection in his famed depiction of lilies and roses in the 19th century. He was able to capture perfectly in the published plates the colour, perspective and charm of his preparatory watercolour work.

In 1793, the year of Marie Antoinette's execution, Redouté was employed (with his younger brother Henri-Joseph) at the renamed Jardin des Plantes to continue the famous series of vellums, a comprehensive collection of botanical and other natural history illustrations. He had weathered the storm and his fortunes continued to rise thanks to the patronage of the next first lady of France, the Empress Joséphine. She employed him to paint the flowers in her fabulously stocked garden at Malmaison.

After Joséphine's death, the fortunes of the 'Painter to the Empress' declined, and his earlier profligacy haunted him. His folio edition of *Les Roses* was beautiful but a financial disaster. Despite formal honours, Redouté struggled until his death from a cerebral haemorrhage, brought on by the news that the French government would not be his patron.

(Opposite) A preliminary sketch of *Quercus coccinea* for Michaux's *The North American Sylva* (1819): even the great master's work was corrected as necessary. (Above) *Oenothera* flowers, a gift from Redouté in 1840.

in print

Changes in printing technology and the graphic arts opened up the potential for illustrated publishing in the 18th century. Industrialization with the steam printing press then created an exponential growth in picture books and other printed matter in the 19th century. If depictions of the botanical world were more readily available, the process still began with sketches and drawings. Alfred Riocreux, Olive Coates Palgrave and Okada Seifuku offer very different kinds of near-perfect drawings for plate and block. Their work was used for books aimed at plant connoisseurs and scholars. Muriel Dawson, Anne Todd Dowden and Violet Emily Graham sketched for children's books, a wonderful use of the creativity of botanical artists in the mass-market world.

ALFRED RIOCREUX

Alfred Riocreux (1820–1912) could have followed his father's career in the floral decorative arts. Denis-Désiré Riocreux was a painter of exquisite work on porcelain at the Sèvres ceramics factory, though by the time his son was born his eyesight had failed him and instead he ran its newly established museum for its director, geologist Alexandre Brongniart. Brongniart's own son, Adolphe, was a notable botanist, with a special interest in fossil plants. Learning of the young Alfred's talent at the factory, Adolphe had him work on illustrations for his important *Histoire des végétaux fossiles* (1837). The drawing of fossil barks was very different from both the demands of the factory and what Riocreux would have been familiar with at the drawing school of Pierre-Joseph Redouté (p. 224), where he was reputedly one of the last pupils. But with these drawings he began a highly successful career as a scientific botanical illustrator, adept with the microscope as well as the pencil and brush.

Very soon after the intricate drawings of fossilized plant parts, he was working on preparatory drawings for the second series of *Herbier général de l'amateur*, edited by the physician and botanist Jean Louis Auguste Loiseleur-Deslongchamps. Some regard Riocreux as the French equivalent of his contemporary, Walter Hood Fitch (p. 156) – in the 1830s they were on a similar career path. The vast growth of the nursery business and the rise of professional plant collectors led to an expanding market for modestly priced illustrated publications that brought reports of new plants to the eager gardening public. It is equally possible to imagine Riocreux's study of a tropical South American/Caribbean orchid on a piece of Sèvres porcelain as it is to see it engraved as a plate in a periodical.

From the ferns of New Zealand to the trees of North America, to the seaweeds of the Mediterranean, Riocreux continued to draw throughout his long life. He stepped neatly between the worlds of high art and science, exhibiting at the Paris Salon and working for the Muséum d'Histoire naturelle before being decorated Chevalier de la Légion d'honneur.

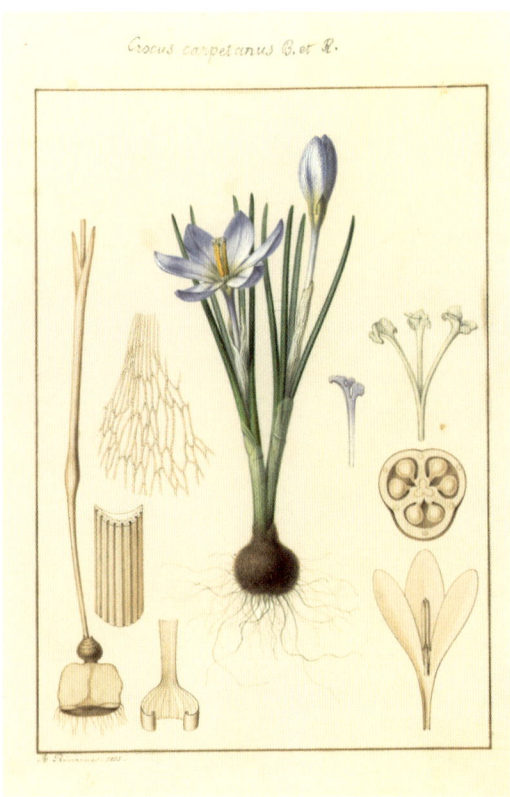

(Left) *Crocus carpetanus*, Riocreux's 1855 drawing for J. É. Gay, a Swiss-French amateur botanist who was also a leading crocologist and commissioned French artists to picture his careful delineation of the genus. (Opposite) *Stanhopea grandiflora* for *Herbier général de l'amateur*.

OKADA SEIFUKU

The beauty of the *Honzō zufu* (Illustrated Manual of Plants) of Iwasaki (Kan'en) Tsunemasa (1786–1842), with its bold woodblock illustrations of Japanese flora, has become increasingly appreciated in recent years. This massive project was born in Edo (Tokyo) early in the 19th century. Iwasaki wrote in the preface that he had taken to the mountains and fields to collect plants for the botanical garden he managed for the Shogun. In addition to these Japanese natives, Iwasaki also illustrated in his work some introduced plants, but for these pictures his models were often illustrations from European books.

Not only was the creation of his project complex, its publication history was also fraught, and cost Iwasaki a great deal of money. Only four of the 92 volumes that had been prepared were published before he died. At great expense, hand-coloured manuscript volumes followed during the 19th century, eventually totalling over 2,000 watercolours. A complete printed woodblock edition followed much later, in 1916–21.

It is likely that Iwasaki had some help with the illustrations. However, while we can trace his career, and that of his book, very little is known about the artist Okada Seifuku (*fl.* 1820s/1830s), who seems to have been responsible for a large series of watercolours on rice paper, some of which appeared later in *Honzō zufu*. Like so many of Iwasaki's, these watercolour drawings are sufficiently botanically accurate to make general identification of the plants easy. This was the scientific goal, but it was married to an aesthetic one. The spontaneous 'boneless technique', with no inked outlines, was driven by colour; a limited palette was repeated throughout the series. The extremely pleasing brush work and arrangement of the plants on the paper have their roots in Chinese flower painting.

'Ryokyou or Chinese ginger' captures the natural flexing of the leaves of the plant through the simple use of two greens and some careful details of veining. The pink of the new shoots is replicated in the emerging petals. Both pages show imperfect leaves, browned and tattered – this must have been executed from life.

(Overleaf) Strawberry geranium (*Saxifraga stolonifera*) and milk thistle (*Silybum marianum*, white-flowered variety), used for tumours and liver complaints in Japanese Kampo medicine.

虎耳草

大薊

OLIVE COATES PALGRAVE

Trees of Central Africa was a family affair. Published in 1956, it reproduced paintings by Olive Coates Palgrave (1889–1963) of the flowers, fruit and leaves of the typical bush trees found in Zimbabwe, Zambia and Malawi. One of her three sons wrote the tree descriptions, while the other two provided additional photographs. Initially issued as a limited edition of 500 copies, the book would go on to become a classic, revised and continued after Olive's death.

Olive Trollip was born in Craddock, Eastern Cape, South Africa. She was descended from the '1820 Settlers', families who were encouraged to emigrate to buffer the border of the Cape colony. Farming difficulties in the 1890s forced her father to move to Southern Rhodesia (Zimbabwe), and after finishing her education Olive returned home. She was inspired by her remarkable botany teacher, Bertha Stoneman (1866–1943), who wrote in her authoritative textbook, *Plants and Their Ways in South Africa* (1906), 'if you have never thought about leaves, you will be surprised to find how many different shapes there are'. It was an observation Olive clearly absorbed.

In 1915 Olive married Sidney Heneage Coates Palgrave, a civil servant, whose father, William, also a civil servant, was a game hunter and amateur butterfly collector as well. The Coates Palgraves were keen that their children should share the family's love of Africa's landscape, and Olive mosquito-proofed the pram and began her watercolours on picnics into the bush when they were babies. As the boys grew, they helped her find the ideal specimen and cut the branches of trees for her to paint. It became a family adventure. Olive Coates Palgrave continued to paint her watercolours for 28 years, and reached nearly a hundred illustrations before she decided to publish. Because the Federation of Rhodesia and Nyasaland had been formed in 1953, she added a few extra ones to make the book more comprehensive. Its enduring success is her legacy.

Flower of the baobab or upside-down tree, *Adansonia digitata* (above), and the flower and fruit of *Gardenia volkensii* subsp. *spathulifolia* (below). In both, Coates Palgrave shaded her background to reinforce the whiteness of the petals. (Opposite) At 12 m (40 ft) tall, the candelabra tree, *Euphorbia ingens*, is a striking succulent brought to the notice of European botanists by the uncle of Isaac Drège (p. 90).

(Overleaf) Spiny *Commiphora africana* (page 232) is recognizable in the bush by its spherical shape, short trunk and low branches. *Widdringtonia whytei* or 'Mulanje cedarwood' (page 233) is a rare species discovered on the Mulanje massif in Malawi in 1891.

MURIEL DAWSON

Muriel Dawson (1897–1974) painted illustrations for a wide range of items – cards, calendars, magazine covers and books – often involving children and animals. But whatever the format or subject, her love of landscapes and the natural world, accurately captured, is always apparent.

Born in Geraldine, New Zealand, where her Scottish family ran a prosperous shop, Dawson, known as 'Toby', was the eldest of four children. The Dawsons later moved back to Scotland and then to Putney, near London. From 1913, Dawson attended three art colleges, graduating from the Royal College of Art, South Kensington, in 1922. A prize took her on a travelling scholarship to Italy and here she converted to Catholicism, remaining deeply religious throughout her life. Children's verse, nursery rhymes and moral tales such as Charles Kingsley's *The Water-Babies* (1863) all suited her whimsical style from the 1920s onwards, and she also worked extensively for the Medici Society, which by the 1930s was a major retailer of high-quality prints and cards.

Dawson always used sketchbooks and loose sheets to record what she saw. Over a thousand drawings made in charcoal, pen and ink, pastel crayons and watercolour survive. While there are many working studies of children, there are also delicate but perceptive depictions of the natural world. These were inspired by her travels around Britain and Ireland and the countryside where she settled – the South Downs, Dartmoor and finally the Shetland Islands. Sometimes she drew a simple flower, leaf and stem, coloured with single tones, with the common name of the plant and the date and location noted on the sheet. Other sketches, often the later ones, were more intricate and composed; the roots might be included, or an enlarged flower part, or she added a drawing showing the plants growing as a clump. Plants and animals, often birds, also featured together in a closely observed landscape, and her notes at this time might record what else was to be found nearby. The sketches are less saccharine than the printed work, but it's always the same assured hand.

'Very tiny Hare Bell', *Campanula rotundifolia*, from Farthing Downs. This open space to the south of London where Dawson sketched in the 1920s is now an area of special scientific interest, with ancient chalky grasslands and wildflower meadows.

A miniature
"Bluebell of Scotland"

Farthing Downs Aug.
Very tiny
Hare Bell
drawing full size.

ANNE TODD DOWDEN

'Newly-weds Plan "Sketchy" Honeymoon' ran a jolly newspaper headline reporting the marriage of Anne Ophelia Todd (1907–2007) and Raymond Baxter Dowden on Easter Day, 1934. It included two of the three most important things in Anne's long life: her art and her husband. The third was her love of the natural world, and plant pollination in particular. In 1955, aged 48, she was finally able to enjoy all three simultaneously. Giving up teaching, she went on to illustrate and write nine books with plant themes, several for children, and collaborated on eleven more, becoming in the process one of North America's most renowned botanical illustrators of the 20th century.

Dowden grew up in Boulder, Colorado. After graduating from Carnegie Tech in 1930 she went to New York seeking a career as an illustrator. It was the height of the Depression and work was scarce; instead she found a part-time teaching job and continued to study. Participation in a mural for the Chicago World's Fair (1934) led to a fifteen-year partnership in the American Design Group. Creating floral chintzes kept up her interest in flowers and provided enough stable income for marriage, and the couple settled in Manhattan.

The Dowdens had no children, but shared their home, including the bathtub, with Anne's flower specimens. She only painted from life and only worked in watercolour; she described her method as the 'world's slowest'. A finished illustration would begin with finding the living plants. This might involve sketching and collecting in the countryside, roaming the city's empty lots or asking colleagues and friends to send flowers by courier (some grown on demand), at precisely the right time. From these she would create her exact, life-sized research paintings, working as fast as the wilting flower demanded. The resulting bank of material was carefully stored so that pencil tracings of the apposite parts could be transferred. The final watercolour was a perfectly designed collage of her studies.

(Above) Dowden often wrote as well as illustrated her books, integrating the text precisely into the composition to satisfy her exacting eye, here a working layout of 'Regular and Irregular Flowers'. (Opposite) Life-size tulip studies.

Atkinson Field 26/III/53
Boraginaceae Cordia nodosa
Fruits in Cymose clusters.
leaves 2-4 together
not quite whorled.
unequal.
15'
P.T.O.
Hollow
(for ants?)
x 3

(Essequibo)
Amaryllidaceae
B. Hymenocallis
declinata
on beach.
Leaves less broad
than A
B
actual
size
6/IX/55
A
A

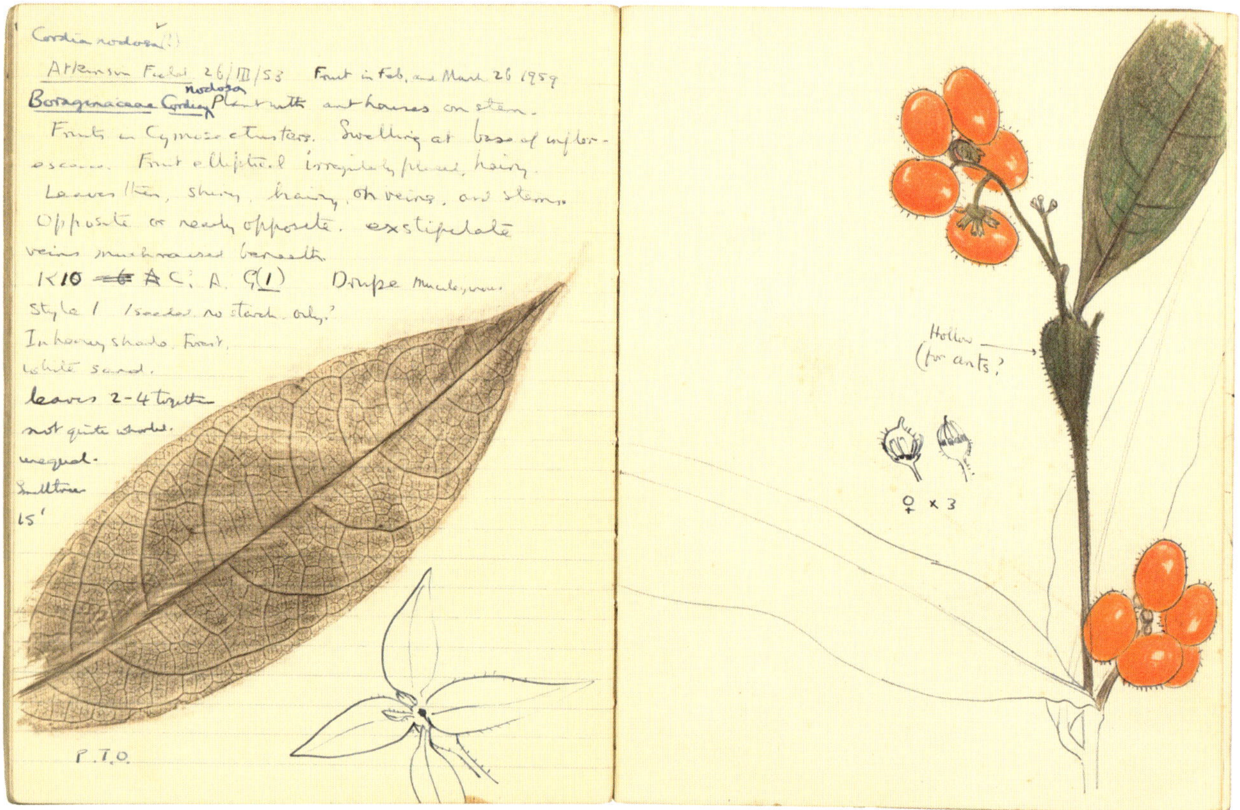

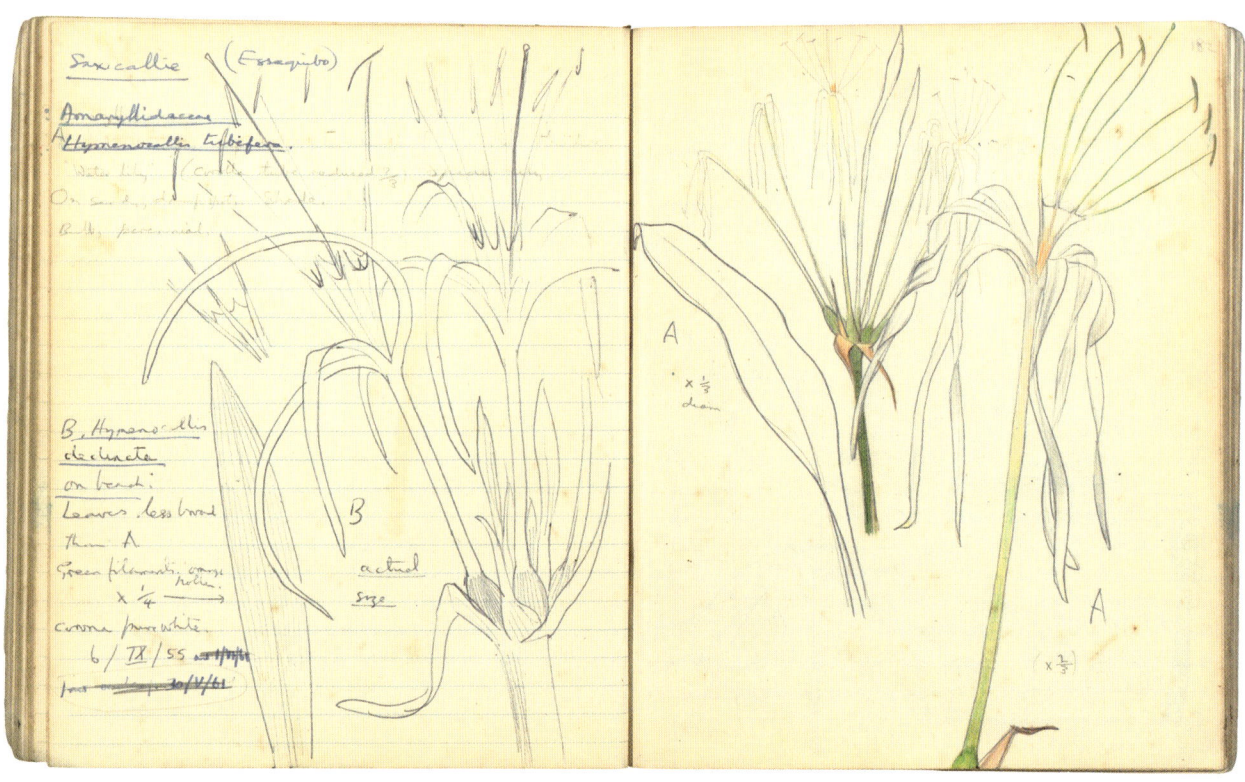

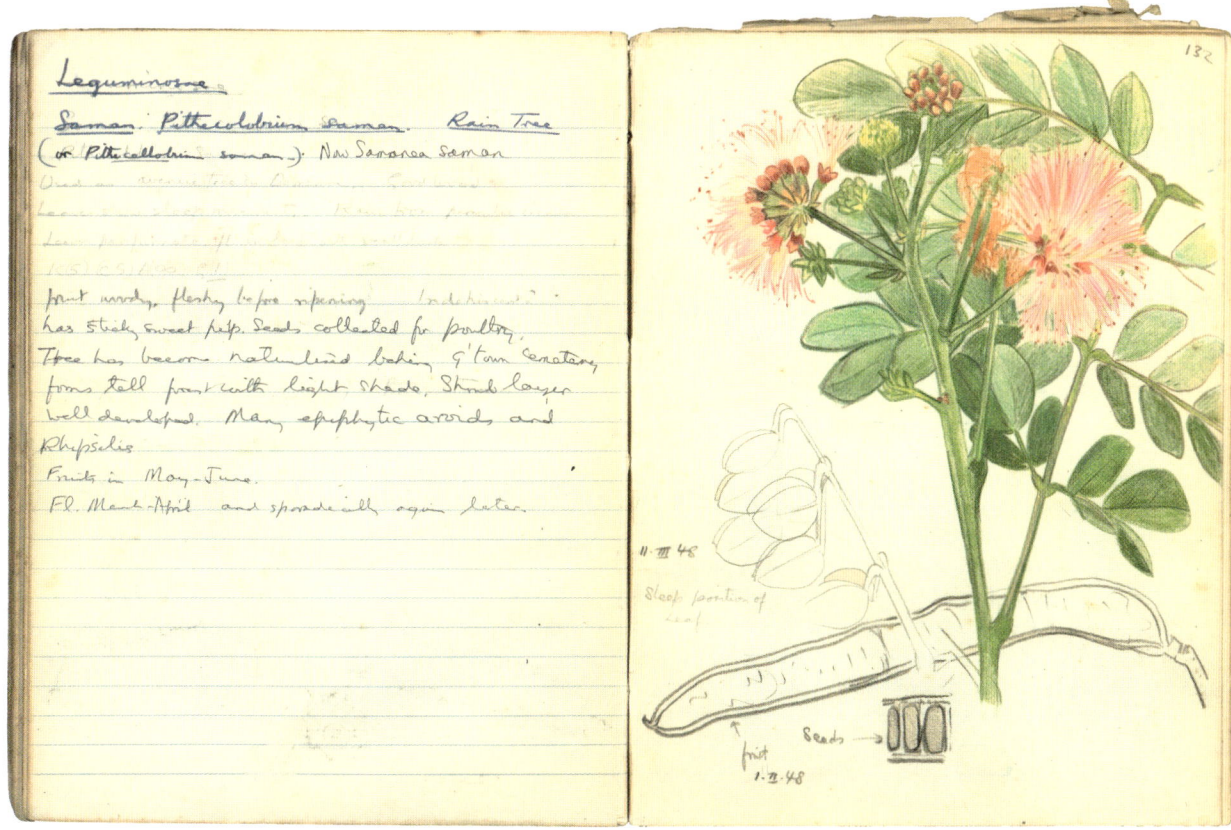

VIOLET EMILY GRAHAM

'I began a nature diary when I was eleven, and now I have many volumes. Each time I look at one of those old diaries it makes me remember exactly what I did in those days. There are hundreds of things there I would have forgotten completely.' So Violet Emily Graham (1911–1991) informed her young readers in *A Primary Nature Study for British Guiana* (1961). This useful little book was one of several she wrote and illustrated based on her experiences teaching, plant collecting and sketching in British Guiana (Guyana) in the mid-20th century. Graham was a biology teacher at the Bishops' High School in Georgetown, then a girl's school in this British colony.

The history of Guyana, like that of much of the Caribbean and northern South America, was bound up with sugar cane and slavery. The 1950s were a troubled period, as the indigenous population sought the right to self-determination and independence. Graham provided a tacit rebuke to the short-sightedness of colonial government when she produced a biology textbook filled with examples from the flora and fauna of the surrounding countryside to replace existing ones that simply relied on the seasons, soils, plants and animals of the temperate world.

In a series of school exercise books – the same as ones she would have issued to her pupils – she made a particular kind of 'nature diary' with a specific purpose in mind. She ranged widely, sketching the flowers of the coastal region of British Guiana and taking her pupils with her on their bicycles if possible. In the accompanying notes she recorded prevalence or size or unusual features, as well as locations. She returned more than once to some places, updating her notes over the fourteen years or so she was busy drawing. The sketches provided a basis for her illustrations, and the school textbooks led to popular educational books after she had retired to England. Graham aimed these at young naturalists in the making. Her kindly advice was always to have a pencil and paper to hand, and remember that 'one of the best ways of observing carefully is to make a labelled drawing'.

(Opposite) A leaf rubbing and sketch of *Cordia nodosa* fruit (above) – Graham noted the hollow in the stem which houses Azteca ants that protect the plant from herbivores – and (below) *Hymenocallis tubiflora* and *H. caribaea*, the Caribbean spider-lily. (Above) *Albizia saman*, or rain tree.

jobbing

To earn a living entirely by making art has always been difficult. To be able to concentrate exclusively on the plant world was a further luxury for those who favoured botanical art. Jobbing artists had to combine the depiction of plants with other subjects. Sydney Parkinson was a general natural history artist; Conrad Martens painted landscapes. Edward Lear wanted to be a landscape artist and although he succeeded in doing so, his cartoons, parrot illustrations and poetry are better known today. John Hill and Edward Minchen had pursued other lines of employment before making their botanical breakthroughs, and in Hill's case difficulties continued. Ferdinand Bauer, for all his brilliance, was employed on a specific project and when it proved uncongenial chose not to renew the contract. Sketching was an unexpected boon to John Doody, a transported convict. Jobbing was insecure, but rarely, it seems, dull.

JOHN HILL

'Sir' John Hill (bap. 1716–1775) was a man of many parts: actor, playwright, editor, poet, novelist, apothecary, wit, artist and botanist, to name only some. He was clever and energetic, but he never seemed to earn money quite as fast as he spent it, or had the means to live up to his ennoblement. His 'knighthood' was actually a decoration from the Swedish king, perhaps because that country appreciated Hill's early adoption of Linnaeus's system of botanical nomenclature.

Hill was said to have learnt his botany on country walks with his father, a clergyman, and it was his most lasting preoccupation. He used plants in various medicinal remedies he devised, such as 'essence of water dock' (not as unorthodox then as it would be now), and sold to help fund his botanical publications, which stand out among the torrents of words and images he produced. His early interest in botany was furthered when the second Duke of Richmond commissioned him to collect plants for him in England and Wales. Hill subsequently took up residence at Goodwood, the Duke's home in Sussex. After a couple of years he returned to London and to acting, writing and probably keeping his apothecary's shop again. He also cultivated the city's scientific elite and was bitter that he failed to achieve his goal of election to the Royal Society. Nevertheless, he continued to publish prolifically in the natural sciences, including volumes on fossils, *materia medica*, trees and gardening.

Finally securing the patronage of Lord Bute, one of King George III's favourites, he embarked on his most ambitious work, *The Vegetable System*, an attempt to classify, describe and illustrate all the known plants. It finally ran to 26 volumes and took sixteen years to complete. If it helped his European reputation, it also cost him financially, particularly after Bute withdrew his support. A bound collection of some of his preparatory sketches (there were 26,000 figures) found its way back to Kew where Hill had been either 'First Superintendent' or merely 'Botanist', depending on who was in charge at the time.

'Radiatae II. Calyce Simplici' and 'Radiatae III. Calyce Duplici' from a folio of Hill's sketches, with examples of the flower types based on the Linnaean artificial classification system.

RADIATÆ II.
CALYCE SIMPLICI.

MILLERIA. XII.

SIGISBECKIA. XI.

RADIATÆ III.
CALYCE DUPLICI.

BELLIS. XIV.

DORONICUM. XIII.

VERBESINA. XVI.

CŒLESTINA. XV.

COTULA. XVIII.

ANTHEMIS. XVII.

RUDBECKIA. XX.

CALENDULA. XIX.

SYDNEY PARKINSON

The sketches made by Sydney Parkinson (*c.* 1745–1771) in his role as natural history artist employed by Joseph Banks on James Cook's first great voyage of 1768–71 would take another two hundred years to be published in finished form. The official purpose of the voyage of the *Endeavour*, sponsored by the Royal Society and enabled by the Admiralty, was to observe the transit of Venus across the sun from the island of Tahiti, only recently encountered by Europeans. The wealthy Banks arranged for himself and his entourage to be taken on the *Endeavour*, and he planned his team carefully.

Parkinson was the son of a Quaker brewer in Edinburgh, but after his father's early death the family moved to London. There Sydney found work not in the woollen trade to which he had been apprenticed, but as a flower painter and art teacher for a fellow Quaker, nurseryman James Lee. Lee's Vineyard nursery in Hammersmith specialized in exotic plants, and it was Lee who first suggested Parkinson to Banks. Following his expedition to Labrador and Newfoundland in 1766, Banks needed watercolours made of his preserved animals. Parkinson was in good company – on this occasion the plants were painted by Georg Ehret (p. 220).

Banks's party on the *Endeavour* also consisted of Linnaeus's protégé Daniel Solander, who served as botanist. Parkinson was the artist for the plants and animals, and Alexander Buchan for the people and places. Such official artists were something new. Both at sea and during landfall, Banks took every opportunity to collect natural history specimens. From these he selected novel or significant examples for Parkinson to draw in the Great Cabin. Buchan suffered from epilepsy, and an attack on Tahiti resulted in his death. Parkinson's workload doubled; he painted in Banks's tent working under a net to prevent the flies eating 'the colour off the paper as fast as he could lay it on'. He made 128 watercolour sketches of plants (113 complete), including the breadfruit made famous by Captain Bligh's later voyage on the *Bounty*.

The astronomy accomplished, on 13 July 1769 the *Endeavour* sailed again for the fabled great southern continent under the secret 'Additional Instructions'. The result was a charting of New Zealand's coasts and possession of New South Wales for the crown. There was of course also much botanizing; Parkinson was overwhelmed. Banks reported that the young artist produced 94 sketches in 14 days in May 1770. Most of Parkinson's earlier drawings were finished, but from New Zealand onwards the majority of his 655 sketches remained as pencil or ink outlines, some with colour descriptions and others partially coloured. Parkinson's plan was to work them up later, but the unhealthy climate of Batavia (Jakarta) told and he died at sea on 26 January 1771. Banks commissioned other artists to finish and engrave his sketches, though they were published in full only in 1990.

Examples of Parkinson's part-coloured sketches from Cook's first voyage of 1768–71. (Opposite) *Ipomoea indica*, blue or ocean morning glory, a pan-tropical species. (Above) *Dampiera stricta* a native of Tasmania and eastern Australia; the notes refer to a previous naming error due to mixing up plant specimens, hardly surprising given the working conditions on the *Endeavour* by the time the ship entered Australian waters.

JOHN DOODY

Penal Australia in the late 18th century was a hive of botanical activity. There were officers with serious botanical goals who wanted to understand, name and classify the newly discovered plants, trophy hunters who looked to make money exporting exciting exotics, and convicts who were employed to draw for the botanically inclined. Forgery was a transportable crime and may have accounted for some of the talent among the early convict artists whose sketches captured the flora and fauna of the country. John Doody (*fl.* 1790s) was sentenced in December 1788 to seven years transportation, but details of his crime are vague.

Doody arrived in Australia on the *Admiral Barrington* in November 1791. Within a matter of days he was back on board ship, this time on the *Kitty* bound for Norfolk Island, around 1,000 nautical miles to the east, as servant of Captain William Paterson (1755–1810) of the New South Wales Corps, who had charge of the troops on this small island. Among the aims of its penal station was the exploitation of the island's plants, particularly pine trees for masts (this failed) and the fibres of the flax plant *Phormium tenax* for sail cloth. On cleared land, food crops were grown to supply the main settlement in Sydney, and it was hoped that the occupation of the island would prevent rival nations seizing it.

Paterson also had an ambitious project to record the natural history of Norfolk Island. He was seeking entry to the elite Royal Society of London and to further his cause he sent seeds, specimens, drawings and descriptions back to its president, Joseph Banks. Doody appears to have been used as a visual amanuensis by Paterson. Perhaps as a trusted

servant, Doody accompanied him when he botanized. It was certainly a far cry from the harsh conditions the convict agriculturalists laboured under. In 1793 Paterson was summoned back to Sydney Cove and Doody left with him. Paterson's project remained unfinished and he had to wait until 1798 for his election as a Fellow of the Royal Society.

Doody's drawings document the plants Paterson recommended to Banks for their utility and beauty. They also are a record of a landscape rapidly being altered by the activities of colonists. Of Doody himself we only know that as a free man, he was awarded 30 acres on the Parramatta River by Paterson in a land grant in 1795, which became Doody's Bay for a time. He may have tried collecting plants for a living, but if he returned to his job as plant artist, nothing has survived.

(Opposite) *Freycinetia baueriana*: Paterson described how the stem of this woody climber 'terminates with the flower on the top as represented'. He reported that the fruit in May which followed the November flowers was popular with the convicts who went bird-hunting in the woods.
(Above) *Phormium tenax*: 'Two drawings of the flax plant the one from a scale of 9ft the other natural size flowers in October.'

FERDINAND BAUER

Ferdinand Bauer (1760–1826) has been called the 'Leonardo of natural history painting', but he remained an artisan and needed to find employment from one project to the next. His first 'job' was for the prior Norbert Boccius. Like Ferdinand's father, Lucas, who was court painter, Boccius served the house of Liechtenstein, but as a doctor. At their mother's request, Boccius became a mentor to her talented sons, Joseph, Francis, also a skilled botanical artist (p. 146), and Ferdinand, after their father's death. Boccius's approach was practical – he had the boys illustrate his herbarium.

It is not always possible to identify which of the brothers created which miniature for Boccius's *Liber regni vegetabilis*, or *Codex Liechtenstein*. Francis and Ferdinand probably worked together on the process, from sketch, through outline pencil drawings to finished watercolour, annotated in ink. Ferdinand later famously used numerically coded pencil drawings with a corresponding colour chart. It was not a new device – Dürer had done the same. During these years, perhaps inspired by Boccius's example, both Francis and Ferdinand relied on this technique. If both had copies of the chart and knew the pigment recipes, one could work up a sketch made by the other.

Ferdinand developed as a natural history illustrator in Vienna, where he lived with the professor of botany, Nikolaus von Jacquin, in his house situated in the botanical garden. When John Sibthorp, newly appointed as Sherardian professor at Oxford, was botanizing through Europe he called there, and Jacquin encouraged his interest in the *De materia medica* by Dioscorides of the 1st century AD. This provided Sibthorp with a mission: to identify all the plants mentioned by Dioscorides and produce a flora, the *Flora Graeca*. And in Ferdinand Bauer, Sibthorp found a botanically literate draughtsman who was able to work accurately at speed. He later wrote 'nothing can be more beautiful & perfect than his drawings – I shall possess a perfect work'.

Bauer travelled with Sibthorp through the Levant from March 1786, frenetically but meticulously recording the flora, fauna, vistas and even the costumes of the inhabitants. He drew multiple species of plants on small sheets of thin paper, used on both sides, often folded once, and had an enhanced 250-shade colour chart. The party returned to England in December 1787, and from this huge resource, and possibly larger field drawings (which have not survived), Bauer produced some 1,500 drawings by 1794. Of these, 966 watercolours of plants were engraved for the *Flora Graeca*.

Tired of Sibthorp's attitude, however, Bauer declined to travel with him again. Instead he signed on to HMS *Investigator* as natural history draughtsman. Captained by Matthew Flinders, with the botanist Robert Brown as naturalist, the ship sailed for Australia in July 1801 to survey (and claim) more of the continent and bring home specimens of its plants and animals. Bauer again worked intensively. An excursion to the Blue Mountains and several months on Norfolk Island were highlights. His colour chart now had 999 shades and he produced over 2,000 sketches (around 1,750 of plants) before returning home in October 1805. To help achieve such a prolific workload he may have used a camera lucida. Back in London, he produced meticulous final watercolours for others, and for his own publication, *Illustrationes Florae Novae Hollandiae* (1813), which was never completed as he intended it, before returning to Vienna in 1814, disillusioned with publishing and his paymasters.

(Opposite) Bauer's pencil sketch, probably of the tall tree fern *Cyathea brownii*, was made on Norfolk Island, where he spent several months in 1804–05. It captures the endemic plants as a community in their island landscape.

(Overleaf) Bauer's early colour chart (attributed on the basis of his handwriting) is surrounded by a larger one created by T. Haenke (1761–1816). The numbers do not correspond to the *Iris germanica* sketch (page 249) prepared during the travels with Sibthorp, though current analysis of the pigments in the chart might reveal more.

CONRAD MARTENS

For a little over a year in 1833–34, Conrad Martens (1801–1878) was an official artist for the surveying ship HMS *Beagle*. The voyage of the *Beagle* (1831–36) has become one of the most famous in history thanks to Captain Fitzroy's gentleman companion, Charles Darwin (p. 118). Anything attached to it has gained a certain cachet, but at the time it brought no special rewards. While Darwin returned to England to ponder the theory of evolution by natural selection, Martens needed to find a way to support himself in Australia, where he settled.

If Martens gained neither fame nor fortune from the *Beagle*, his skills as an artist and his way of seeing the world were changed by the constant work, the need for accurately recording topography and the scientific interests of those around him. Darwin referred to him as 'full up to the mouth with enthusiasm', a spirit he carried with him now. Martens had been taught by the distinguished landscape artist Copley Fielding (as had John Ruskin; p. 206). In Australia, he combined a telling combination of Romanticism with his newfound attention to the analytical detail of landscape objects such as rock formations and plants.

Martens arrived in Sydney in 1835 via Tahiti and New Zealand, steeped in the alien landscapes and vegetation he had been sketching throughout his travels. Australia provided fresh challenges. He was immediately at work recording his first impressions of the new shapes and colours he found in the plant life. He began teaching in Sydney, but also made extensive tours in New South Wales. The views of Sydney's harbour from the North Shore fascinated him. The uplifted sandstone had been steeply dissected by rivers, creating microclimates with diverse vegetation. Inland to the east, the undulating Cumberland Plain provided a different geology, soil and flora, to which he was particularly attuned.

During the depression of the 1840s Martens turned his favourite views of Sydney into lithographs, some of which were hand coloured, but he persisted with his landscape art, gaining considerable renown for his ability to convey the light of New South Wales as well as its vistas.

(Opposite) A palm, *Archontophoenix cunninghamiana*, and tree fern, from 'Sketchbook of views and botanical studies in the Illawarra district', 1835. (Above) 'Scene in the Blue Mountains N.S. Wales' (*c.* 1835). All capture Marten's very early experience of the Australian flora.

many of my best flowers — but I have just now a beautiful show of Daturas, 3 sorts of Hibiscus, Abutilons, Solanums, Kennedyas &c &c in bloom, & a famous Bougainvillea coming into blossom. But Calamity has come upon me in the shape of a Monster Hotel, built I regret to say by T. Hanbury of Mortola, (who has promised me for years past that he would not build on his land close below mine — though he would not sell it to me,) & which I fear will totally shut out all my Sea Terrace view. At æt 66½ it is wise to make the best of disagreeables, & I suppose I ought to be glad that a very wealthy Quaker Druggist has been able to add perhaps a hundred or two to his large income at the expense of my poor little property.

So I am buying up (at 3 francs apiece,) all the biggest Cypresses I can lay my hands on, & planting them along the bottom Terrace. They are over 20 feet high, & there be who predict that they will all die presently. — others however say the ground is so saturated with rain that they may live.

I suppose my dear old friend Mr Bell comes no more to London nowadays.

Please to give my compliments & remembrances to Lady Hooker; I hope she is well, — also your latest member of the family.

Believe me, Dear Sir Joseph,
Yours sincerely,
Edward Lear.

1. Common Banian Tree. (Ficus Indicus?)
2. Mango.
3. Papaya —
4. Breadfruit tree
5. Traveller's tree —
6. Jambool —
7. Babool — or Mimosa — very general in NW Provinces about Delhi
8. Peepul —
9. Poinciana Regia — grows from Narkunda upward towards Thibet (Name rightly spelt? Poinciana?)
10. Deodara — grows all about Simla.

leaf of Papaya — grows abundantly on the Mahabaleshwur Hills. much resembles a laurel. Bears a berry, eaten by the natives.

Villa Emily. Sanremo.
2. December 1878.

My dear Sir Joseph,

By an odd coincidence, just as I had written the envellope of this letter & had made the above remarkable drawings, Sir Graham Briggs left his card & your letter of October 30. I called on Sir Graham & Lady Briggs as soon as I could, & have seen them both yesterday & to day; & I will do all I can to enliven their stay by books &c &c. I have a good Library. They are very interesting & nice people, — & all the more interesting to me as Barbadians, because

Quilándi.
Nov. 3. 1874. 4–5 PM.

EDWARD LEAR

Mention the name Edward Lear (1812–1888) and most people today will think of 'The Owl and the Pussycat' and his nonsense verse. Lear's word play included many early limericks and 'nonsense' alphabets that he also illustrated. He even drew a nonsense botany – 'Sketches of new and rare plants discovered in Braneland', complete with made up Linnaean nomenclature. Lear's caricatures form part of the prehistory of the modern comic book, but he was also a serious landscape artist, working in pencil, watercolours and oils, mostly on location, in his lonely career of wandering.

Lear was an epileptic and suffered from asthma and near sightedness. As a young man, he developed his talent for nature painting, especially birds, including his renowned parrot illustrations. Early on he prepared his own lithographs, but failing eyesight made it difficult. His plant studies were often executed in the service of his landscapes, and he was an inveterate sketcher, always travelling with his tripod and drawing materials. He lived most of his adult life in the Mediterranean, writing and illustrating travel books, seeking commissions and organizing occasional exhibitions in London, mostly of his studio work.

In 1873 Lear travelled to India and found it overwhelming: 'crimson rhododendrons bewilder by their beauty … great numbers of trees covered with white roses'. Even the Mediterranean and Levant had hardly prepared him for the sights and sounds he encountered here, and his sketches document the botanical luxuriance of form, even if the colours are muted. Travel in India for a plump, middle-aged man was not easy, and at one point he had to stop painting after his sketching stool collapsed and he was hurt.

Queen Victoria admired Lear sufficiently to invite him to give her drawing lessons, but he spent his life mostly on the fringes of society. Lear's most ambitious painting, a study of cedars of Lebanon painted in 1861, almost 3 m (9 ft) long, sold for less than a third of its asking price. It is now lost, but appreciation of Lear as a landscape artist has grown enormously.

(Opposite) In 1878 Lear wrote to Joseph Hooker to ask for his help to ensure he had correctly identified his Indian trees after a commission to draw them (above). At Quilandi (Koyilandy), northern Malabar Coast, India, Lear annotated his palm frond sketch (below) with notes on the different greens, including an old favourite, 'bright parrot green'. (Above) 'Tigerlillia Terribilis' from 'Braneland'.

(Overleaf) 'Rattan' in a landscape (above); and (below) sketches of plants and trees with hastily written names clearly the work of the nonsense poet – 'Vulgar or Pumptious tree' and 'semi-Genteel or Shamble tree' growing near the village of 'Churnbutter', a transliteration of Chunabhatti. (Page 255) Landscape of Ootacamund, made on 7 October 1874 at 5 p.m. – the time of day affecting the colours (above); and (below) 'Nil=gherri plant & his flower', with extensive colour notes.

EDWARD MINCHEN

Among the trees and shrubs of Australia, the eucalypts, casuarinas and banksias are some of the most quintessential antipodean species. Such popular exotics were sometimes added to early landscape sketches sent home by artists to be worked up, even if they were not present in the original scene. As Australians developed their own identity, and began to understand and exploit the natural flora, these plants also came to be appreciated for their scientific and commercial, rather than simply exotic, interest.

In his final job as lithographic artist for the Government Printer of New South Wales, Edward Minchen (or Minchin; 1852–1913) would sketch many of these trees and shrubs for possible eventual reproduction in publications written by botanists, horticulturists and foresters also working for the government. In this way, he was able to combine his love of nature with a stable position that suited his talents.

Born in Perth to a couple who had both emigrated to Australia as children, Minchen moved to Melbourne with his family while still a boy. He inherited his artistic talent and perhaps also his temperament from his mother; he was later described as diffident and sensitive. Although artistically inclined, it took him some years to find his true vocation. He tried several careers, including a life at sea and on the stage. The turning point came when he decided to improve his art and took classes at the National Art Gallery in Melbourne. After a job with the Melbourne Lands Department, in 1879 he left for Sydney, where he worked as draughtsman in the Survey Office before transferring to the Government Printer.

Minchen also became involved in founding the Art Society of New South Wales in 1880. This period was a coming of age for Australian art. He was honorary secretary, helping to hang the pictures for the first exhibition, and served on the committee, which was divided into amateur and professional members. Minchen was listed as an amateur, but produced pleasing landscapes and miniature watercolours in addition to the botanical sketches of his day job.

(Above) *Banksia serrata*, 'Old Man's Banksia', named in honour of Joseph Banks. (Right) On this drawing of *Telopea speciosissima* small faint ticks indicate those elements included in the published print, which featured the familiar brilliant red 'flower' rather than the fantastic architecture and rich browns of the ripened seed pods seen here in Minchen's sketch. (Opposite) *Eucalyptus eugenioides*, with 'stringy bark'. Minchen's use of grey in the central area sharpens the contrast with the delicate white flowers in this pencil and watercolour sketch.

A Stringybark
Eucalyptus Eugenioides Near Liverpool

IV A Pleasing Occupation

Sketchers everywhere know the intense pleasure that comes from practising their art. It can be done almost anywhere with little more than a sheet of paper and a pencil. The sketches here record moments and moods, as well as documenting places and plants. John James distracted himself from the misery of captivity by Barbary pirates. John Traherne Moggridge also sought escapism, but his confinement was caused by a debilitating and eventually terminal illness. Francis Nicholls created a unique, idiosyncratic manuscript flora of British plants. In India, Burma and China, Laura King and Annie Morse achieved something similar in an exotic and colonial setting. The Shelley sisters filled a period of their lives in a typically Victorian way, sketching in the fields and gardens that surrounded their house. Anne Stebbing sketched all her life and celebrated it in her old age. After a settled career in Britain, in her retirement in South Africa, Marianne Mason exulted in life outdoors among the plants. John Day nurtured his orchid obsession in ten greenhouses and thousands of sketches – surely a pleasing occupation.

JOHN DAY
(Opposite) *Vanda coerulea*, the famous 'blue orchid', introduced to the orchid market in the mid-19th century. John Day bought this specimen in June 1880 and painted its delicate and unusual blueness on 18 December that year. Below is '*Aerides fieldingii*' (*A. rosea*) from the Khasi Hills (then part of Assam), a popular orchid-hunting ground. Day was lucky to have obtained this plant (and many others) through family connections: his nephew, Major Williamson, was on the spot serving the imperial machine.

JOHN JAMES

On 8 February 1661 the diarist Samuel Pepys spent the afternoon drinking in the Fleece tavern in London. His companions were sea captains, and over their wine they talked about the conditions of the slaves held by the corsairs or pirates of the Barbary Coast in Algeria. Some spoke from personal experience of the privations they had endured there. One other such captive was the naval surgeon John James (*fl.* 1680s), who left a remarkable record of his period of captivity. Many of the slaves were put to work in the galleys or on land, but James was fortunate and passed some of his nearly twenty years in captivity sketching the flora of the North African coast.

Working only in ink, he was still able to convey rich detail by careful shading and crosshatching. With his written descriptions he also included some phonetic renderings of the 'Moorish' names. Knowledge of the flora from this part of the world was not widespread in the Britain James had left behind, but he cleverly described the features of the unfamiliar plants by reference to the colours or leaf shapes of commonplace plants back home.

Back in England, James's drawings found their way into the hands of the magpie James Petiver (*c.* 1665–1718). Trained as an apothecary, Petiver had a professional interest in plants and an eclectic desire for all things relating to natural history. Having amassed an impressive collection of specimens and supporting materials, he began publishing plates and descriptions. *Gazophylacium naturae et artis* (1702–09) featured several plants reproduced from James's drawings. They proved a rich legacy of a most unfortunate experience.

(Opposite) Plants 'E' and 'G' (above) featured in Petiver's *Gazophylacium*, making identification easier. 'E' is probably a species of *Globularia*; 'G' is perhaps *Cynomorium coccineum*, known as Tarthuth (pronounced tar-thooth), a much prized fungus at the time of his captivity. 'F' was likened to lamb's cress in his notes. (Below) James called 'CCC' a willow, describing its leaves and stems, and a 'bunch of flowers in colour reasonably like the Damask Rose', one of which featured in the sketch, although the number of the petals was changed in the notes from four to five. It could have been a *Nerium*. 'DDD' is a narcissus. To help with the identification of the plant 'EEE', which he was unfamiliar with, James referred to its 'Linaria like leaves'.

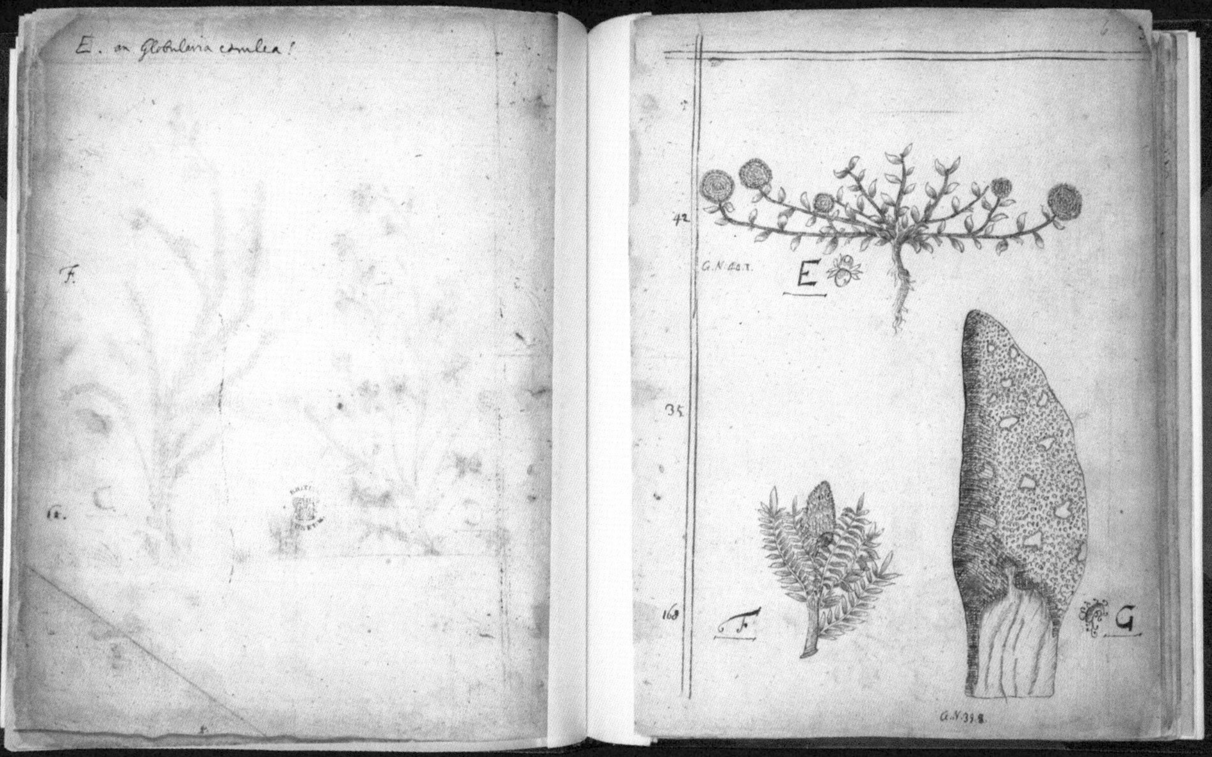

E. or Globularia coerulea?

E
F
G

CCC
DDD
EEE

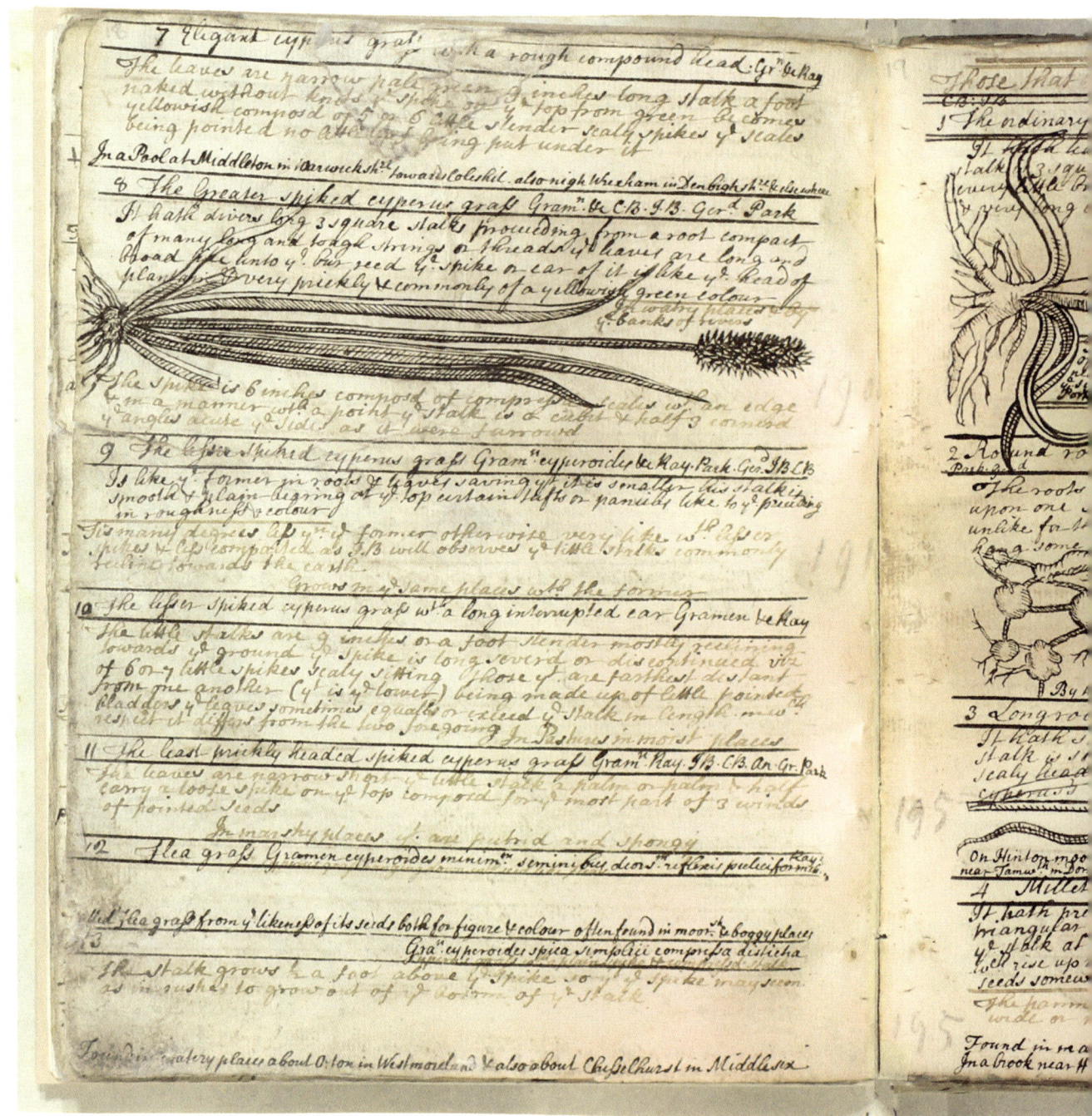

FRANCIS NICHOLLS

An Oxford student and lecturer, 'Frank' Nicholls (1699–1778) dissected and taught anatomy for several years before embarking on a scientific Grand Tour of Europe in the early 1720s. After a short period in Cornwall he arrived in London, where he taught lucrative anatomy classes. In 1743 he married the daughter of the famous and influential physician Richard Mead, who helped his practice – Nicholls was appointed a physician to King George II in 1753. Of the couple's five children two survived, and Nicholls returned to Oxford to educate his son before retiring to Epsom, Surrey.

Although a successful and busy physician, at some point Nicholls also began collecting botanical notes and making sketches of native British plants. He used these materials to create two surviving notebooks, in a complex process of recording that involved writing a new manuscript in darker

ink followed by its systematic enhancement in paler ink. He also relied on earlier notes and sketches made on the back of used paper that he cut to shape, sometimes pasted in and sometimes left between the appropriate pages waiting to be fixed into the spaces. Interwoven with the text are the idiosyncratic ink drawings. Not all plants are illustrated, perhaps not all were seen – there are references to key botanical texts in the headings – but he includes location notes for some, and these indicate that botanizing was a lifelong hobby.

Nicholls would have learnt botany during his medical education. His notes mostly describe a plant's form and habitat. The rhizome of the 'sweet Cyperus or English Galingale' (top right) had a traditional use in perfumery and he commented on its 'sweet pleasant smell when broken'.

HELLEN SHELLEY & MARGARET SHELLEY

A famous sibling often dominates, and can devastate, a family. This was certainly the case for the Shelleys, whose *enfant terrible* was the Romantic poet Percy Bysshe Shelley (1792–1822). Field Place, Horsham, Sussex, was home to the baronet Sir Timothy and his family; Percy was the eldest child. The estate was entailed, meaning that Percy would automatically inherit. Disgusted by his son's behaviour and knowing that after his early death the house and land would pass to Percy and Mary Shelley's son, Percy Florence, the baronet allowed Field Place and the surrounding farms to become dilapidated.

Percy had five siblings: Hellen (1799–1885) and Margaret (1801–1887) were the youngest of the girls. They never married and continued to live at Field Place until 1844, when they moved to Elcot Park, Berkshire, with their widowed mother. Hellen's letters, written in the 1850s, provide details of Percy's childhood, otherwise little documented. Information of a different kind comes from the two volumes of watercolour sketches Hellen and Margaret compiled together. Most are unsigned, so it's not possible to be sure which sister created which picture.

There are some 210 paintings of cultivated garden natives and wildflowers of the fields and ponds around Field Place. Sketching and rambles in pursuit of flora, thus engaging with the elements of the popular 'language of flowers', were typical activities of so many women of their class and situation at the time. Typical perhaps, yet their paintings are a useful record of the local plant life, especially of the once common water meadows that tended to make Field Place damp when the weather was wet. The sisters sketched around where they had grown up: Warnham Mill Pond, Broadbridge Heath and Mill. Further afield they painted at Backlands Farm and Enfield Mill, an hour or two away by horse and trap. They also sometimes drew from dried specimens, as noted on a sketch of *Silene maritima* collected at St Leonards-on-Sea. Some of the watercolours are dated 1839–43, while there are also two dated from 1851 after the move to Berkshire, so the sisters' gentle pursuit continued.

'Fly Orchis, *Orchis Muscifera*' (*Ophrys insectifera*; left) and '*Epipactis Grandiflora*, Large White Helleborine' (*Cephalanthera damasonium*; opposite) are both woodland species. The helleborine is now rare due to habitat loss.

Epipactis Grandiflora
Large White Helleborine

JOHN DAY

Obsessions can tend towards the negative, while passions are more positive, but it's a fine line between the two. Perhaps having adequate time and money to pursue an interest helps to keep it on the safer side. Fortunately, John Day (1824–1888) inherited his father's business as a London wine merchant, and this funded his passion: collecting, growing and sketching orchids.

A visit to Tottenham to see Day's collection, held in ten orchid houses organized by species including the *Cattleya*, *Vanda*, *Phalaenopsis*, *Masdevallia* and *Odontoglossum*, involved walking at least 90 m (300 ft) through thousands of plants. Fine specimens were displayed on benches and in baskets hung overhead, all maintained in media and environments – temperature, humidity and light – that suited their needs. Day was very reliant on his gardeners.

He bought his first orchids in 1852, the year commercial orchid-grower Benjamin Williams published *The Orchid-Grower's Manual*. Orchids were still elite plants, if no longer exclusively aristocratic. Specimens now flooded on to the market as plant hunters raided the tropics and subtropics, auction houses and nurseries retailed them and clever hybridizers added to the variety. It became known as orchidelirium.

Day began to sketch in January 1863, after first paying to have pictures of his orchids made and subsequently for lessons. Initially he used ink, and then later, after borrowing a paintbox, watercolour. Day drew plants both at home and in other private and public orchid houses. From the early 1860s he also travelled to the tropics and subtropics where orchids abounded, filling his scrapbooks with glorious images, details and notes.

The sale of his collection in 1881 (he was sadly in poor health) lasted ten days and raised around £7,000 (approximately £680,000 today). And his 3,000 watercolour and 500 ink sketches filled 2,800 pages of 53 scrapbooks. These were more than picture books – they recorded the acquiring, growing, recording and revisiting of the objects of his passion, and form a unique visual history of mid-Victorian orchid mania.

'*Grammatophyllum ellisii*' (*Grammangis ellisii*), endemic to Madagascar, first came to notice in Britain through William Ellis, a missionary with natural history interests. This plant came via Frenchman Léon Humblot, a gardener for the Muséum d'Histoire naturelle who collected on a botanic mission to the island – an example of the plant-collecting world that Day had links to.

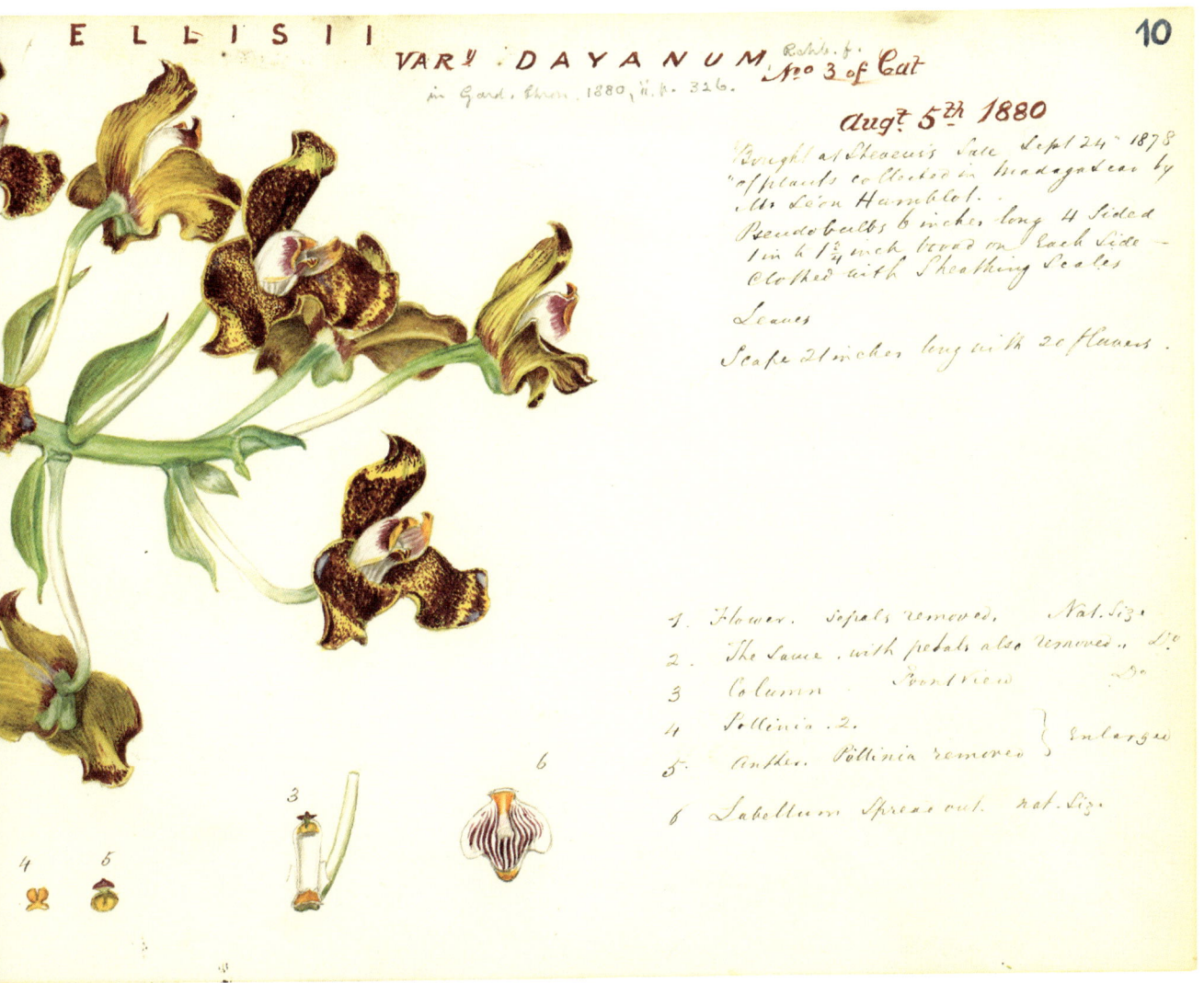

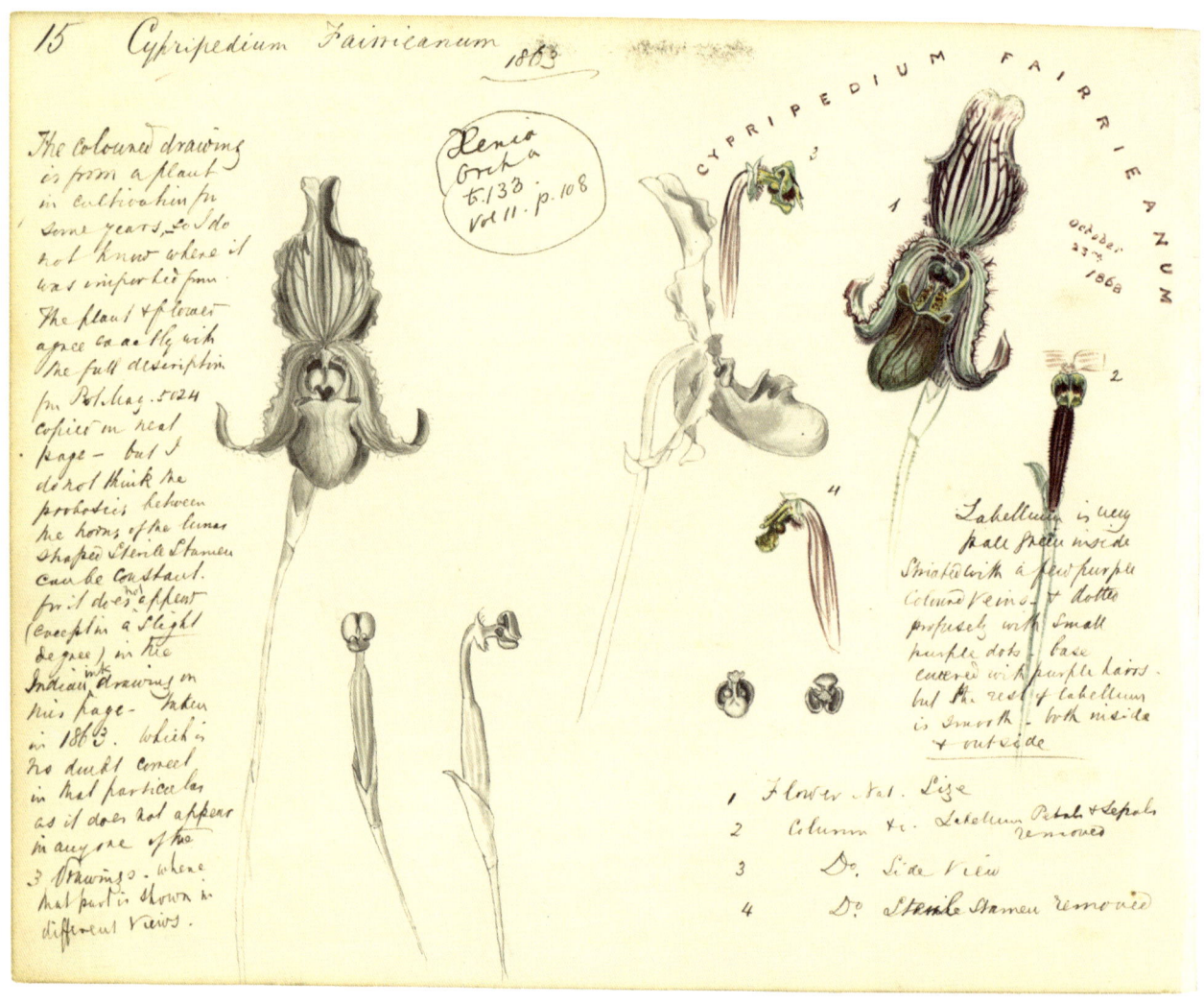

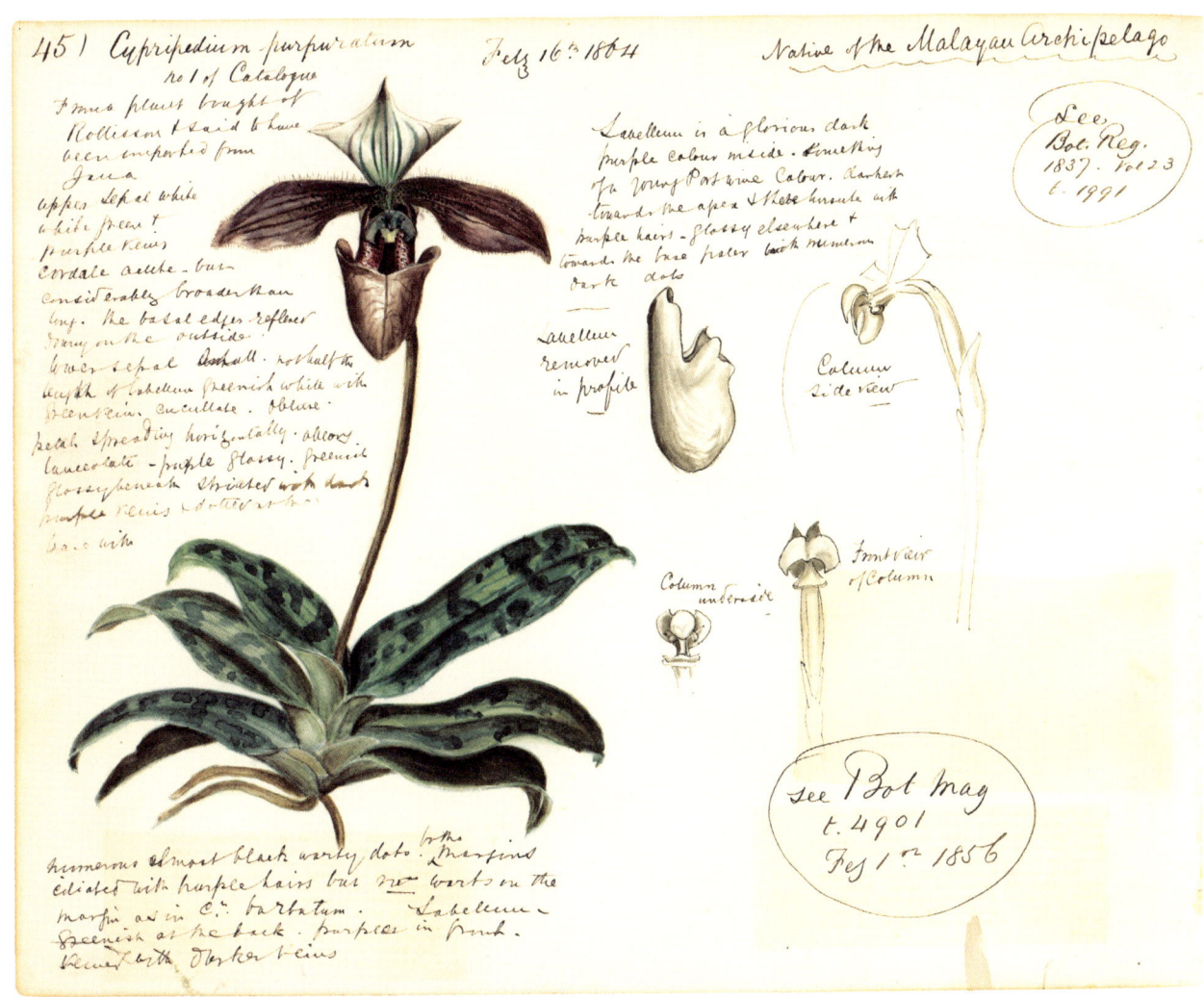

(Opposite) '*Cypripedium fairrieanum*' (*Paphiopedilum fairrieanum*). Day supplemented an early ink drawing from 1863 with a watercolour five years later. (Above) '*Cypripedium purpuratum*' (*Paphiopedilum purpuratum*): Day thought his plant had come from Java, and probably encountered the description 'Native of the Malayan Archipelago' in the *Botanical Register* and *Curtis's Botanical Magazine*. Its native range is parts of China and Vietnam, where it is critically endangered.

(Opposite) '*Orchis latifolia*' (*Dactylorhiza incarnata*): for once out of the hothouse, Day drew 'this splendid specimen of a British orchid' in June 1884, but confessed to distorting the proportions of the flower spike, 'being rather tired of the undertaking' and wanting the time to include the leaves. Even obsessives can struggle on occasion. (Above) An early watercolour of *Anguloa clowesii* and details of '*A. ruckeri*' (*A.* × *ruckeri*; a natural hybrid). From Venezuela and Colombia, these are known as Tulip Orchids. The first was Day's own plant, while the details were drawn at a nursery a few days later.

ANNE STEBBING

In May 1924, at the age of 83, Anne Stebbing (1841–1925) was still sketching. She proudly recorded her age and the date on an ink line drawing of a conifer branch; unusually, she also signed her picture. Earlier, in the late 1888s and 1890s as her children were growing up, she had been engaged on a project sketching British fungi. Each watercolour was annotated in pencil with the date and place the specimen had been found. Other notes recorded characteristics of the skin, flesh and gills. She was keen on textures, colours and sometimes the smells, 'earthy' or 'savoury', that accompanied the picking.

Stebbing's artistic skills were augmented by her sister-in-law Mary Anne Stebbing (p. 180) – their husbands were brothers. It was botanist Mary Anne Stebbing, also keenly interested in fungi, who provided many of the identifications, and her handwriting appears on the sketches alongside Anne's.

While the generous grounds of Frith Park, the Stebbing home at Walton on the Hill, Surrey, provided much of the material for Anne's drawings, she also travelled with her paper and watercolours and made visits to well-connected friends. Mosses were painted in the Lake District, North Wales and, rather more glamorously, in Italy. Later her son, the forester Edward Percy Stebbing, supplied her with conifers. In the 1920s Stebbing set about reviewing and arranging her years of drawings in a series of albums. They form a social as well as a botanical document, recording her privileged way of life.

Pages from Stebbing's albums of mosses (above, *Polytrichastrum formosum*), conifers (opposite above, *Pseudotsuga menziesii*) and fungi (opposite below, *Boletus luridus*, now *Suillellus luridus*).

Abies Menziesii
Sep. 1897 Silver Fir

Boletus Luridus
October 3. 1899

IV A Pleasing Occupation

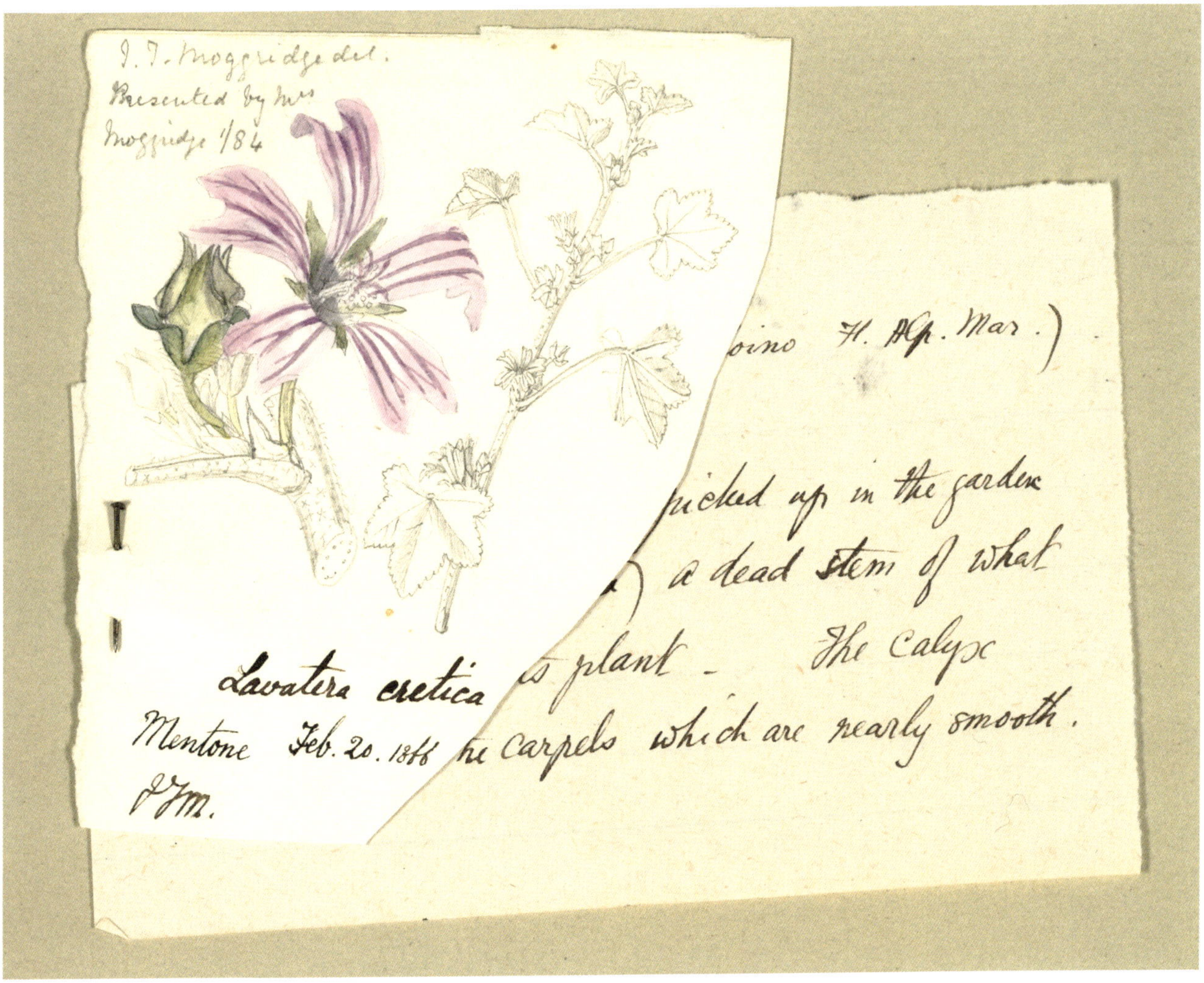

JOHN TRAHERNE MOGGRIDGE

'If the lodgings could be near your headquarters, it would be a great additional comfort to us, as my son is not able to walk very far.' It must have been painful for Fanny Moggridge to write this. Her son Traherne (1842–1874) was suffering from tuberculosis and spent the final years of his short life as an invalid. Joseph Hooker had offered to meet the young man, a skilled naturalist, and assist in his botany.

Sickness had prevented Moggridge from finishing his studies at Trinity College, Cambridge. But his family, also involved in natural history, rallied round him, and their comfortable circumstances allowed him to cultivate his interest in botany while trying to improve his health. At that time, those who could afford it travelled overseas for a better climate, and from the early 1860s the Moggridges regularly overwintered in Menton (Mentone) on the French Riviera. This offered sea-air and ready access to the slopes of the lower Maritime Alps, a wonderful place for plants.

'Craving employment in weary satiety of absolute rest', as he wrote, Moggridge published a beautifully illustrated *Contributions to the Flora of Mentone* (1864, 1871, 1874), encouraging others to continue the work. When he was too sick to collect, his family and friends supplied him with specimens. He became interested in the crocus-like *Romulea* genus, working out differences between the species and recording the subtle variations in their flowering patterns. As the plants are easily transported as a corm, the family garden contained species from Cannes, Biarritz, Genoa and Corsica – places Moggridge could only dream of visiting.

Lavatera olbia and '*Lavatera cretica*', the sheets cut by herbarium staff after Mrs Moggridge donated Traherne's papers. (Overleaf) *Romulea bulbocodium* and *R. ramiflora* both featured in Moggridge's *Flora*.

Romulea Bulbocodium Seb. et M.
Feb. 3 1870
Originally from Pegli near Genoa
Now cult. in Garden at Mentone.

J. T. Moggridge del.
Presented by Mrs. Moggridge.

Lower bract of spathe almost entirely herbaceous,
upper membranous with two broad confluent lines of
herbaceous texture about the middle.
Peduncle semicylindrical, almost winged.

Feb. 6. Bud nearly open shewing stamens which are
yellow throughout. Styles & Stigmas white in upper half.

Feb. 7. Bud ready to expand now measures 1½ inch
from base of tube to apex of segments, & the outer
segs. 1¼ in.

Outer segs lanceolate acute, fine mauve col.
in upper half & in golden yellow below, yellow
outside with dusky purplish veins; inner
segs. lanc. acute shorter, outer
mauve in uppermost third golden in lower two thirds

Feb. 13. 1870.
A second flower commencing
to expand on same scape with that
drawn. The corolla was slightly
shorter measuring only 1⅓ inch; ft.
otherwise similar.
Feb. 22. a third fl. expanded, slightly smaller
than 2nd fl. but otherwise accurately similar.

Romulea Bulbocodium S&M,

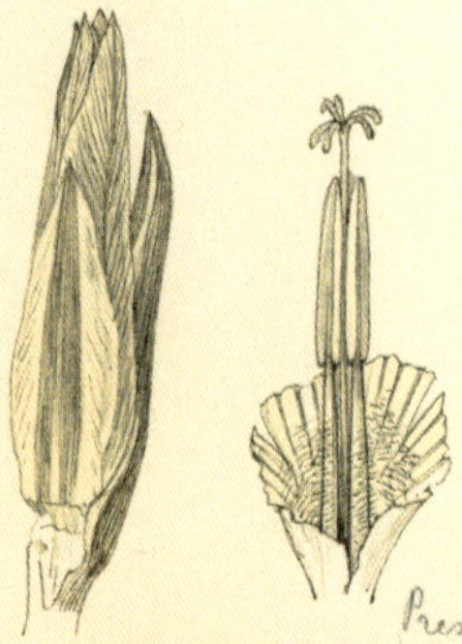

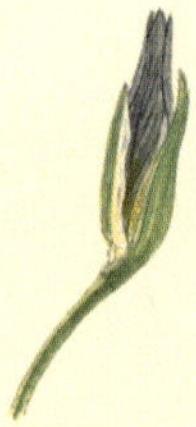

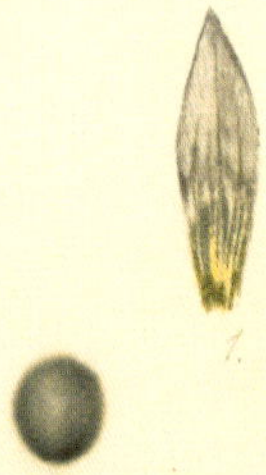

J. T. Moggridge del.
Presented by Mrs. Moggridge 1/84

Originally rec'd from Biarritz Ap.5 1869.
since cult in garden. fld March 11 1870 *Romulea* Bulbocodium var. Lusitan fed.

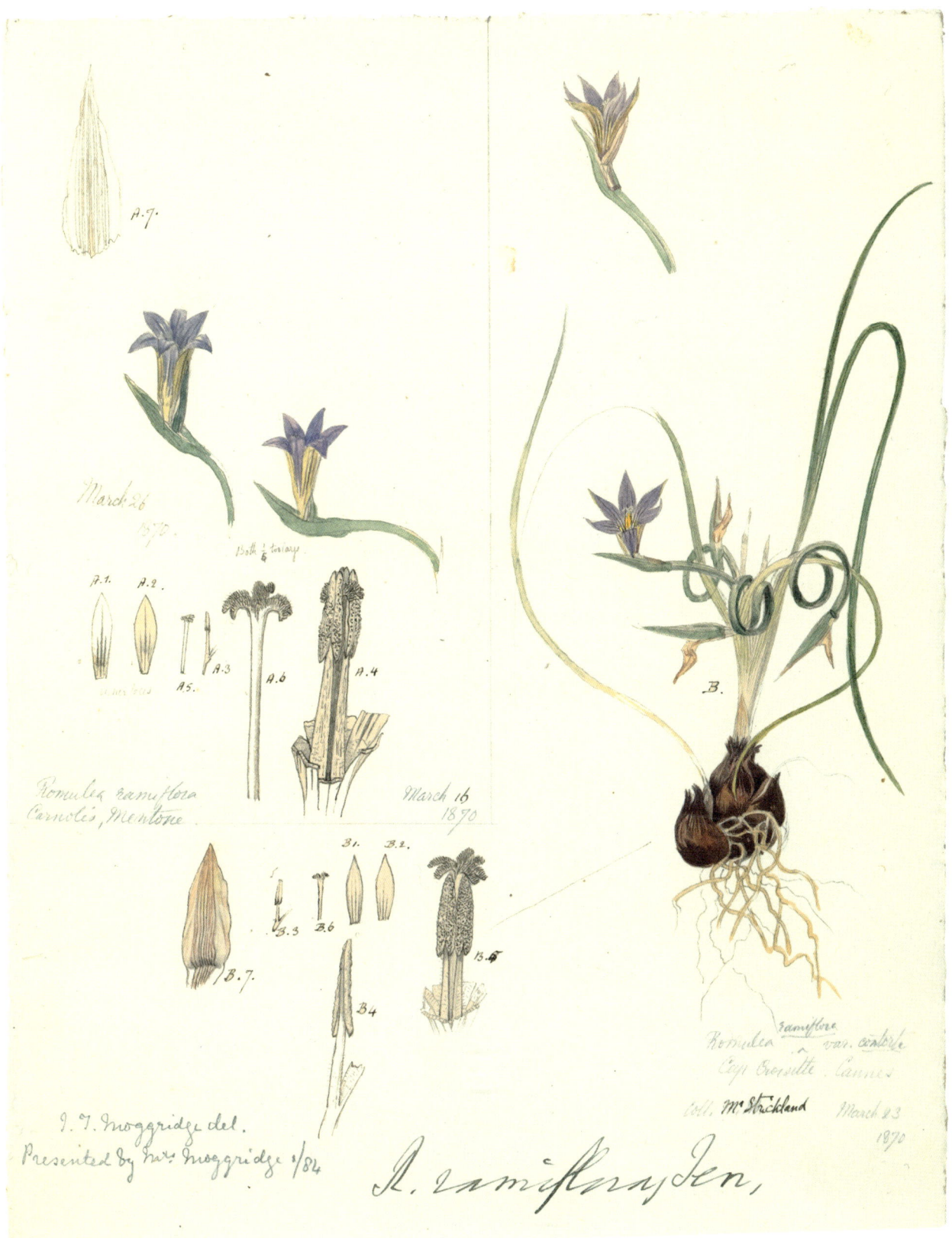

MARIANNE HARRIET MASON

The young 'Mitty' Mason (1845–1932) wanted to be a singer, but despite her talent and the singing lessons her family paid for, this was an unthinkable profession for the stolidly middle-class Masons. She was, however, allowed to volunteer for social work, supervising and most importantly scrutinizing the conditions of locally fostered children. In 1885 as Inspector of Boarded-out Children she became the first senior woman civil servant.

Mason never married, and flower painting became her relaxation of choice from the pressures of work. It was a passion she indulged after retirement in 1910 in the Transkei in South Africa, where one of her younger brothers, Canon Edward Mason, ran St Bede's College for Native Clergymen. A planned stay of six months turned into two years. Later she lived in Rondebosch.

Views from the veranda at St Bede's and its gardens provided an array of exotic plants for her watercolour sketches. But this was just the beginning. 'Interesting as is botany, and delightful as are gardens, nothing, to me, comes up to the joy of nature itself, and of finding flowers growing wild in country.' She travelled 645 km (400 miles) with her brother by Cape cart, rejoicing in the freedom to stop, sketch and collect as it suited her. More distant forays in southern and eastern Africa, taking in the Victoria Falls and Zambezi River, involved slow trains, the better to appreciate the great swathes of wild flowers. Harriet found the urge to sketch the 'strange forms and wonderful colours' irresistible. She considered herself no flower painter – there were no dissections to reveal 'minute botanical details' – instead her bold, delightfully untutored pictures, often drawn on her knees in trains and carts, were made 'simply to show the flower as it grew, and alive'.

The landscape with *Acacia horrida* (above) and the smaller and larger flowers (opposite) were created directly in watercolour, with pencil touches only in '*Lasiosiphon anthylloides*'. The fading tubular flowers of the three *Kniphofia* species and prickled leaves of '*Stobaea acanthopoda*' (*Berkheya acanthopoda*) (page 280 and page 281, right) make dynamic compositions.

Kniphofia aloides — Umtata River
K. sarmentosa — Guthrie's Farm
K. rufa — between Cala and Zichengeni

Helichrysum foetidum & Stobaea acanthopoda   Ngadu Forest. Transkei

LAURA KING

Memsahibs in British India often earned a bad reputation, appearing content that simply by being there they contributed to the empire's 'civilizing mission'. With cheap domestic help and ayahs for the children, it was possible to spend their time on never-ending rounds of visits, shooting parties and balls. The higher their husband's rank, the better the social life. But there were other ways to spend free time, and Laura King (1847–1918) spent hers sketching plants.

She was married to Walter Gawen King (1851–1935), a doctor in the Indian Medical Service who rose to prominence during the famine years of 1876 and 1896. He also reorganized the administration of sanitation and vaccination departments in what was then known as the Madras Presidency, and created the King Institute of Preventative Medicine in Madras (Chennai). His final posting was to Rangoon (Yangon) in Burma (Myanmar). As sanitary commissioner and, later, inspector-general of civil hospitals he travelled widely, and Laura went too, to sketch. By 1910, when he retired, she had created over 900 drawings, many of them carefully mounted in nine albums.

Laura King was keen to identify her plants as well as draw them. They were sourced from jungles, at altitude in the Nilgiri Hills and along the famed Malabar Coast, long a plant collector's haven. She used the great published floras such as Robert Wight's *Icones plantarum Indiae Orientalis* (1840–53), illustrated by indigenous artists. Still wanting to know more, she turned to a local *hakim*, a practitioner of unani medicine in Kurnool (Andhra Pradesh), who gave her an illustrated book of 'medicinal plants used by Mahomedans'.

While on leave in England in 1908, the Kings approached Kew Gardens for further help with sorting out the Burmese plants. A miscommunication led to their rebuff; it seemed the returned drawings were thought 'crude in artistic work'. Colonel King pointed out, on his wife's behalf, that the drawings were not being gifted, merely loaned for assistance with identification, and suggested he would pay for the work. After Laura's death, her husband offered the results of her botanical energies to Kew, and this time the answer was 'yes'.

(Opposite) From the Burmese period '*Dillenia pulcherrima*' and *D. indica* were drawn at Bassein (Pathein) on 12 January 1910, the final year the Kings were in Asia. (Above) Despite all efforts these two watercolours of '*Colocasia* sp.?' were not further identified.

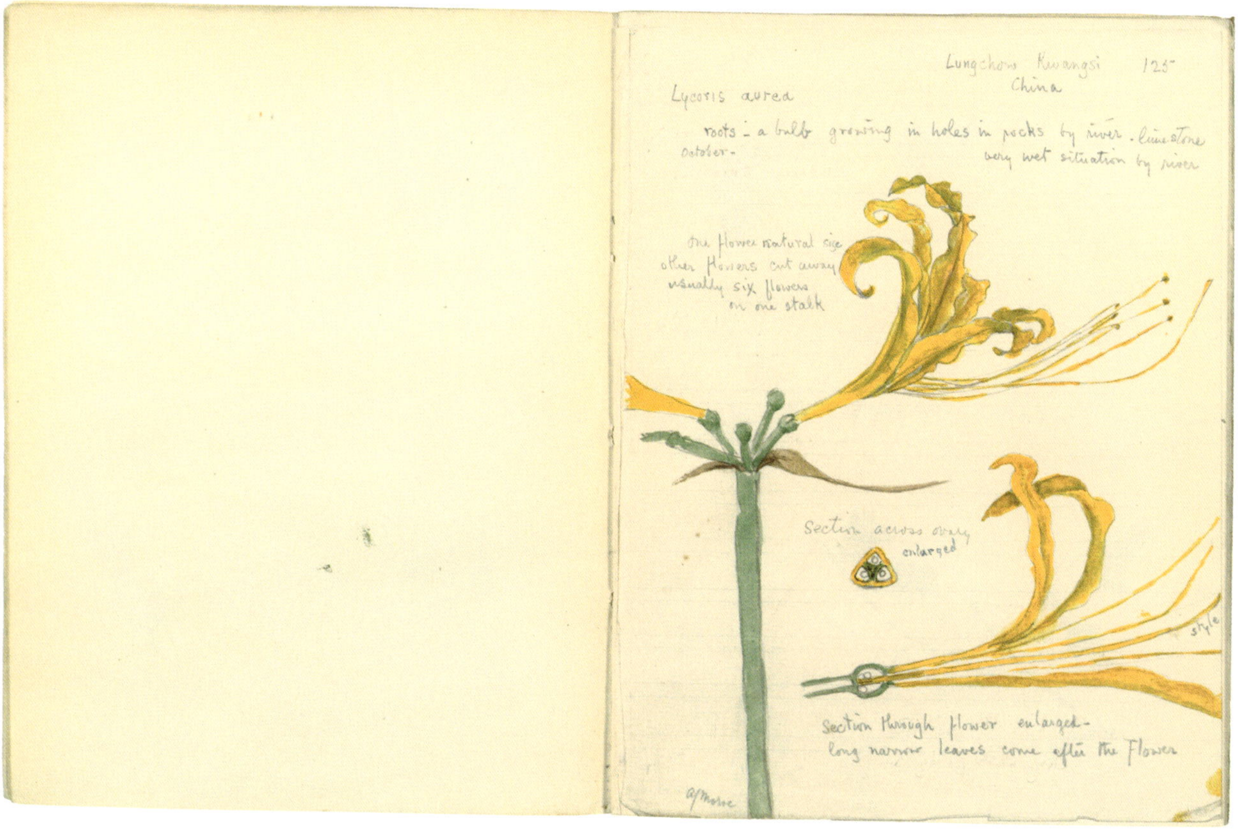

Lycoris aurea Lungchow Kwangsi 125
China

roots – a bulb growing in holes in rocks by river – limestone
october –   very wet situation by river

one flower natural size
other flowers cut away
usually six flowers
on one stalk

Section across ovary
enlarged

style

Section through flower enlarged –
long narrow leaves come after the flower

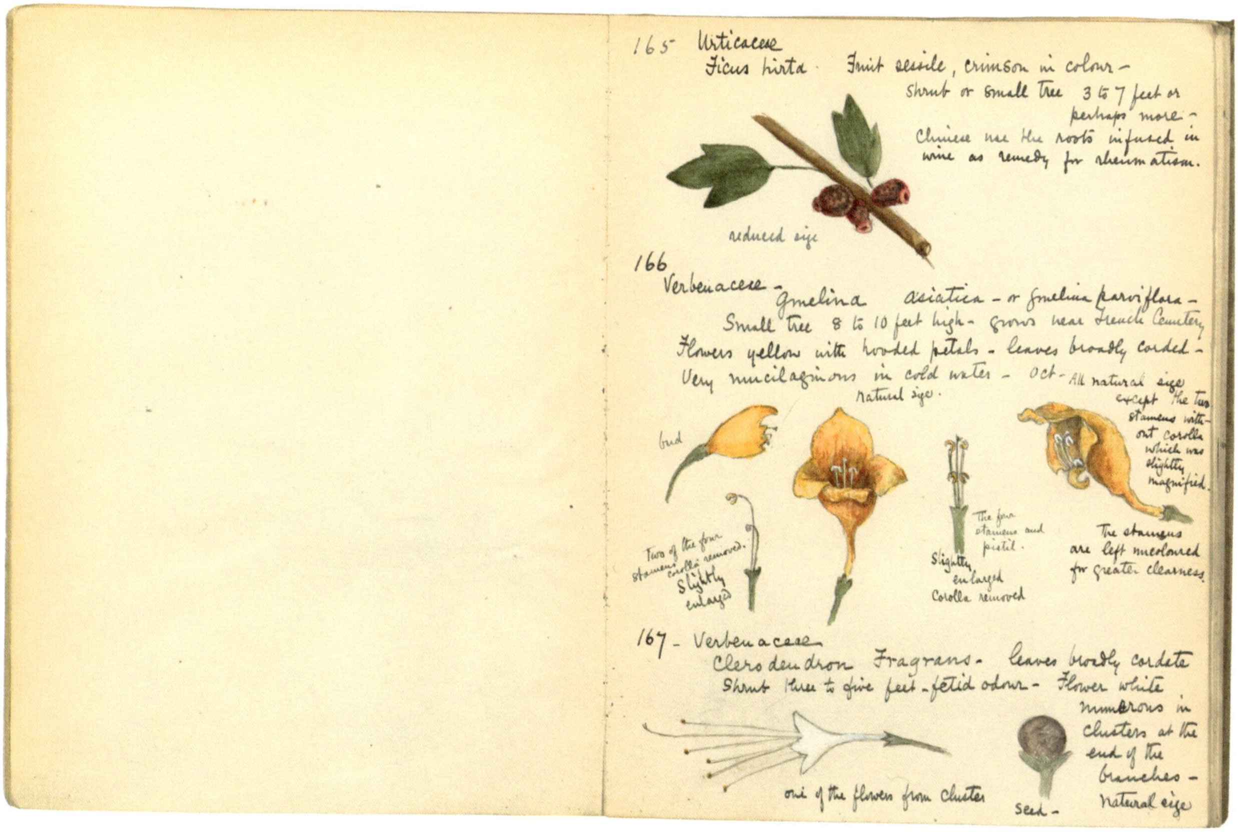

---

165 — Urticaceae
Ficus hirta — Fruit sessile, crimson in colour –
Shrub or small tree 3 to 7 feet or perhaps more –
Chinese use the roots infused in wine as remedy for rheumatism.

reduced size

166 — Verbenaceae — *Gmelina asiatica* – or *Gmelina parviflora* –
Small tree 8 to 10 feet high – grows near French Cemetery
Flowers yellow with hooded petals – leaves broadly cordate –
Very mucilaginous in cold water – Oct – All natural size
natural size.

bud

Two of the four stamens with corolla removed. Slightly enlarged

The four stamens and pistil.

Slightly enlarged Corolla removed

except the two stamens without corolla which was slightly magnified.

The stamens are left uncoloured for greater clearness.

167 — Verbenaceae
Clerodendron fragrans – leaves broadly cordate
Shrub three to five feet – fetid odour – Flower white numerous in clusters at the end of the branches – natural size

one of the flowers from cluster   Seed –

ANNIE MORSE

Mr and Mrs Morse had time on their hands. Hosea Ballou Morse had been promoted to acting commissioner in the Chinese customs service at Tamsui (now part of New Taipai City) in 1892. His office duties filled the working day, but with only a small number of Europeans for company, the Morses turned to natural history in their leisure time.

Annie 'Nan' Welford (1855–1940) and Hosea (1855–1934), both born in North America, had married in 1881, and she settled into being a colonial wife. In the quiet treaty port of Pakhoi (Beihai) on the Gulf of Tonkin, she gardened and desultorily collected plants and painted. From the Taiwan period this evolved into a highly organized activity that yielded a valuable collection of dried plants and sketches. Devoted to her husband, and without the distraction of their own children, Morse threw herself into their botanical enterprise. She credited Hosea as the collector, but it is her sketches that appear on the herbarium sheets at Kew.

On Taiwan, the Morses encountered the Ulsterman Dr Augustine Henry, also in the customs service though on his way to becoming a dendrologist and one of the great plant collectors of central China. He helped with plant identification and continued to do so when the Morses moved to Lung Chow (Longzhou) near the Chinese–Vietnam border in 1896.

Although the couple botanized themselves, Hosea also trained a Chinese collector. From 1896 to 1898 they processed their finds systematically. Nan assigned a number to a specimen and 'hastily scratched' her notes and drawings into notebooks, sometimes a customs office account book. Morse pressed the plants and they sent a duplicate and Nan's subsequent sketches to Henry by 'postal coolies', who walked over the mountains, nearly 645 km (400 miles), to Mengzi, Yunnan. Henry sent the names of the plants by return.

Years later, after the Morses retired to England and the plants had gone to Kew, Nan was widowed. She returned to her sketches, still adding notes about colours and remembering how fever had kept them from collecting.

Morse's initial pencil sketches and notes (below) were enhanced or remade later in colour (opposite and overleaf) when the plants were processed. As well as size, form and habit, she recorded Chinese names and uses for the plants and their meaning in folklore. She came to dislike China, but still caught its beauty in the little landscape (overleaf), perhaps painted on a visiting card.

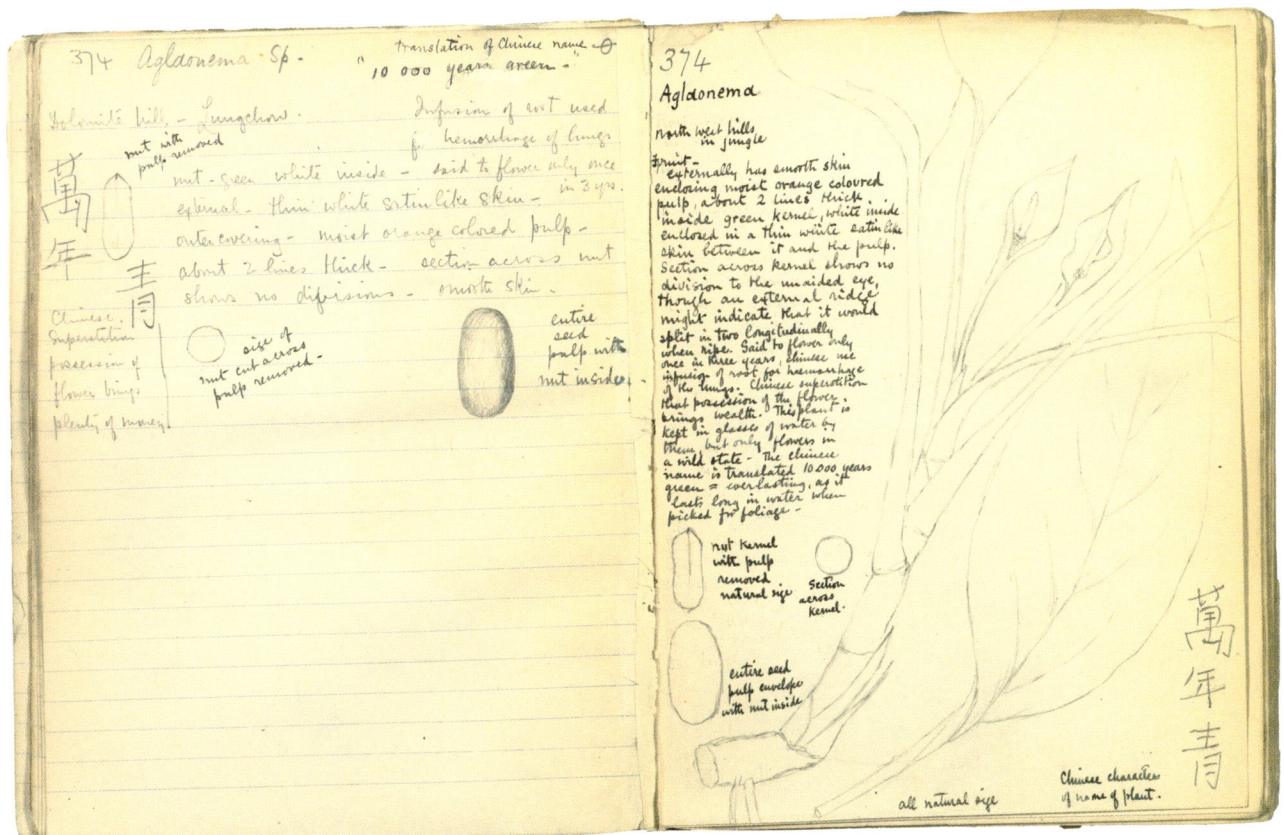

Lungchow
South West Hills &
Sun Kee river

259 Primulaceae

Androsace saxifragæfolia - Bunge
leaves arranged in rosettes
white flower in appearance
resembling forget-me-nots -
Plentiful, also in North China
Frequently found in fields of
Chinese graves -
A finished water colour drawing
of this has been sent to Kew by
me with others - I believe also found
light pink
Plants 4 to 6 inches high, about natural size

natural size

one leaf from rosette

260 Liliaceae - Smilaceae
Peliosanthes teta - Andr.
In jungle on hills - Feb

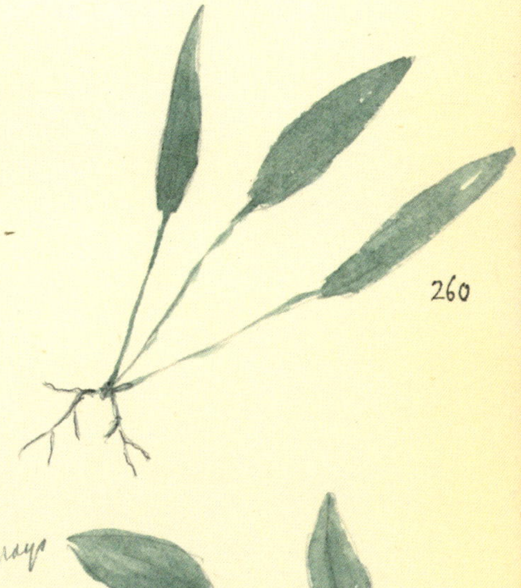

reduced

260

261 Polygonum tinctorium? Lour.
White flowers in light
feathery sprays -
Flowers minute
weedy plant -

In jungle of hills
    February

stalks of flower sprays
flowers removed

261 probably reduced

finding out more

Rather than a full bibliography we have compiled a list of useful publications and online collections about many of the people featured in this book, together with some of their own publications, as places to start to learn a little more about who they were. Those titles listed in the general section are also often useful for the leading names of botanical art in this book, and are not repeated for individual artists.

General

Attenborough, David, et al., *Amazing Rare Things* (London: Royal Collection Trust; New Haven: Yale University Press, 2007).

Blunt, Wilfrid, *The Art of Botanical Illustration* (Woodbridge: Antique Collectors' Club, 2000).

Desmond, Ray, *Kew: The History of the Royal Botanic Gardens* (London: Harvill Press, with the Royal Botanic Gardens, Kew, 1995).

Desmond, Ray, *Great Natural History Books and Their Creators* (London: British Library; New Castle, DE: Oak Knoll Press, 2003).

Egmond, Florike, *Eye for Detail: Images of Plants and Animals in Art and Science, 1500–1630* (London: Reaktion Books, 2016).

Fairman, Elisabeth R. (ed.), *Of Green Leaf, Bird and Flower: Artists' Books and the Natural World* (New Haven and London: Yale University Press, 2014).

Hart, Andrea, *Women Artists. Images of Nature* (London: Natural History Museum, 2014).

Jardine, N., et al. (eds), *Cultures of Natural History* (Cambridge and New York: Cambridge University Press, 1996).

Jenkins, Alan C., *The Naturalists: Pioneers of Natural History* (London: Hamish Hamilton, 1978).

Magee, Judith, *Art of Nature: Three Centuries of Natural History Art from Around the World* (London: Natural History Museum, 2009).

Rice, Tony, *Voyages of Discovery: Three Centuries of Natural History Exploration* (London: Natural History Museum/Scriptum, 2000).

Rix, Martyn, *The Art of Botanical Illustration* (London: Bracken Books, 1989).

Rix, Martyn, *The Golden Age of Botanical Art* (London: Andre Deutsch; Chicago: University of Chicago Press, 2013).

Saunders, Gill, *Picturing Plants: An Analytical History of Botanical Illustration* (Berkeley: University of California Press, in association with the Victoria & Albert Museum, 1995).

Curtis's Botanical Magazine is available online at the Biodiversity Heritage Library: http://www.biodiversitylibrary.org/bibliography/706#/summary

I Made on Location

adventurers

MARK CATESBY
Catesby, Mark, *The Natural History of Carolina, Florida and the Bahama Islands* (London, 1731–1743; reprint ed. G. Frick, Savannah: Beehive Press, 1974).

Nelson, E. Charles and David J. Elliott (eds), *The Curious Mister Catesby* (Athens: The University of Georgia Press, 2015).

THOMAS BAINES
Baines, Thomas, *Explorations in South-west Africa* (London: Longman & Co., 1864; reprint Salisbury, Rhodesia: Pioneer Head 1973, intro. by Frank R. Bradlow).

Carruthers, Jane and Marion Arnold, *The Life and Work of Thomas Baines* (Vlaeberg: Fernwood Press, 1995).

Stevenson, Michael (ed.), *Thomas Baines: An Artist in the Service of Science in Southern Africa* (Christies: London, 1999).

JAMES AUGUSTUS GRANT
Grant, James Augustus, *A Walk Across Africa* (Edinburgh, 1864).

Grant, James Augustus and Daniel Oliver, *The Botany of the Speke and Grant Expedition…*, Transactions of the Linnean Society of London, 29 (1875), 103–90.

JOHN KIRK
Goyder, David, 'Lectotypification of *Musa Livingstoniana* (Musaceae)', *Kew Bulletin* 69 (2014), 9529.

Jeal, Tim, *Explorers of the Nile* (London: Faber and Faber, 2010).

Jeal, Tim, *Livingstone* (New Haven and London: Yale University Press, 2013).

Liebowitz, Daniel, *The Physician and the Slave Trade. John Kirk, the Livingstone Expeditions and the Crusade Against Slavery in East Africa* (New York: W. H. Freeman, 1999).

JOHN MUIR
Muir, John, *Journeys in the Wilderness: A John Muir Reader*, intro. by Graham White (Birlinn Ltd: Edinburgh, 2009).

Worster, Donald, *A Passion for Nature: The Life of John Muir* (New York and Oxford: Oxford University Press, 2008).

http://www.pacific.edu/Library/Find/Holt-Atherton-Special-Collections/Digital-Collections/John-Muir-Drawings.html

FREDERICK ANDREWS WALPOLE
http://www.huntbotanical.org/art/show.php?13

MARGARET MEE
Morrison, Tony (ed.), *Margaret Mee: In Search of Flowers of the Amazon Forests* (Woodbridge, Suffolk: Nonesuch Expeditions, 1988).

Stiff, Ruth (ed.), *Margaret Mee: Return to the Amazon* (London: Stationery Office, 1996).

collectors

WILLIAM BARTRAM
Magee, Judith, *The Art and Science of William Bartram* (London: Natural History Museum; University Park: Pennsylvania State University Press, 2007).

Wulf, Andrea, *The Brother Gardeners: Botany, Empire and the Birth of an Obsession* (London: William Heinemann, 2008).

Wulf, Andrea, *The Founding Gardeners: The Revolutionary Generation, Nature, and the Shaping of the American Nation* (London: William Heinemann; New York: Alfred A. Knopf, 2011).

FRANCIS MASSON
Fraser, Mike and Liz, *The Smallest Kingdom: Plants and Plant Collectors at the Cape of Good Hope* (Kew: Royal Botanic Gardens, 2011).

Masson, Francis, 'An account of three journeys from the Cape Town…', *Philosophical Transactions of the Royal Society of London* 66 (1776), 268–317 (reprint, ed. F. R. Bradlow, Cape Town: Tablecloth Press, 1994).

Masson, Francis, *Stapeliae novae…* (London, 1796, 1797).

WILLIAM BURCHELL
Castell, Robin, *William John Burchell (1781–1863): St Helena (1805–1810)* (St Helena: Castell Collection, 2011).

MARIA GRAHAM CALLCOTT
Carl Thomson, Nottingham Trent University, has an excellent site on Callcott: http://www4.ntu.ac.uk/apps/research/groups/2/home.aspx/project/154085/overview/maria_graham_project

ALFRED RUSSEL WALLACE
Hemming, John, *Naturalists in Paradise: Wallace, Bates and Spruce in the Amazon* (London and New York: Thames & Hudson, 2015).

Wallace, Alfred Russel, *The Malay Archipelago* (London: Penguin Classics, 2014).

http://wallace-online.org
and the Wallace correspondence project
http://www.nhm.ac.uk/research-curation/scientific-resources/collections/library-collections/wallace-letters-online/index.html?utm_source=wallacelettersonline-short-url&utm_medium=wallacelettersonline-short-url&utm_campaign=wallacelettersonline-short-url

FRIEDRICH CARL LEHMANN
Cribb, Phillip, 'The orchid collections and illustrations of Consul Friedrich C. Lehmann', *Lankesteriana* 10 (2–3) (2010), 1–215.

botany on the side

FRANCIS HALL
Hall, Francis (W. J. Hooker ed.), 'Excursions in the neighbourhood of Quito', *Journal of Botany* 1 (1834), 327–54; *Companion to the Botanical Magazine* 1 (1835), 26–29, 52–80.

JOHN EYRE
Barretto, Gloria, Philip Cribb and Stephen Gale, *The Wild Orchids of Hong Kong* (Kota Kinabalu, Malaysia, Hong Kong Natural History Publications (Borneo); Kadoorie Farm and Botanic Garden, 2011).

ROBERT SCHOMBURGK
The Guiana Travels of Robert Schomburgk 1835–1844, 2 vols (Peter Rivière ed.) (London: Ashgate for The Hakluyt Society, 2006).

JOHN CHAMPION
Troyer, James R., 'The natural history publications of John George Champion (1815–1854), soldier and botanist', *Journal of the Society for the Bibliography of Natural History* 9 (2) (1979) 125–31.

Troyer, James R., 'An early record of secondary plant succession: the description by John George Champion', *Archives of Natural History* 13 (2) (1986) 175–78.

CHARLES PARISH
Clayton, Dudley, 'The Reverend Charles Samuel Pollock Parish – plant collector & botanical illustrator of the orchids from Tenasserim Province, Burma', *Lankesteriana* 13 (3) (2014), 215–27.

imperial projects

HENDRIK VAN RHEEDE
Fournier, Marian, 'Enterprise in botany: Van Reede and his *Hortus Malabaricus*', *Archives of Natural History* 14 (2), 123–58; 14 (3) (1987), 297–338.

Manilal, K. S. (ed.), *Botany and History of Hortus Malabaricus* (Rotterdam: Balkema, 1980).

JUAN DE LA CERDA & ATANASIO ECHEVERRÍA
McVaugh, Rogers, *Botanical Results of the Sessé & Mociño Expedition (1787–1803) VII. A Guide to Relevant Scientific Names of Plants* (Pittsburgh, PA: Hunt Institute for Botanical Documentation, Carnegie Mellon University, 2000).

The Torner collection of Sessé and Mociño (CD ROM).

JOHN REEVES
Magee, Judith, *Chinese Art and the Reeves Collection. Images of Nature* (London: Natural History Museum, 2011).

Whitehead, P. J. P., *Chinese Natural History Drawings Selected from the Reeves Collection in the British Museum (Natural History)* (London: British Museum (Natural History), 1974).

WILLIAM SWAINSON
Swainson, Geoffrey, *William Swainson FRS, FLS, naturalist & artist: family letters & diaries 1809–1855: final destiny New Zealand* (Palmerston North, New Zealand: Geoffrey Marshall Swainson, 1992).

JOHN CATHCART
Illustrations of Himalayan Plants chiefly selected from the drawings made for the late J. F. Cathcart ... by J. D. Hooker (London: Lovell Reeve, 1855).

II Doing Science

primus inter pares

CARL LINNAEUS
Blunt, Wilfrid, *The Compleat Naturalist: A Life of Linnaeus* (Collins: London, 1971).

Fara, Patricia, *Sex, Botany and Empire: The Story of Carl Linnaeus and Joseph Banks* (Cambridge: Icon, 2003).

https://www.linnean.org/education-resources/who-was-linnaeus

CHARLES DARWIN
Browne, Janet, *Charles Darwin: Voyaging & the Power of Place*, 2 vols (London: Jonathan Cape, 1995, 2002).

Darwin, Charles, *Voyage of the Beagle* (London: Penguin Classics, 1989).

http://darwin-online.org.uk
https://www.darwinproject.ac.uk

naturalists

CONRAD GESNER
Zoller, Heinrich, et al., *Conradi Gesneri Historia plantarum* (Dietikon-Zürich: Urs Graf-Verlag, 1972–80), 8 volumes of facsimiles of his drawings.

MARIA SIBYLLA MERIAN, JOHANNA HELENA HEROLT & DOROTHEA MARIA GSELL
Reitsma, Ella, *Maria Sibylla Merian & Daughters: Women of Art and Science* (Los Angeles: J. Paul Getty Museum; Zwolle: Waanders, 2008).

HARRIET SCOTT & HELENA FORDE
Olsen, Penny, *Collecting Ladies* (Canberra: National Library of Australia, 2013).

http://australianmuseum.net.au/a-biography-of-the-scott-sisters

BEATRIX POTTER
Jay, Eileen, et al., *A Victorian Naturalist: Beatrix Potter's Drawings from the Armitt Collection* (London: F. Warne & Co., 1993).

Lear, Linda, *Beatrix Potter: A Life in Nature* (London: Allen Lane, 2007).

http://armitt.com/armitt_website/beatrix-potter/

from the botanical garden

FRANCIS BAUER
Lack, H. W., *Franz Bauer: The Painted Record of Nature* (Vienna: Naturhistorisches Museum Wien, 2008).

Stewart, J. and W. T. Stearn, *The Orchid Paintings of Franz Bauer* (London: The Herbert Press in association with the Natural History Museum, 1993).

WILLIAM JACKSON HOOKER
Allan, Mea, *The Hookers of Kew 1795–1911* (London: Michael Joseph, 1967).

WALTER HOOD FITCH
Lewis, Jan, *Walter Hood Fitch: A Celebration* (London: HMSO, 1992).

botanists

JOHN STEVENS HENSLOW
Russell-Gebbett, Jean, *Henslow of Hitcham* (Lavenham: Dalton, 1977).

Walters, S. M. and E. A. Stow, *Darwin's Mentor: John Stevens Henslow, 1796–1861* (Cambridge: Cambridge University Press, 2001).

JOSEPH DALTON HOOKER
Desmond, Ray, *Joseph Dalton Hooker: Traveller & Plant Collector* (Woodbridge: Antique Collectors' Club with Royal Botanic Gardens, Kew, 1999).

Endersby, Jim, *Imperial Nature: Joseph Hooker and the Practices of Victorian Science* (Chicago and London: University of Chicago Press, 2008).

Griggs, Pat, *Joseph Hooker: Botanical Trailblazer* (London: Kew Publishing, 2011).

MARY ANNE STEBBING
Le-May Sheffield, Suzanne, 'Gendered Collaborations: Marrying Art and Science', in Ann B. Shteir and B. Lightman (eds), *Figuring It Out: Science, Gender and Visual Culture* (Lebanon: Dartmouth College Press, 2006), 240–64.

ARTHUR HARRY CHURCH
Mabberley, David, *Arthur Harry Church: The Anatomy of Flowers* (London: Merrell and the Natural History Museum, 2000).

http://www.nhm.ac.uk/nature-online/art-nature-imaging/collections/art-themes/drawingconclusions/more/geranium_more_info.htm

III Making Art

nature in art

LEONARDO DA VINCI
Emboden, William A., *Leonardo da Vinci on Plants and Gardens*, Historical, Ethno- & Economic Botany Series, vol. 1 (Portland: Dioscorides Press, 1987).

Reeds, Karen, 'Leonardo da Vinci and botanical illustration: Nature prints, drawings, and woodcuts ca. 1500', in Jean A. Givens et al. (eds), *Visualizing Medieval Medicine and Natural History, 1200–1500* (Burlington, VT and Aldershot: Ashgate, 2006), 205–37.

ALBRECHT DÜRER
Salley, Victoria, *Nature's Artist* (Munich, New York and London: Prestel, 2003).

White, Christopher, *Dürer: The Artist and His Drawings* (London: Phaidon, 1971).

JOHN CONSTABLE
Fleming-Williams, Ian, *A Private World: John Constable: Landscape Drawings, Watercolours, Oil Sketches, & Paintings* (Toronto: Art Gallery of Ontario, 1995).

Parris, Leslie, et al., *Constable: Paintings, Watercolours & Drawings* (London: Tate Gallery Publlications, 1976).

SAMUEL PALMER
Butlin, Martin (ed.), *Samuel Palmer: The Sketchbook of 1824* (London: Thames & Hudson, 2007).

Grigson, Geoffrey, *Samuel Palmer: The Visionary Years* (London: Kegan Paul, 1947).

Grigson, Geoffrey, *Samuel Palmer's Valley of Vision* (London: Phoenix House, 1960).

JOHN RUSKIN
Batchelor, John, *John Ruskin: No Wealth But Life* (London: Pimlico, 2001).

http://www.lancaster.ac.uk/users/ruskinlib/Flora/Flora.html

CHARLES RENNIE MACKINTOSH
Robertson, Pamela, *Charles Rennie Mackintosh: Art is the Flower* (London: Pavilion, 1995).

patrons' dependents

SEBASTIAN SCHEDEL
Barker, Nicholas, *Hortus Eystettensis: The Bishop's Garden and Besler's Magnificent Book* (London: British Library; New York, H. N. Abrams, 1994).

GEORG DIONYSIUS EHRET
Calmann, Gerta, *Ehret: Flower Painter Extraordinary* (Oxford: Phaidon, 1977).

PIERRE-JOSEPH REDOUTÉ
Lawrence, G. H. M., *A Catalogue of Redouteana Exhibited at the Hunt Botanical Library* (Pittsburgh, PA: Hunt Botanical Library, Carnegie Institute of Technology, 1963).

Rix, Martyn and Alison, *The Redouté Album* (London: Studio Editions, 1990).

in print

ANNE TODD DOWDEN
Crowell, Robert and Anne Dowden, *The Lore and Legends of Flowers* (New York: Thomas Crowell, 1982).

Dowden, Anne, *The Secret Life of the Flower* (New York: Odyssey Press; London: Paul Hamlyn, 1964).

Dowden, Anne, *Look at a Flower* (New York: T. Crowell; London: Constable, 1965).

VIOLET EMILY GRAHAM
Graham, Violet, *A Primary Nature Study for British Guiana* (London: Macmillan & Co., 1961).

Graham, Violet E., *Activities for Young Gardeners* (Amersham: Hulton, 1972).

jobbing

JOHN HILL
Rousseau, George, *The Notorious Sir John Hill: The Man Destroyed by Ambition in the Era of Celebrity* (Bethlehem, Pa.: Lehigh University Press, 2012).

SYDNEY PARKINSON
Parkinson, Sydney, *A Journey of a Voyage to the South Seas* (London: 1773; reprint London: Caliban, 1984) also available online at http://southseas.nla.gov.au/journals/parkinson/title.html

JOHN DOODY
Anemaat, Louise, *Natural Curiosity: Unseen Art of the First Fleet* (Sydney: NewSouth Publishing, 2014).

Coyne, Peter, *Norfolk Island's Fascinating Flora* (Belconnen: Petaurus Press, 2011).

FERDINAND BAUER
Lack, H. W., *The Bauers: Joseph, Franz & Ferdinand: Masters of Botanical Illustration* (Munich: Prestel 2015).

Lack, H. W., with David Mabberley, *The Flora Graeca Story. Sibthorp, Bauer, and Hawkins in the Levant* (Oxford: Oxford University Press, 1999).

CONRAD MARTENS
A voyage round the world http://www.lib.cam.ac.uk/exhibitions/Darwin/sketchbooks.html

Ellis, Elizabeth, *Conrad Martens: Selected Sketches 1835–1872* (Sydney: State Library of New South Wales, 1994).

EDWARD LEAR
Dehejia, Video, *Impossible Picturesqueness: Edward Lear's Indian Watercolours, 1873–1875* (New York: Columbia University Press; Ahmedabad: Mapin Publishing, 1989).

Murphy, Ray (ed.), *Edward Lear's Indian Journal* (London: Jarrolds, 1953).

Noakes, Vivien, *Edward Lear: The Life of a Wanderer* (Stroud: Sutton Publishing, 2006).

IV A Pleasing Occupation

HELLEN & MARGARET SHELLEY
Seymour, Miranda, *Mary Shelley* (London: John Murray, 2000)

On Field Place see https://www.rc.umd.edu/reference/misc/shelleysites/england/Fieldplace/Fieldplace.html

JOHN DAY
Cribb, Philip and John Tibbs, *A Very Victorian Passion: The Orchid Paintings of John Day* (London: Blacker and the Royal Botanic Gardens, Kew, 2004).

JOHN TRAHERNE MOGGRIDGE
Moggridge, John Traherne, *Contributions to the Flora of Mentone* (London: Lovell, Reeve & Co., 1874).

ANNIE MORSE
Fairbank, John, et al., *H. B. Morse Customs Commissioner and Historian of China* (Lexington: The University Press of Kentucky, 1995).

index of people and places

Page numbers in *italics* refer to illustrations

Abbásí, Shafi' 218–19, *218–19*
Afghanistan 169
Africa 14, 17, 23, 27, 42, 60, 61, 91, 230, 260, 278
Aiton, William 42
Alaska 30, 32, 105
Algeria 42, 260
Amazon basin 14, 36
Amsterdam 98, 102, 128
Anderson, Alexander 151
Aristotle 119
Assam 7, 169
Australia 17, 102, 110, 136, 243, 244, 245, 246, 250, 256
Austria 146, 186

Baines, Thomas 16–21, *16–21*
Banks, Joseph 42, 108, 146, 151, 152, 220, 243, 244, 245
Barbary Coast 260
Bartolozzi, Francesco 223
Bartram, John 40
Bartram, William 40–41, *40–41*, 220
Batavia (Jakarta) 243
Bauer, Ferdinand 146, 246–49, *247–49*,
Bauer, Francis 146–49, *147–49*, 246
Bauer, Joseph 146, 246
Bauer, Lucas 146, 246
Beihai 285
Berlin-Dahlem Botanical Garden 55
Besler, Basilius 212
Blake, William 204
Bligh, William 151, 243
Boccius, Norbert 246
Bolívar, Simón 69
Boussingault, Jean-Baptiste 69
Brazil 36, 44, 49, 52, 110
British Library, London 98
Brongniart, Adolphe 224
Brongniart, Alexandre 224
Broom, Robert 91
Brown, Nicolas 160–61, *160–61*
Brown, Robert 146, 246
Buchan, Alexander 243
Burchell, William 44–47, *44–47*
Burma (Myanmar) 7, 85, 169, 182
Bute, Lord 240

Calcott, Harriet 136
Calcutta (Kolkata) Botanical Garden 85, 169
Callcott, Augustus Wall 49
Callcott, Maria Graham 2–3, 48–51, *48–51*
Cambridge, University of 66, 166, 275
Canada 30, 69
Candolle, Augustin de 105
Canton (Guangzhou) 108

Cape Town 42
Caribbean 72, 94, 105, 151, 224, 239
Carolina 14
Carson, Joseph 142
Casearius, Johannes 98
Catatumbo River 94
Catesby, Mark 8, 14–15, *14–15*, 220
Cathcart, John 112–15, *112–15*
Central America 105, 142
Cerda, Juan de la 104–07, *104–07*
Ceylon (Sri Lanka) 79
Champion, John 72, 78–83, *78–83*
Chapman, James 17
Chelsea Physic Garden 151, 220
Chennai 282
Chile 49
Chimborazo 69
China 10, 72, 108, 181, 269, 285
Church, Arthur Henry 190–91, *190–91*
Clifford, George 118, 220
Cochin (Kochi) 98
Coleridge, Samuel Taylor 40
Collinson, Peter 40, 220
Colombia 8, 55, 94, 271
Colonna, Fabio 126–27, *126–27*
Colorado 236
Colville, Frederick 32
Constable, John 163, 198–99, *198–99*
Cook, James 42, 243
Cortés, Santiago 8, 94–97, *94–97*
Cranston, Catherine 208
Crimea 27, 79
Cuba 105
Cunningham, Allan 155
Curtis William 66

Darbangha, Maharaja of 184
Darjeeling 10, 112
Darling River 136
Darwin, Charles 52, 118, *119*, 166, 172, 250
Dawson, Muriel 234–35, *235*
Day, John 258, *259*, 266–71, *266–71*
Doody, John 244–45, *244–45*
Dorat, Charles 142–43, *143*
Dowden, Anne Todd 236–37, *236–37*
Dowden, Raymond Baxter 236
Drège, Isaac 90–93, *90–93*, 230
Dreyer, Richard 66–67, *67*
Durban 17
Dürer, Albrecht 196–97, *196–97*, 246

Eastern Cape 91, 230
Echeverría, Atanasio 104–07, *104–07*
Ecuador 12, 55, 69
Edinburgh 27, 49, 112, 151, 243
Ehret, Georg Dionysius 14, 220–21, *220–21*, 243
Ellis, William 267
Ellys, Richard 127
El Salvador 142

Essequibo River 77
Eyre, John 72–75, *72–75*

Fairchild, Thomas 14
Faulkner, Helen 60–65, *60–65*
Fielding, Copley 250
Fisher, John 199
Fitch, John Nugent 156
Fitch, Walter Hood 23, 112, 116, *117*, 152, 156–59, *156–59*, 172, 224
Flinders, Matthew 246
Florence 133, 194
Florida 14, 40
Forde, Edward 136, 138, *141*
Forde, Helena 136–41, *136–41*
Fothergill, John 40
France 69, 105, 120, 194, 220, 223, 275
Frankfurt 128

Gay, J. É. 224
Gemmingen, Johann Conrad von (Bishop of Eichstätt) 212
Genoa 275
Georgetown 239
Georgia 14, 40
Germany 55, 128, 196, 212, 220, 246
Gesner, Conrad 120–25, *121–25*
Glasgow 152, 156, 208
Glasnevin, National Botanical Gardens 55
Goedkint, Antoni Jacobs 98
Graff, Johann 128
Graham, Thomas 49
Graham, Violet Emily 238–39, *238–39*
Grahamstown 91
Grant, James Augustus 22–25, *22–25*, 156
Great Britain 17, 27, 30, 32, 40, 42, 44, 49, 52, 55, 60, 66, 72, 85, 145, 152, 234, 240, 260, 272
Greece 110, 246
Grenada 42
Grierson, Mary 162–65, *162–65*
Griffith, William 6, 8, 168–71, *168–71*, 172
Gronovius, Jan F. 118
Grossweiler, John 60
Gsell, Dorothea Maria 128–31, *130*
Gualtieri, Niccolò 132–35, *132–35*
Guangzhou 108
Guatemala 142
Guyana 77, 151, 239
Gwalior, Maharaja of 184

Hall, Francis 13, 68–71, *68–71*
Hanbury, Daniel 142
Harare 61
Hawaii 163
Henry, Augustine 285
Henslow, George 184
Henslow, John Stevens 166–67, *167*, 184
Herolt, Johanna Helena 128–31, *130*
Hill, John 240–41, *241*

Himalaya 172
Hindu Kush 169
Hong Kong 66, 72, 79
Hooker, Joseph Dalton 10, *11*, 112, 156, 166, 169, 172–79, *172–79*, 186, 253, 275
Hooker, William Jackson 49, 69, 79, 108, 110, 146, 152–55, *152–55*, 156, 172
Humblot, Léon 267
Humboldt, Alexander von 69
Hunter River 136
Huxley, Thomas H. 119

Iceland 152
India 10, 23, 49, 85, 98, 112, 169, 184, 219, 253, 282
Indonesia 52, 269
Iran 186, 187, 188, 219
Ireland 55
Isfahan 219
Italy 110, 127, 133, 194, 272
Iwasaki Tsunemasa 227

Jacquin, Joseph von 146
Jacquin, Nikolaus von 146, 246
Jakarta 243
James, John 260–61, *261*
Jameson, William 69
Japan 10, 102, 184, 201, 227
Jardin du Roi 223
Jardine, David 72
Jefferson, Thomas 40
Joséphine, Empress 223

Kerala 98
Kew, Royal Botanic Gardens 8, 12, 23, 27, 42, 44, 55, 61, 72, 79, 85, 91, 116, 145, 146, 152, 156, 161, 163, 172, 186, 187, 223, 240, 275, 282, 285
King, Laura 282–83, *282–83*
King, Walter Gawen 282
Kingstown 151
Kirk, John 26–29, *26–29*
Kochi 98
Kyoto 201

L'Héritier, Charles-Louis 223
Lake District 145, 271
Lear, Edward 252–55, *252–55*
Lee, James 243
Lehmann, Friedrich Carl 54–59, *54–59*
Leiden 102, 118
Leonardo da Vinci 8, 194–95, *195*
Levant 246, 253
Lindley, John 108, 146
Linnaeus, Carl 8, 66, *118*, 119, 216, 220, 240, 243
Liverpool Botanical Garden 116
Livingstone, David 17, 27
Loiseleur-Deslongchamps, Jean Louis Auguste 224
London 8, 14, 40, 110, 145, 146, 199, 204, 208, 220, 234, 243, 246, 262, 266
Longzhou 285
Low & Co., Hugh 55, 85

291

Low Countries 223
Lucknow 23
Lung Chow (Longzhou) 285

Macao 108
McIntosh, Charles 145
Mackintosh, Charles Rennie 208–11, *208–11*
Mackintosh, Margaret 208
M'Clelland, John 169
Madras (Chennai) 282
Madrid 105, 156
Malabar Coast 98, 253, 282
Malawi 230
Malay Archipelago 52, 269
Malaysia 52
Malta 110
Marie Antoinette 223
Maries, Charles 184–85, *184–85*
Marrel, Jacob 128
Martens, Conrad 136, *137*, 250–51, *250–51*
Martyn, Thomas 166
Maruyama Ōkyo 201
Mason, Marianne Harriet 278–81, *278–81*
Massee, George 144, 145
Masson, Francis 42–43, *42–43*
Mawlamyine 85
Mee, Greville 36
Mee, Margaret 36–39, *36–39*
Melbourne 256
Menton(e) 275
Merian, Maria Sibylla 14, 102, 128–31, *129–31*
Merian, Mattäus 128
Mexico 105
Michaux, Andrew 223
Micheli, Pier Antonio 133
Miller, Philip 220
Milne-Redhead, Edgar 61
Milton, John 204
Minchen, Edward 256–57, *256–57*
Mociño, José Marino 105
Mocuba 60
Moggridge, John Traherne 260, 274–77, *274–77*
Montpellier 105
Morse, Annie 284–87, *284–87*
Morse, Hosea Ballou 285
Moscow 102
Moulmein (Mawlamyine) 85
Mozambique 60
Muir, John 30–31, *30–31*
Muséum d'Histoire naturelle 223
Mwambeni 60
Myanmar 7, 85, 169, 182

Naples 127
Nash, John 163
National Herbarium, USA 32
National Tropical Botanical Garden, Kauai 163
Natural History Museum, London 145
New South Wales 136, 243, 244, 250, 256
New York Botanical Garden 94

New Zealand 110, 172, 234, 243, 250
Nicholls, Francis 8, 262–63, *262–63*
Nightingale, Florence 79
Norfolk Island 244, 245, 246
North America 14, 30, 32, 40, 69, 105, 236, 285
Nuremberg 128, 196, 212, 220

Okada Seifuku 226–29, *226–29*
Oliver, Daniel 23
Oregon 32
Orinoco River 77
Oxford 191, 207, 246, 262
Oxford University Botanic Garden 220

Pakhoi (Beihai) 285
Palgrave, Olive Coates 230–33, *230–33*
Palgrave, Sydney 230
Palmer, Samuel 204–05, *204–05*, 207
Paris 60, 120, 224
Parish, Charles 84–89, *84–89*
Parkinson, Sydney 242–43, *242–43*
Parramatta River 245
Pasmore, Victor 36
Paterson, William 244–45
Pearl River 108
Pennsylvania, University of 142
Pepys, Samuel 260
Persia (Iran) 186, 187, 188, 219
Perth 236
Peru 69
Peter the Great 128
Petiver, James 260
Philadelphia 40
Pichincha 69
Pisa 133
Pittsburgh 236
Polak, Jakob 187
Popayan 55
Port Elizabeth 91
Portland 32
Portugal 42
Potter, Beatrix 7, 144–45, *144–45*
Pretoria, National Herbarium 61
Prussia 77
Puerto Rico 105

Quindio 94
Quito 12, 69

Rangoon (Yangon) 169, 282
Ray, John 14
Redouté, Pierre-Joseph 8, 222–23, *222–23*, 224
Reeves, John 108–09, *108–09*
Regensburg 220
Reichenbach, Heinrich Gustav 55
Reigate 161, 181
Rheede, Hendrik van 98–101, *99–101*
Richmond, Duke of 240
Riocreux, Alfred 192, *193*,

224–25, *224–25*
Riocreux, Denis-Désiré 224
Rio de Janeiro 36
Robert, Nicolas 128
Rome 194
Rondebosch 278
Roscoe, Henry Enfield 145
Ruskin, John 32, 206–07, *206–07*, 250
Russia 102, 128, 219

Sachs, Julius von 10
St Helena 44
St Lucia 151
St Petersburg 128
St Vincent Botanic Gardens 151
Salisbury (Harare) 61
Sander, Frederick 55
San Francisco 30
São Paulo 36
Saunders, William Wilson 159, 161, 181
Schedel, Sebastian 212–17, *212–17*
Schomburgk, Robert 76–77, *76–77*
Schongauer, Martin 8, 9, 196
Schönland, Selmar 91
Scott, Alexander 136, *137*
Scott, Harriet 136–41, *136–41*
Seemann, Berthold 72
Sessé, Martin de 105
Sèvres 223
Shelley, Hellen 264–65, *264–65*
Shelley, Margaret 264–65, *264–65*
Shelley, Percy Bysshe 264
Shiraz 188
Shoreham 204
Sibthorp, John 246
Sicily 110
Sloan, Junius R. 32
Sloane, Sir Hans 130, 220
Smith, Annie Lorrain 181
Smith, James Edward 66
Solander, Daniel 243
Sommelsdijk, Cornelis van 128
South Africa 17, 42, 44, 61, 91, 102, 112, 156, 161, 162, 230, 278
South America 36, 44, 49, 55, 69, 77, 94, 110, 118, 128, 151
South Carolina 40
Sowerby, James 66
Spaendonck, Gerard von 223
Spain 105
Speke, John Hanning 23, 156
Splijnter, Marcelis 98
Sri Lanka 79
Stapf, Otto 186–89, *186–89*
Stebbing, Anne 181, 272–73, *272–73*
Stebbing, Edward Percy 272
Stebbing, Mary Anne 159, 161, 180–83, *180–83*, 272
Stebbing, Thomas R. R. 181
Sterkfontein 91
Stoneman, Bertha 230
Stour Valley 199
Suffolk 66, 152, 166, 199, 208
Surinam 128

Swainson, William 110–11, *110–11*
Sweden 119
Switzerland 120, 220
Sydney 136, 244, 256
Syme, John T. Boswell 161

Tahiti 243, 250
Taipai 285
Tamsui (Taipai) 285
Tanganyika (Tanzania) 60
Tasmania 110, 243
Thiselton-Dyer, William 186
Thomson, Thomas 23
Thoreau, Henry David 30
Thunberg, Carl Peter 42
Tokyo 227
Tonkin, Gulf of 285
Torquay 181
Tournefort, Joseph Pitton de 133
Transkei 278
Transvaal 17
Trew, Christoph Jacob 220
Tunbridge Wells 181
Turner, Dawson 152
Turner, J. M. W. 207
Tyley, John 150–51, *150–51*

Utrecht 98

Vatican Botanical Garden 127
Veitch & Sons, James 184
Venezuela 69, 94, 271
Venice 196
Verrocchio, Andrea del 194
Victoria, Lake 23
Victoria, Queen 253
Victoria Falls 17, 278
Vienna 146, 186, 246
Vietnam 269
Virginia 14
Vlamingh, Willem de 102
Vogel, Theodore 178

Walberswick 208
Wallace, Alfred Russel 52–53, *53*
Wallich, Nathaniel 169
Walpole, Frederick Andrews 32–35, *32–35*
Washington, DC 32
Weinmann, Johann 220
West Indies 42, 77, 151
Wight, Robert 282
Williams, Benjamin 266
Witsen, Nicolaes 102–03, *102–03*
Wordsworth, William 40

Yangon 169, 282
Yosemite 30
Yoshikawa Kokei 200–03, *200–03*
Young, George 151
Yunnan 285

Zambezi 27, 278
Zambia 230
Zanzibar 27
Zimbabwe 61, 230
Zurich 120

index of plants

Page numbers in *italics* refer to illustrations; common names included if they have been used in the text or caption

Acacia horrida 278
Acacia longifolia 138, *140*
Acer sp. *202*
aconite see *Aconitum* sp.
Aconitum napellus 208, *209*
Aconitum sp. 202, *203*
Adansonia digitata 230
Adonis annua 66, *67*
Aerides fieldingii see *Aerides roseum*
Aerides roseum 258, *259*
Aeschynanthus ceylanicus 82, *83*
Agaricus velutipes see *Flammulina velutipes*
Agathis australis 110
Aglaonema sp. 285
Albizia saman 239
alder see *Alnus* sp.
Alexandria imperatricis see *Vellozia tubiflora*
Alnus sp. 208, *211*
Aloe barberae 20
Androsace umbellata 287
Angraecum eburneum 27
Anguloa clowesii 271
Antirrhinum majus 208
Archontophoenix cunninghamiana 250, *251*
Arisaema propinquum 178, *179*
Aristolochia 36, *38*
Artabotrys zeylanicus 83
Arum sp. 133, *134–35*
Asclepiadaceae 161
Asclepiadae 169, *171*
Asparagus officinalis 181

'Balsam of Peru' see *Myroxylon pereirae*
Banksia serrata 256
banyan 79
Bauhinia forficata 12, *13*
Begonia roxburghii 112, *113*
Berkheya acanthopoda 278, *281*
Billbergia 49, 295
black bryony see *Dioscorea communis*
Blandfordia nobilis 138, *139*
Blechnum punctulatum 156, *157*
Blighia unijugata 61
Boehmeria nivea 184
Boletus luridus see *Suillellus luridus*
Bombax pentondium see *Ceiba insignis*
Bowiea volubilis 156
breadfruit 151, 243
Bunias erucago 132, *133*
Burmannia championii 79

cabbage palm see *Livistona australis*
Calamus wightii 168, *169*
Callicarpa tomentosa 72, *74*

Calluna vulgaris 206, *207*
Campanula rotundifolia 34, 35, 234, *235*
candelabra tree see *Euphorbia ingens*
Carduus nutans 1, *4*
Caribbean spider-lily see *Hymenocallis caribaea*
Carica papaya 130, *131*
casellore see *Bunia erucago*
Cassiope tetragona 32
Castanea sativa 163, *165*
Catasetum macrocarpum 36, *37*
Ceiba insignis 48
Centaurea montana 207
Cephalanthera damasonium 264, *265*
Chinese cinnamon see *Cinnamomum aromaticum*
Christmas Bells see *Blandfordia nobilis*
Cinchona sp. 151, 220, *221*
Cinnamomum aromaticum 124, *125*
Citrullus 22, 295
Cleome foliosa 178
Cleome sp. 112
Clerodendron chinense 284
Clusia sp. 106–07, 295
cobra lily see *Arisaema propinquum*
Colocasia sp. 283
Commiphora africana 230, *232*
conchalagua see *Schkuhria* sp.
Conophytum sp. 160–61
Coprinus sp. 187
Cordia nodosa 238, *239*
Cordia sp. 106–07, 295
cornflower, perennial see *Centaurea montana*
Corymbia citriodora 137
Corypha umbraculifera 98, 100–01
crab apple see *Malus* sp.
cranberry see *Vaccinium oxycoccos*
crape myrtle see *Lagerstroemia indica*
Crassula 24–25, 295
Crataeva sp. 97, 295
Crinum crassicaule 19, *20*
Crocus carpetanus 224
Cryptolepis dubia 169
Cucumis sativus 112, *114–15*
Curatella americana 106–07, 295
Cussonia thyrsiflora 90, *91*
Cyathea brownii 246, *247*
Cyathea dealbata 110, *111*
Cycnoches ventricosum var. *chlorochilon* 104, *105*
Cynomorium coccineum 260, *261*
Cyperus articulatus 142, *143*
Cyperus longus 262–63
Cypripedium fairrieanum see *Paphiopedilum fairrieanum*
Cypripedium purpuratum see *Paphiopedilum purpuratum*
Cyrilla racemiflora 150, *151*

Dactylopsis digitata see *Mesembryanthemum digitatum*
Dactylorhiza incarnata 270, *271*
Dalbergia championii 79
Dampiera stricta 243
Daphne striata 122, *123*
Dasylirion glaucophyllum 35
Datura stramonium 216, *217*
Daucus carota 180, 181
Dendrobium albosanguineum 89, 295
Dendrobium formosum 85, *89*
Dendrobium tortile 89, 295
Dendrosenecio 22, 295
Desmodium sp. 80, *83*
Diclis reptans 279
Dieffenbachia seguine 166, *167*
Dieffenbachia seguinum see *Dieffenbachia seguine*
Dillenia aurea 282, *283*
Dillenia indica 282
Dillenia pulcherrima see *Dillenia aurea*
Dionysia sp. 187
Dioscorea communis 122
Diplosoma luckhoffii 42, 295
Draba aretoides 69, *70*
Dracula radiosa 55, *57*
Dracunculus vulgaris 130
dragon fruit see *Hylocereus triangularis*

Elaeocarpus montanus 78, *79*
Ensete livingstonianum 26, *27*
Ephedra 186
Epidendrum sp. 59
Epipactis grandiflora see *Cephalanthera damasonium*
Eria ornata 85
Erica cerinthoides 93, 295
Eucalyptus eugenioides 256, *257*
Euphorbia sp. 161
Euphorbia cereiformis 90, *91*
Euphorbia ingens 230, *231*
Euphorbia polygona 91
evening primrose see *Oenothera grandiflora*
Exostema sanctae-luciae 151

Fagraea obovata 98, *99*
Felicia echinata 93, 295
Ficus carica 124
Ficus hirta 284
Ficus religiosa 10, *11*
Ficus sp. 200, *201*
fig see *Ficus* sp.
Flammulina velutipes 144, *145*
fly orchis see *Ophrys insectifera*
Fockea angustifolia 90, *91*
Freycinetia baueriana 244, *245*
Fuchsia sp. 181, *183*

gadigalbudyari see *Blandfordia nobilis*
galingale see *Cyperus longus*
Gardenia volkensii 230
Gavilea patagonica 118, *119*
Gentiana ciliata 122, *123*
Gentiana pneumonanthe 122, *123*
gentians see *Gentiana* sp.

giant Colombian blackberry see *Rubus nubigenus*
gigantic rata see *Metrosideros robusta*
Globularia sp. 260, *261*
Gloriosa superba 220
Gmelina asiatica 284
Gnidia anthylloides 278, *279*
Grammangis ellisii 266–67, *267*
Grammatophyllum ellisii see *Grammangis ellisii*
grape hyacinth 188, 295
Grevillea robusta 154, *155*

harebell see *Campanula rotundifolia*
Helichrysum foetidum 281
Heliconia 49
helleborine, large white see *Cephalanthera damasonium*
Heloniopsis orientalis 202
Heteropterys chrysophylla 152
Hibiscus pusillus 279
Hippocratea volubilis 97, 295
Hodgsonia macrocarpa 176–77, 178
Huernia reticulata 42, *43*, 295
Hura crepitans 94, *95*
Hydrangea quercifolia 40, *41*
Hylocereus triangularis 108
Hymenocallis caribaea 238, *239*
Hymenocallis tubiflora 238, *239*
Hymenocardia acida var. *mollis* 60
Hymenocardia mollis see *Hymenocardia acida* var. *mollis*
Hypericum calycinum 191
Hypericum laricifolium 69
Hyphaene coriacea 27, *29*
Hyphaene petersiana 20, *21*

Ilex buxifolia 81, *83*
Indian red water lily see *Nymphaea rubra*
Ipomoea biloba see *Ipomoea pes-caprae*
Ipomoea indica 242, *243*
Ipomoea pes-caprae 44, *46*
Ipomoea pterygocaulis see *Merremia pterygocaulos*
Iris germanica 246, *249*

Jack fruit 163
jar plum see *Syzygium cumini*

kale 204
Kauri pine see *Agathis australis*
Knautia arvensis 180, 181
Kniphofia aloides see *Kniphofia uvaria*
Kniphofia rufa 280
Kniphofia sarmentosa 280
Kniphofia uvaria 280
knobcone pine see *Pinus attenuata*

Lagerstroemia indica 102
Langsdorffia hypogaea 77
larch see *Larix decidua*

Larix decidua 124
Larix griffithii 172
Lasiosiphon anthylloides see *Gnidia anthylloides*
Lavatera cretica see *Malva linnaei*
Lavatera olbia 274, 275
Leucanthemum vulgare 180, 181
lianas 163, 164
ling see *Calluna vulgaris*
Lipotriche 23, 295
Litchi chinensis 109, 295
Livistona australis 138, 141
Loasa tricolor 12, 13
Lycoris aurea 284
Lygodium microphyllum 85, 86–87

Magnolia championii 72, 75
Magnolia odoratissima see *Magnolia championii*
Magnolia virginiana 14, 15
Malmea depressa 106–07, 295
Malus sp. 208, 210
Malva arborea 122
Malva linnaei 275
Mangifera indica 109, 184, 185, 295
Mangifera sp. 109, 184, 185
mango see *Mangifera* sp.
maple see *Acer* sp.
marine algae/seaweed 4, 133, 155
Masdevallia callichroma 55, 56
Merremia pterygocaulos 27, 28
Mesembryanthema 161
Mesembryanthemum digitatum 43, 295
Mesembryanthemum simplex see *Dipsoloma luckhoffii*
Metrosideros robusta 110, 111
Microloma linearis see *Microloma tenuifolium*
Microloma tenuifolium 92
milk parsley see *Peucedanum palustre*
milk thistle see *Silybum marianum*
Monocera hookeriana see *Elaeocarpus montanus*
Moreton Bay bignonia see *Pandorea jasminoides*
Mucor sp. 144
Mucuna urens 36, 39
Mulanje cedarwood see *Widdringtonia whytei*
Myroxylon pereirae 142

Narcissus sp. 128, 129, 260, 261
nasturtium see *Tropaeolum* sp.
Nauclea 27, 28
Nerium sp. 260, 261
Nidularium innocentii 36
nodding thistle see *Carduus nutans*
Norway spruce see *Picea abies*
Nuphar lutea 198, 198, 199
Nuphar polysepala 35
Nymphaea polysepala see *Nuphar polysepala*
Nymphaea rubra 190, 191

oak 204
oak-leaved hydrangea see *Hydrangea quercifolia*
Oenothera grandiflora 40
Oenothera sp. 223
Old Man's banksia see *Banksia serrata*
Oncidium hallii 68
Oncidium mirandum 55
Oophytum nanum 42, 295
Ophrys insectifera 264
orchids 12, 13, 36, 37, 54–59, 68, 72, 84, 85, 88, 89, 104, 105, 106, 224, 225, 258, 259, 264, 265, 266–71, 295
Orchis latifolia see *Dactylorhiza incarnata*
Orchis muscifera see *Ophrys insectifera*
Ornithogalum umbellatum 194
Otoglossum palaciosii 12, 13
ox-eye daisy see *Leucanthemum vulgare*

Paeonia officinalis 8, 9
Paeonia sp. 8, 9, 201
Pancratium tenuifolium 18, 20
Pandorea jasminoides 138
papaya see *Carica papaya*
Paphiopedilum fairrieanum 268, 269
Paphiopedilum purpuratum 269
Papilionanthe teres 84, 85
Pararchidendron pruinosum 138, 140
Parnassia palustris 122, 123
Passiflora ligularis 220, 221
Pelargonium diadematum 192, 193
Peliosanthes sp. 287
peonies see *Paeonia* sp.
Persicaria tinctoria 287
Pescatoria Lehmanii 54
Peucedanum palustre 120, 121
Phialodiscus unijugatus see *Blighia unijugata*
Philodendron 36
Pholiodota advena 85, 88
Phormium tenax 244, 245
Photinia glabra 202
Picea abies 124
Picea sp. 196
pine see *Pinus* sp.
pineapple 49, 50
Pinus attenuata 32
Pinus cembra 124
Pinus pinea 124
Pistia stratiotes 158, 159
Pisum sativum 182, 295
Pithecolobium pruinosum see *Pararchidendron pruinosum*
Polygonatum sp. 216
Polytrichastrum formosum 272
Portaea paradoxa see *Cycnoches ventricosum* var. *chlorochilon*
Proboscidea althaeifolia 105
Prosthechea cochleata 106–07, 295
Protea neriifolia 91

Protea sp. 63, 64–65
Pseudotsuga menziesii 272, 273
Puccinia graminis 146, 147
Punica granatum 109, 295

Quercus coccinea 222, 223

Rafflesia 146
Ranunculus flammula 66, 67
Renanthera coccinea 72
Rhododendron falconeri 172, 175
Rhododendron grande 172, 174
Rohdea japonica 102, 103
Romulea bulbocodium 275, 276
Romulea ramiflora 275, 277
Rosa sp. 212, 214–15, 219, 223
Rothmannia sp. 63
Rubus nubigenus 69
Ryokyou see *Zingiber* sp.

sacred lily of Japan see *Rohdea japonica*
Sadleria cyatheoides 162, 163
St John's wort see *Hypericum calycinum*
Sansevieria aethiopica 17
Sassafras albidum 14, 15
sassafras see *Sassafras albidum*
Saxifraga stolonifera 227, 228
Schkuhria 142, 143
Schoenoplectus acutus 32, 33
Scirpus lacustris occidentalis see *Schoenoplectus acutus*
Scolopendrium krebsii see *Blechnum punctulatum*
Scrophularia maior see *Scrophularia nodosa*
Scrophularia nodosa 126–27
Selenicereus wittii 36
Senna alata 51
Sequoiadendron giganteum 30
Sikkim larch see *Larix griffithii*
Silene maritima 264
silver leaf fern see *Cyathea dealbata*
Silybum marianum 227, 229
skunk cabbage see *Symplocarpus foetidus*
snap dragon see *Antirrhinum majus*
solomon's seal see *Polygonatum* sp.
spruce see *Picea* sp.
Stanhopea grandiflora 224, 225
Stapelia reticulata see *Huernia reticulata*
Star of Bethlehem see *Ornithogalum umbellatum*
Sterculia africana 16, 17
stinkwood see *Terminalia prunioides*
Stobaea acanthopoda see *Berkheya acanthopoda*
strawberry geranium see *Saxifraga stolonifera*
Strophanthus sp. 62, 63
Suillellus luridus 272, 273
suntule see *Cyperus articulatus*
sweet bay see *Magnolia virginiana*

sweet chestnut see *Castanea sativa*
sweet cyperus see *Cyperus longus*
Symplocarpus foetidus 14, 152, 153
Syzygium aromaticum 124
Syzygium cumini 151

Tacca leontopetaloides 159
Talipariti tiliaceum 69, 71
tarthuth see *Cynomorium coccineum*
Taxus baccata 149
Telfairia occidentalis 116, 117
Telopea speciosissima 256
Terminalia prunioides 16, 17
Thalictrum flavum 66, 67
Torikabuto see *Aconitum* sp.
Trapa bicornis 109, 295
tree mallow see *Malva arborea*
Triticum 186
Tropaeolum sp. 130
Tulbaghia alliacea 279
tule see *Schoenoplectus acutus*
Tulipa sp. 236, 237

Vaccinium oxycoccos 120, 121
Vanda coerulea 258, 259
Vanda teres see *Papilionanthe teres*
Vellozia tubiflora 76, 77
Verbascum thapsus 66, 67
Victoria amazonica 77
Viola lutea 66, 67
Viola sp. 187, 194, 195, 218, 219
Viola tricolor 66, 67

Wahlenbergia burchellii 44
water lettuce see *Pistia stratiotes*
water lily 35, 77, 198
white mountain Arctic heather see *Cassiope tetragona*
Widdringtonia whytei 230, 233
Wightia speciosissima 10, 11

Xylopia championii 79

yew see *Taxus baccata* 149

Zea mays 212, 213
Zingiber sp. 72, 73, 92, 226, 227
Zinnia multiflora see *Zinnia peruviana*
Zinnia peruviana 279

note on plant names

Where possible we have tried to identify the plants that are featured in the sketches at least to the genus level. If they are unnamed or their current name does not appear in the caption, they are listed here. We are extremely grateful for the help we have received with identifying the plants; any errors are our responsibility.

p. 22 (above) *Dendrosenecio* sp.; (below) *Citrullus* sp.
p. 23 *Lipotriche* sp.
p. 24–25 *Crassula* sp.
p. 42 these proved very difficult to identify: (left) *Oophytum nanum*; (right) *Diplosoma luckhoffii*
p. 43 (above) *Dactylopsis digitata* now *Mesembryanthemum digitatum* (below) *Stapelia reticulata* now *Huernia reticulata*
p. 45 (above) *Musa × paradisiaca* (left); *Canna indica* (right)
p. 47 (bottom) possibly *Dicksonia arborescens*
p. 49 (above) possibly a *Billbergia* sp.
p. 89 (above left) *Dendrobium tortile*; (below) *D. albosanguineum*; (others) *D. formosum*
p. 93 *Microloma linearis* now *M. tenuifolium* (left); *Erica cerinthoides* (centre); *Felicia echinata* (right)
p. 97 possibly (left) a *Crataeva* sp., *C. tapia*; (right) a *Hippocratea* sp., *H. volubilis*
p. 106–07 clockwise from top left *Prosthechea cochleata*, *Clusia* sp., *Malmea depressa*, *Cordia* sp., *Curatella americana*
p. 109 other fruit are plums, peaches and apricots, all *Prunus* sp., *Punica granatum*, *Litchi chinensis*, water chestnut *Trapa bicornis*, mango *Mangifera indica*
p. 130 *Tropaeolum* sp.
p. 160 (above) species include: 1. *Conophytum jucundum* (*C. gratum*); 2. *C. minutum*; 3. *C. wettsteinii*; 4. *C. calculus*; 5. *C. pearsonii* (*C. minutum* var. *pearsonii*); 6. *C. pearsonii* var. *minor* (*C. minutum* var. *pearsonii*)
p. 160 (below) *Conophytum truncatum* subsp. *viridicatum*
p. 161 *Conophytum pageae*, *C. translucens* (*C. truncatum*)
p. 183 *Pisum sativum* var *umbellatum*
p. 188 the grape hyacinth collected by Otto Stapf in the Kew herbarium is now known as *Leopoldia tenuiflora*
p. 197 identified species include common yarrow (*Achillea millefolium*), dandelion (*Taraxacum officinale*), meadowgrass (*Poa pratensis*) and greater plantain (*Plantago major*)
p. 214–15 Plants include *Rosa* sp. *Dianthus*, *Bellis*, Cyclamen
p. 221 plants include *Jasminum* sp., *Passiflora ligularis*, *Cinchona* sp.
p. 236 (left) *Sisyrinchium angustifolium*, *Lobelia* sp., *Dicentra cucullaria*, *Scutellaria galericulata*, *Viola* sp.; (right) *Rubus* sp., *Anemone coronaria*, (Carrion flower), (Lizard tail); *Centaurea cyanus*
p. 279 Using Mason's numbers: 1. *Tulbaghia alliacea*; 2. *Zinnia multiflora* now *Zinnia peruviana*; 3. *Lasiosiphon anthylloides* now *Gnidia anthylloides*; 4. *Hibiscus pusillus*; 5. *Diclis reptans*.
p. 280 *Kniphofia aloides* now *K. uvaria*, *K. sarmentosa*, *K. rufa*.
p. 282 *Dillenia pulcherrima* now *D. aurea*,
p. 284 (above) *Lycoris aurea*; (below) Morse's numbers: 165. *Ficus hirta*; 166. *Gmelina asiatica*; 167. *Clerodendron fragrans* (*C. chinense*)
p. 285 *Aglaonema* sp.
p. 287 Morse's numbers: 259. *Androsace saxifragaefolia* (*A. umbellata*); 260. *Peliosanthes* sp.; 261. *Polygonum tinctorium* (*Persicaria tinctoria*)

illustration credits

Every reasonable attempt has been made to identify owners of copyright. Errors or omissions will be corrected in subsequent editions.

All images are © The Board of Trustees of the Royal Botanic Gardens, Kew, except the following:

1 Universitätsbibliothek Erlangen-Nürnberg, MS 2386; 9 The J. Paul Getty Museum, Los Angeles; 14, 15 British Museum, London; 30, 31 John Muir Papers, Holt-Atherton Special Collections Department, University of the Pacific Library, Stockton, C.A. ©1984 Muir-Hanna Trust; 32, 33, 34, 35 Courtesy of Hunt Institute for Botanical Documentation, Carnegie Mellon University, Pittsburgh, P.A.; 40, 41, 53 Mary Evans Picture Library/Natural History Museum, London; 67 By permission of the Linnean Society of London; 99, 100–01, 103 British Library, London; 104, 105, 106–07 Courtesy of Hunt Institute for Botanical Documentation, Carnegie Mellon University, Pittsburgh, P.A./Torner Collection of Sessé & Moficio Biological Illustrations; 108, 109 Mary Evans Picture Library/Natural History Museum, London; 118 By permission of the Linnean Society of London; 121, 122, 123, 124, 125 Universitätsbibliothek Erlangen-Nürnberg, MS 2386; 126 National Trust Images; 129 Universitätsbibliothek Johann Christian Senckenberg, Goethe-Universität Frankfurt; 130, 131 British Museum, London; 132, 133, 134–35 Courtesy of Hunt Institute for Botanical Documentation, Carnegie Mellon University, Pittsburgh, P.A.; 136, 137, 138, 140, 141 State Library of New South Wales, Sydney; 143 Courtesy of Hunt Institute for Botanical Documentation, Carnegie Mellon University, Pittsburgh, P.A.; 144, 145 The Armitt Trust, Ambleside; 147, 148, 149 Mary Evans Picture Library/ Natural History Museum, London; 150, 151, 167 Courtesy of Hunt Institute for Botanical Documentation, Carnegie Mellon University, Pittsburgh, P.A.; 190, 191 Mary Evans Picture Library/Natural History Museum, London; 193 Botany Libraries, Harvard University Herbaria, Cambridge, M.A.; 195 Mary Evans Picture Library/Alinari Archives, Florence; 197 Mary Evans Picture Library/Imagno; 196, 198, 199 British Museum, London; 200, 201, 202, 203 Courtesy of Hunt Institute for Botanical Documentation, Carnegie Mellon University, Pittsburgh, P.A.; 204, 205 British Museum, London; 207 Ruskin Centre, University of Lancaster; 206 Mary Evans Picture Library/Ashmolean Museum, Oxford; 208, 209 Reproduced courtesy of the National Library of Ireland; 210, 211 Sotheby's; 218 British Museum, London; 219 Brooklyn Museum, Gift of Mr. and Mrs. Charles K. Wilkinson; 220, 221 Mary Evans Picture Library/Natural History Museum, London; 223 Courtesy of Hunt Institute for Botanical Documentation, Carnegie Mellon University, Pittsburgh, P.A.; 225 Botany Libraries, Harvard University Herbaria, Cambridge M.A.; 226–27, 228–29 Courtesy of Hunt Institute for Botanical Documentation, Carnegie Mellon University, Pittsburgh, P.A.; 235 Mary Evans Picture Library/© The Muriel Dawson Collection; 236, 237 Courtesy of Hunt Institute for Botanical Documentation, Carnegie Mellon University, Pittsburgh, P.A.; 242, 243 Mary Evans Picture Library/Natural History Museum, London; 244, 245 State Library of New South Wales, Sydney; 247 Mary Evans Picture Library/Natural History Museum, London; 248 Archivio del Real Jardin Botanico CSIC, Madrid; 249 Bodleian Library, University of Oxford; 250, 251 State Library of New South Wales, Sydney; 252 below, 253, 254, 255 Houghton Library, Harvard University, Cambridge, M.A.; 256, 257 State Library of New South Wales, Sydney; 261 British Library, London; 262–63 By permission of the Linnean Society of London; 264, 265 Courtesy of Hunt Institute for Botanical Documentation, Carnegie Mellon University, Pittsburgh, P.A.

acknowledgments

Botanical Sketchbooks has taken us on many adventures. Just as our artists went far and wide to find plants to sketch we have visited a large number of libraries and owe a great deal to all the staff in these institutions who have helped us along the way by dealing with our requests and sharing our enthusiasm. We looked at much more than we could use. We must begin with the Royal Botanic Gardens, Kew: the Library, Art and Archives is a treasure trove and has been our primary source of material. Julia Buckley has been a pleasure to work with again and her infinite patience and knowledge of the collection are much appreciated. We are sure she has done much more than we are aware of. Thanks to Trishya Long for her timely advice on Eyre. The Directors' Correspondence is a remarkable project. Thanks to the DC Team and Helen Hartley for teaching me how to negotiate the letters on JSTOR. Similarly the Joseph Hooker Correspondence has yielded bounty, and here Ginny Mills deserves the plaudits. Thanks also to past and present staff more generally, who all contributed in different ways: Craig Brough, Lorna Cahill, Alice Evans, Anne Marshall, Christopher Mills, Lynn Parker, Kiri Ross-Jones. The archives and illustrations teams never groaned publicly about creating our huge trolleys of material, nor the desk staff who had to hand it out and take it back. Beyond the library thanks to Frances Cook, Lydia White, Masumi Yamanaka. Photographer Paul Little made the images and Georgie Hills masterminded this side of things. Various scientists in the Herbarium have very kindly given their time to help identify plants figured in the sketches: Bente Klitgård and the Americas Team, Andre Shuitman and above all David Goyder. The inclusion of the Kirk material is due to David's energy in revealing the herbarium sketches, and his help with names of African plants and understanding what we have been up to with this book have been greatly appreciated. The encyclopaedic Martyn Rix took on the last remaining puzzles, expertly and with great speed, thank you. It has also been a pleasure to work again with Gina Fullerlove, Head of Publishing at Kew – thank you for wanting to take this partnership on again.

Lugene Bruno curator and scholar at the Hunt Institute for Botanical Documentation has felt like a co-researcher for the images that come from this wonderful collection in Pittsburgh. We have had some frustrating dead-ends, but the live ones are of the highest quality. It's been a rich collaboration along the way and we are so grateful for her vivacity and expertise. Thanks to Carrie Roy at the Hunt as well. Elaine Charwat at the Linnean Society library, John Gandy at The National Trust's Blickling Hall library, Judith A. Warnement and Lisa DeCesare at the Botany Library of Harvard University Herbaria deserve our thanks. So too Carrie, at our local Beccles Library. The Armitt Collection; Australian Museum collections; the British Library; British Museum Prints and Drawings collection; Houghton Library, Harvard; the Mary Evans Picture Library; the Natural History Museum library and image information service; National Library of Ireland; Ruskin Library at Lancaster University; State Library of New South Wales; Suffolk Libraries, UCL libraries, Warburg Institute Library and Wellcome Library – all have helped to make this book possible. The Biodiversity Heritage Library is an amazing resource, which we have used almost daily.

While many of our artists travelled, some stayed at home and worked locally, and likewise from our computers in Suffolk we have reached out and found help the modern way via Twitter from Bill Baker, Dale Dixon, Tim Entwistle, Steven Hammer, Suzanne Mace, David Middleton, Tom Mulholland, Colin Walker, @BioDivLibrary. We would also like to thank Peggy Edwards and members of the Bishops' High School alumni at Toronto for sharing their memories of Violet Graham via email, Arnab Chakraborty and Keiko Sudo.

Friends are another source of help and inspiration, and in particular we thank Janet Fisher for friendship and meticulous genealogical research, Yunah Lee for sharing the love of plant pictures and exploring Asian possibilities, Bettina Bryan for her native German and for asking what it was all about, Caroline Tonson-Rye for her excellent Spanish and interest in plants too, Keith and Nicole Roberts for the discussion on Mackintosh and Anna Marie Roos for fielding all sorts of questions magnificently and by return. Emma and Kathleen know why too.

Besides our own digging around, our picture researcher Sally Nicholls has been marvellous in balancing everything and bringing all the images for the book together when they seemed to be all over the place in our minds.

At Thames & Hudson the book looks beautiful because of Sarah Praill's fantastic design work. Her pressing us for images rich in 'materiality' changed the way we saw the book. Rachel Heley's production skills are meticulous. Sarah Vernon-Hunt is a most remarkable editor, to whom we owe so much. Final thanks go to Colin Ridler, who gave us the idea for this book and started us off on the journey. It is dedicated to him, with affection and gratitude.

about the authors

Helen Bynum studied at University College London and the Wellcome Institute for the History of Medicine before lecturing in medical history at the University of Liverpool. She is now a freelance writer, speaker and editor. She is the co-author with William Bynum of *Remarkable Plants* (2023), author of *Spitting Blood: The History of Tuberculosis* (2012), co-editor with William Bynum of *Dictionary of Medical Biography* (2007) and *Great Discoveries in Medicine* (2022), and co-editor of the *Biography of Diseases* series.

William Bynum received his MD from Yale University and his PhD from the University of Cambridge. A Fellow of the Royal College of Physicians of London, he is professor emeritus of the history of medicine at University College London. His numerous books include *A Little History of Science* (2013), *The History of Medicine: A Very Short Introduction* (2008), and, as editor, *Companion Encyclopedia of the History of Medicine* (1993; with Roy Porter) and *The Oxford Dictionary of Scientific Quotations* (2005).